CAPITALISM AND AGRICULTURE IN THE HAOUZ OF MARRAKESH

CAPITALISM AND AGRICULTURE IN THE HAOUZ OF MARRAKESH

Paul Pascon

Translated by
C. Edwin Vaughan and Veronique Ingman

Edited with an Introduction to the English Edition
by John R. Hall

KPI

London, New York and Sydney

First published in English in 1986 by KPI Limited
11 New Fetter Lane, London EC4P 4EE

Distributed by
Routledge & Kegan Paul, Associated Book Publishers
11 New Fetter Lane, London EC4P 4EE

Routledge & Kegan Paul, Methuen Inc
29 West 35th Street, New York, NY10001, USA

Routledge & Kegan Paul
c/o Methuen Law Book Company
44 Waterloo Road
North Ryde, NSW 2113
Australia

Produced by Worts-Power Associates

Set in Times
by Margaret Spooner Typesetting, Bridport, Dorset
Printed in Great Britain by Dotesios Printers Ltd.,
Bradford-on-Avon Wiltshire

© *KPI 1986*

No part of this book may be reproduced in any form without permission from the publisher, except for the quotation of brief passages in criticism

ISBN 07103 0189 8

Table of Contents

List of Maps, Tables and Figures	vii
Author's Acknowledgements	xi
Translators' and Editor's Acknowledgements	xiii
Editor's Introduction by John R. Hall	15
CHAPTER 1: THE PENETRATION OF CAPITALISM INTO THE HAOUZ OF MARRAKESH	41
1 Weakness of the Merchant and Manufacturing Economy in the Pre-colonial Haouz	42
2 Seizure of Domestic and Foreign Trade	46
3 Attempts at Development of Commercial Agriculture	58
4 Resistance to Foreign Intervention	71
CHAPTER 2: DEVELOPMENT OF CAPITALISM UNDER THE PROTECTORATE	79
1 The Occupation of the Land	81
2 The Problems	120
3 The Results	139
4 Half-hearted Attempts at Modernizing the Moroccan Peasantry	154
CHAPTER 3: THE PROGRESS OF CAPITALISM AFTER INDEPENDENCE	163
1 The Partial Liquidation of the Caidal System	165
2 The Decline of Colonial Farming	175
3 Social Structure Today	197
4 Transition or Composite?	213
Afterword	215

Notes	217
Glossary of Arabic and Berber Terms	227
Glossary of Government Agencies	231
Bibliography	233
Index	243

Maps, Tables and Figures

Maps

A	The Maghreb and Northwest Africa	24
B	Morocco during the Protectorate	26
C	The Haouz of Marrakesh	34

Tables

1.1	Trade Balance for Mogador (Essaouira), 1911-1917	54
1.2	Trade Balances (value per ton)	54
1.3	Export and Import Products, 1913 (by percent of value)	55
1.4	Number of Protégés and Partners Associated with German Firms, 1901-1910	69
2.1	Acquisition of Land Through Colonization Before 1928	84
2.2	Distribution of Land and Water in the Tamesguelft	116
2.3	Population of Domanial Lands by Groups, 1946	117
2.4	Land Transactions Between Moroccans and Europeans, 1942-1950	118
2.5	European Acquisitions and Sales of Moroccan Land, 1952-1954	119
2.6	Evolution of the Surface Area of Farms Following Abandonments	123

2.7	Irrigation Allotment per Farm by Sector, Over Time	124
2.8	Irrigated Land and Irrigation Allotments in Selected Tributary Basins of the Haouz	135
2.9	Distribution of Water by Seguia, Khettara, and Pumping	136
2.10	Agricultural Production Characteristics for Official Colonization Farms in Selected Irrigation Sectors	142
2.11	Selected Farm Characteristics and Indices of Productivity by Irrigation Sector	144
2.12	The Volume, Capacity and Supply Sources of Companies Engaged in Apricot Processing, 1960	147
2.13	The Volume, Capacity and Supply Sources of Companies Engaged in Olive Processing, 1960	148
2.14	The Volume, Capacity and Supply Sources of Companies Engaged in Citrus Processing, 1960	149
2.15	Surface Areas of Cultivations of Selected Crops by Moroccans and Europeans, 1915	151
2.16	Percent Cultivations of Types of Crops by Moroccans and Foreigners, 1960	153
2.17	Comparison of the Gross Product of Moroccan and Foreign Agriculture, According to Type of Crops	153
2.18	Full-time Equivalent Working Days of Salaried Occasional Workers in the Haouz, by Blocks of Length of Employment	159
3.1	Devolution of Haouz Lands Obtained by the State in the Sequestration of 1958	169
3.2	The Leasing of Lands Formerly Belonging to Haj Thami el-Glaoui, 1959-1960	172
3.3	Estate Income and Its Allocation According to Means and Relations of Production	173
3.4	Devolution of Colonization Lands in the Haouz of Marrakesh, 1 December, 1974	181
3.5	Length of Existence of Government Agencies Charged with the Management of Repossessed Lands	188
3.6	Allotment of Repossessed Land, 1969-1974	190
3.7	Distribution of Land of all Statuses in the Central Haouz by Size of Landholding, 1974	200
3.8	Characteristics of Olive Production and Distribution	203

Figures

2.1	Acquisition of Lands by the Colonization in the Haouz of Marrakesh, 1910–1930	82
2.2	Employment on Colonization Farms in the Haouz	160
3.1	Changes in Ownership of Former Colonization Lands in the Haouz of Marrakesh, 1957–1974	178

Author's Acknowledgements

My first thought goes to those who live in the Haouz. This is not a stylistic bow aimed at popularity. I have spent nine years trying to understand the people of the Haouz. My work was not possible without their tacit support. And yet, after having read this book over again, I am left with the impression of not having spoken about them, but rather across them, above, below, beside them. During my defense Jacques Berque remarked: 'This is a metathesis!' True! I have understood the groups, sequences and practices better than the behavior of individuals. For me the individuals are still elusive, oscillating between so many solutions and possibilities, filled with so many riches, worthy of so much care, that I have been unable to conceptualize them. Nevertheless, they did not hold back information — the Haouz people are talkative; they know a great deal; they express themselves with cloquence, and their hospitality is proverbial.

I am also indebted to the authorities of my adopted country, who have allowed me both to do applied work and to study. Where and in what country can one find a sociologist in charge of coordinating studies for hydraulic planning, who then is placed at the head of an office for development, and who finds himself, in short, 'in the hot seat' and on the activist side of social practice? Thus I found myself, and I thereby naturally developed a well-intended, but nevertheless persistent and lively questioning attitude, as much orally as in writing. For what purpose would social research serve if it did not debunk?

My professors gave me good advice: Jean Dresch directly, Jacques

Berque through his work and his demands; without them and their support, I would have undertaken neither to write so extensively nor to publish.

Even so, it was a question of finding the time in the field. During the survey period I put aside a day a week to collect the raw data. After nine years of gathering data, the time came to organize the materials and write about them. This endeavor would not have succeeded without the support of Abdallah Bekkali, Director of the Institut Agronomique et Vétérinaire Hassan II. Without interrupting my duties, I was able to take advantage of certain liberties: the entire work was written in eight months.

Have I forgotten someone? Of course: all my colleagues, my friends, my family. Is it possible to mobilize one's time in such a way without affectionate discussions, without support, without profound comprehension?

And for the reader I will add this: the preparation of a thesis all too often depends on a phantom. This has its good and bad sides. One has a score to settle with oneself. Too often, there is pain involved, and the quality suffers from it. I thank the reader in advance for making the effort to understand me.

Translators' and Editor's Acknowledgements

The translators would like to express their appreciation to the various persons who contributed to this project. Marguerite Green of Stephens College, and Richard Riddle and Jere Gilles of the University of Missouri-Columbia gave valuable assistance with special problems encountered during the translation. In addition to his introduction, John Hall made very important contributions to the translation. Kenneth Brown of the University of Manchester, England, reviewed a draft of the manuscript in English, and his comments were much appreciated. Paul Pascon and his associate, Timothy Dottridge, responded several times to specific questions and to our effort in general, and their assistance was invaluable.

The editor wishes to thank those who helped in the editorial effort and those who unselfishly gave critical advice and support. Richard Riddle provided the service of a *khalifa* in various editorial tasks, including the preparation of tables and a bibliography. Maps are the work of Bhupinder S. Marh. Those who acted as a sounding board through critical readings of the introduction in an earlier draft include Richard Riddle, George Primov, C. Edwin Vaughan, Veronique Ingman, and Rex Campbell — all of the University of Missouri-Columbia; Phillip D. Schuyler of Columbia University; Daniel Chirot of the University of Washington, and Paul Pascon. Obviously those who have helped me so much still cannot be held responsible if I did not always follow their good advice!

Secretarial assistance for both translation and editorial phases of the project was provided by Gerry Burke, Liz Keller, Kerry Henley, Barbara Barman and Sharon Watson. We are all very grateful for their unflagging efforts.

We would also like to express our appreciation to the Graduate School, the College of Arts and Science, and the College of Agriculture Experiment Station of the University of Missouri-Columbia for the financial support which made this endeavor possible.

Editor's Introduction

Today the push of world events is forcing the peoples of developed countries to become aware, however dimly, that their own development involves dependency on fragile economic and diplomatic relations with less developed countries, while the peoples on the periphery of the world economy see the world turn toward new alignments which, once again, promise little more than to leave them on the margins. The post-colonial era has come to another parting of the ways.

The occasion of world political and economic change and, perhaps, the emergence of new forms of international relationships, is an appropriate time to reflect upon what has come before. Paul Pascon's study of the *Haouz* — the fertile plain between the Moroccan city of Marrakesh and the Atlas Mountains to the south — is one recent effort in that direction. It is an attempt to understand the colonial dimension of European capitalism and its post-colonial legacy in a peripheral society of the capitalist world economy. Because of its scope and detail, Pascon's work should be inherently interesting to students of the *Maghreb* — the western Muslim countries bordering the Mediterranean. The broader relevance of the present volume can be understood best by briefly considering recent discourse on development and social change.

For the past decade or so, we have witnessed concerted and timely efforts to supplant modernization theory within an analysis of development which focuses both on economic and political relations between nation-states, and on the ways in which these relations shape the nexus between class formation and state formation in economically dependent countries.[1] The foremost recent studies of economic dependency have focused on societies which were incorporated into the capitalist world-economy with little or no effective political and cultural resistance among the indigenous populations.[2] Thus, the colonizers of the Americas were able to establish colonial states largely of their own design. By contrast, Europeans traded in the Arab-dominated world much earlier than in the Americas, but European capitalist penetration of Muslim societies came much later and met greater local resistance. It is reasonable to suggest that this alternative pre-colonial history of Muslim societies has affected the course of European colonization itself. Therefore, Muslim societies have received a different treatment in the analysis of long-term, or secular, social change; and as subjects of study, they differ from the South American cases in the problems they have posed for recent attempts to recast theories of development.

The two classic accounts of the origins of European capitalism — those of Karl Marx and Max Weber — differ somewhat in their explanations of the crucial causes of the emergence of modern capitalism in western Europe. But they nevertheless share a negative case analysis of Muslim societies which is intended to demonstrate conditions under which capitalism does *not* develop. For Weber and Marx alike, the societies of the Arab-dominated world were resistant to self-sustained development because of the relation of the political superstructure to tribal pastoralism and peasant agricultural economies. Prebendal patrimonialism[3] and the so-called asiatic mode of production[4] are each key terms of analyses which try to explain the *absence* of economic change. They do so by positing an entrenched but often unstable political class which directly engages in appropriation of economic surplus. The supposed results are conditions which discourage independent entrepreneurial action and channel economic and other power aspirations through the political sphere, leaving unchanged the spheres of economic production and distribution.

Bryan Turner recently has argued that both Marx's and Weber's assessments of Arab-dominated societies are pervaded by a set of 'orientalist' assumptions which are basically ideological in nature. The outcome of western orientalist analysis fulfills the prophecy of its assumptions — according to Turner, it holds that:

> Islam's civilization is static and locked within its sacred customs, its formal moral code, and its religious law. The stationary quality of its culture is reinforced by the authoritarianism and despotism of its political system.[5]

In the orientalist view attacked by Turner, any movement toward change within the realm of Islam would be subverted by other actors within the traditional order. The conclusion of the orientalist ideology is clear: 'progress' must come from the outside. Like the European capitalists, Marx and Engels embraced this view. Given their evolutionary framework, they too regarded internal resistance to change in Arab societies as reactionary. Whatever the validity of the orientalist assumptions, in the works of Marx and Engels they buttressed the assertion that capitalist colonialism was necessary to the world of Islam as a stage of modernization.[6] Incorporation of Arab-dominated societies into the capitalist world-economy would pave the way for the advent of socialism in those societies.

The historical process by which one Muslim society, Morocco, has been incorporated within the capitalist economy is a major theme of the present volume. But the process described herein raises questions about the shape of a marxist theory of economic transformation in peripheral societies. In marxist terms, the process of colonial transformation has to do with a capitalist appropriation of economic surplus, with the articulation of traditional and modern technical methods and social organizations of production, with the emergence of new economic classes tied to the new mode of production, and with the fate of previously established economic classes which must adjust to the new conditions. Of course such a transformation is not simply a material process: it transpires in crosscutting webs of political intrigue, religious sanctions, and ethnic alliances. How marxist theory is to handle the coexistence of two or more modes of production within a single, subordinated (colonial) social formation is far from clear. The tidy solution is to posit a single mode of production, for example, the colonial mode of production.[7] But Pascon's analysis of the Haouz draws this theoretical solution into question.

Dependency theory and the world economy perspective might

seem more appropriate than either modernization theory or marxism for explaining the ambiguous colonialism of Arab societies. Yet dependency theorists have concentrated on analyzing capitalist domination of relatively weak societies, and world economy theorists have yet to give their full attention to questions which emerge when Arab and other culturally resilient societies are considered. They are not predisposed to deal with the kinds of questions which the colonial histories of Arab societies call forth, namely: To what extent can indigenous politics shape the local articulation of capitalism? How effectively can an entrenched political class maintain its grip on certain channels of surplus appropriation, while capitalism seizes others and develops new channels of surplus appropriation? Is capitalism itself necessarily preeminent, even when various kinds of labor mobilization and surplus appropriation coexist?[8] If there is no inherent next stage for Arab societies, what are the paths and sequences whereby change likely occurs; how do political, economic, and religious forces come to the fore in these developments; and how do these developments affect the nature of the world economy? In short, what are the nature and direction of transformation?

Paul Pascon's analysis of capitalism and agriculture in a specific region of Arab society — the Haouz of Marrakesh — does not pretend to answer definitively the questions sketched above, but the attention he gave to detail will likely provide a good deal of ammunition for the debate. Pascon employed land usage as a key axis of analysis in order to contend with the play of social forces in the Haouz as a concrete region, over an extended period of time, from the pre-colonial era to post-colonial movements toward land reform and state-owned agribusiness. The regional focus allows a detailed look at a particular formation of a mode of production and social and political relations in the face of shifting tides of European colonialism and the advance of industrial technology — all of this in a region dominated by the long-established social forms of segmented lineage 'tribalism', caidalism, Islam, and the centralized Arab governmental administration, the *Makhzen*.

Pascon's delimited regional and topical focus develops a rich and culturally diverse set of historical sources; these allow social actors and their concrete organizations to take their due, in place of anonymous historical forces like capitalism, which too often are substituted in theoretical discussions for a lack of substantive detail.

While theorists can maintain discourse at the level of models and streamlined sequences of development, Pascon was forced by his choice of a regional and historical analysis to contend with the complex play of diverse, interpenetrating phenomena. Because Pascon actually confronted the occupation and exploitation of land over time, he was able to comprehend the ways in which small changes in land tenure compel tribal groups to shift their strategies of economic want satisfaction, or how colonialists were able to undercut indigenous agriculture by expropriating irrigation resources and exploiting them more efficiently. Because Pascon has detailed the shifting interests of various social strata historically, his analysis brings to light the patterns of social interaction whereby the French colonial interests — especially those corporations which came to be allied with the State — were able to penetrate the Moroccan agricultural economy. Because Pascon was familiar with the specific pieces of land held at various times and worked by tribespeople, by tenants of *caids* ('feudal' lords with origins in tribal groups), by French colons, agricultural corporations, state corporations, and beneficiaries of land reform, he could delineate the relationship between surface geology and hydrology, technical means of production, class relations of production, and the fate of various social strata. These sorts of investigations provide a substantive standard by which to assess theoretical discourse on social change in peripheral societies.

Social analysts of all kinds — both those concerned with theoretical debates and with practical intervention for agricultural, economic, and socio-political change — will have to contend with the central theme of these investigations on the Haouz of Marrakesh. By carefully detailing the whole fabric of Haouz society over a period of history during which the region went through major changes, Pascon implicitly, and at times explicitly, has drawn into question the central theoretical concept which is a keystone of practically the whole gamut of theories of change, namely the concept of *transition*.

Transitions — whether they take the form of stages, movements along a continuum, cycles, or other motifs — are a mainstay of sociological discourse. Thus we hear about the transition (or transitions) from feudalism to capitalism, just as surely as we hear about stages of modernization.[9] No matter how the clash of different modes of production has been viewed in the debates about penetration of capitalism into new territories, the phenomenon has been depicted as involving an irreversible shift, in which the new economic framework undercuts the old ways and sets in motion the transition to a new form.

In his conclusion, Pascon has placed before us an alternative, more syncretic model based on his studies of the Haouz. This he has termed *composition*. In contrast to transition, composition involves the dynamic interplay of diverse social, cultural, and economic forms, in the context of political domination. These coexist with one another over time, while each retains some of its own internal coherence. The idea of dynamic composition does not suggest that these various forms and structures do not undergo change. But the change they undergo may involve more adjustment and articulation to each other, rather than necessarily an overall transition.

In this view, for example, tribalism, the power of caids, traditional irrigation technologies, feudalistic sharecropping, and the like are not simply vestiges of archaic and necessarily doomed social formations. Nor is their present form explained solely by their relationship to a new and overarching capitalist mode of production. Instead, they sometimes persist in their own right, changed here and there by the ways they articulate with the new realities, but by the same token, influential in channeling the ways in which the alien forms take hold. Indeed, in some spheres, they remain absolutely predominant in defining the forms and limits of social action.

To me, the concept of composition suggests that there is no straightforward transition, and, thus, certainly no final direction to history; instead, there is a shifting constellation of sociologically distinct elements, the composition of which at one time sets up ranges of future possibilities. Thus, future developments do not necessarily stem from the predominance of any single element. History involves a dialectic not only of classes and material transformations, but of social structures in play with one another. Given the multiple axes on which shifting composition occurs, history has a checkered course.

It is worth wondering why Pascon arrived at his distinctive understanding of composition, when other analysts have not. While the question is really a chapter in the sociology of knowledge, some preliminary comments on Pascon's life may be suggestive, at the same time introducing the reader to Pascon's mode of analysis and to the historical and social character of Morocco.

Paul Pascon was born in Fez, Morocco, in 1932. He died in 1985, tragically and before his time, in an automobile accident while conducting research in Mauritania. Pascon's grandparents were all French colons. In Pascon's words, they were 'not the grand colons of classic imagery', but small-scale colons who, debt-ridden, abandoned agriculture for other callings well before the independence of Morocco from the French Protectorate in 1956. While Pascon's grandparents may not have been major beneficiaries of French colonialism, his parents, on the other hand, were its victims. They experienced harsh treatment at the hands of the French administration during World War II: while Pascon was still a young boy, they were relocated in Moroccan detention centers for resistance to the German-allied Vichy regime. During that period, Pascon himself was distanced from the French colonial milieu in Morocco and immersed in the native Moroccan *lycée* culture. There he began to learn Arabic. It is probably safe to say that the biographies of Pascon's forbears and his own childhood experiences shaped his interest in both agriculture and the Moroccan people. The young Pascon found himself far more conversant in the ways of Moroccan life than most members of the French colonial enclave. By the same token, his ability to see patterns of composition between different social forms subsequently was enhanced. It is not surprising that Pascon opted for Moroccan, rather than French, citizenship after Independence.

Pascon received undergraduate training in experimental science at Rabat; he went on to earn two *licences*, somewhat more advanced French equivalents of Bachelor's degrees — one in natural sciences from the Sorbonne in 1956, and the second in sociology at Bordeaux in 1958. When Pascon returned to Morocco he devoted himself to research and management in the fields of irrigation and rural development in the Haouz, between 1962 and 1970. Out of that experience and from the information he gathered beginning in that period, Pascon's study of the Haouz emerged as a doctoral thesis at the Sorbonne (Paris VII) in 1975.

The thesis was forged out of diverse and rarely combined intellectual concerns and practical experiences. It carefully describes the geography, climate and traditional and modern technologies of irrigation in the Haouz. The mutual influences of these are woven together with considerations of 'tribalism', Muslim religious brotherhoods and their lodges (*zaouias*), and the conquests of the 'feudal' barons called grand caids. By this procedure, Pascon had already mapped the character of pre-Protectorate Moroccan society before he embarked on the subject of the present volume — pre-Protectorate, Protectorate, and post-independence periods of capitalist agriculture in the Haouz.[10]

How did Pascon view himself and his work? He saw his own intellectual biography as a kind of composition, in a way like that he found in the Haouz. Thus, he identified three major influences: (1) classical orientalism, the legacy of his French nativity and education; (2) empiricism derived from early education in the natural sciences and imported from there to sociological analysis; and, finally, (3) a neo-marxist influence deriving both from post-World War II French intellectual culture and from his own social activism in Morocco. Pascon regarded these currents as very much in play with one another, because 'none of them seems capable by itself of resolving the theoretical problems which practice poses'.[11]

Given Turner's critique of orientalist assumptions in sociological and marxist theories, the heterogeneous sources of Pascon's approach are no doubt a healthy sign, but one which calls for an assessment of Pascon's work as a whole, in relation to more familiar brands of scholarship. If we seek to locate Pascon's style of synthetic analysis in a single intellectual current, the *Annales* school immediately comes to mind. The *Annalistes* — the French school of historical analysis — have reconstructed the character of historical explanation by moving beyond purely political, economic, and diplomatic history to a broader social history which incorporates both qualitative and statistical data on the whole sweep of phenomena influential in human affairs. Pascon's treatment of themes as diverse as soil composition and erosion, migrations and the character of 'tribalism', hydraulic development and capitalism, would seem to fit this mold. The parallel is not completely fortuitous. But Pascon was not directly connected with the *Annales* school, though he was well aware of their work. His own intellectual development — his immersion in the diversity of Maghreb culture from birth, his early interest in natural science, his marginal status in French colonial society, and his career experiences in the Haouz — these ingredients seem to have propelled him to an analysis which could not partition off a narrow set of archival sources from the diverse and rich information to be gained from the lifeworld itself. With these influences, it is easy to see why Pascon refused to set limits to discourse at the boundaries of one or another discipline. Though he may be understood as an *Annaliste* by the nature of his work, he arrived at that position in part on the basis of influences independent of the *Annales* school.

Still, the parallel raises an important question about the present translation: if Pascon's analysis is of the *Annales* style, why have the translators provided only an English edition of his analysis of European capitalism and the Haouz, and left untranslated his prior treatments of geography, climate, irrigation, and traditional social structure? This decision was based on the resources, areas of training, and sociological interests of the translators and editor. We think the present volume dealing with the capitalist penetration of the Haouz is significant in its own right. J.H. Hexter once remarked, in discussing Fernand Braudel's epic account of *The Mediterranean*, that Braudel basically developed a comprehensive geological, geographic, climatic, social, and economic history of the region, and then proceeded to tack political history on top of all this, without really establishing its connections to the rest of the analysis.[12] Hexter was faulting Braudel for failing to live up to the *Annales* claim to show the interconnections between different levels of history. With respect to the Haouz, the point is well taken: capitalism in the Haouz does not stand on its own; indeed, its articulation with geography, irrigation, and traditional social structure is a main theme of the present volume. But whether Hexter is correct in pointing to a disjuncture in Braudel's treatment of the Mediterranean, in Pascon's work, the separation of topics of analysis does not involve a disjuncture, only a division of labor in scholarship. In the present translation, the advent and phases of capitalism provide a reasonable periodization for the analysis of historical events, while the focus on capitalism establishes a criterion of relevance for the consideration of other ecological, economic, and social phenomena. At the outset, however, the non-specialist may find the following description of pre-Protectorate Morocco and the Haouz of Marrakesh useful as background for reading the text itself.[13]

The part of the world now known as Morocco has held a strategic place in the history of the western world since ancient times, mainly because of its location at the northwest corner of Africa, bordering both the Mediterranean Sea and the Atlantic Ocean, and connecting Africa with the European continent across the Straits of Gibraltar. Of

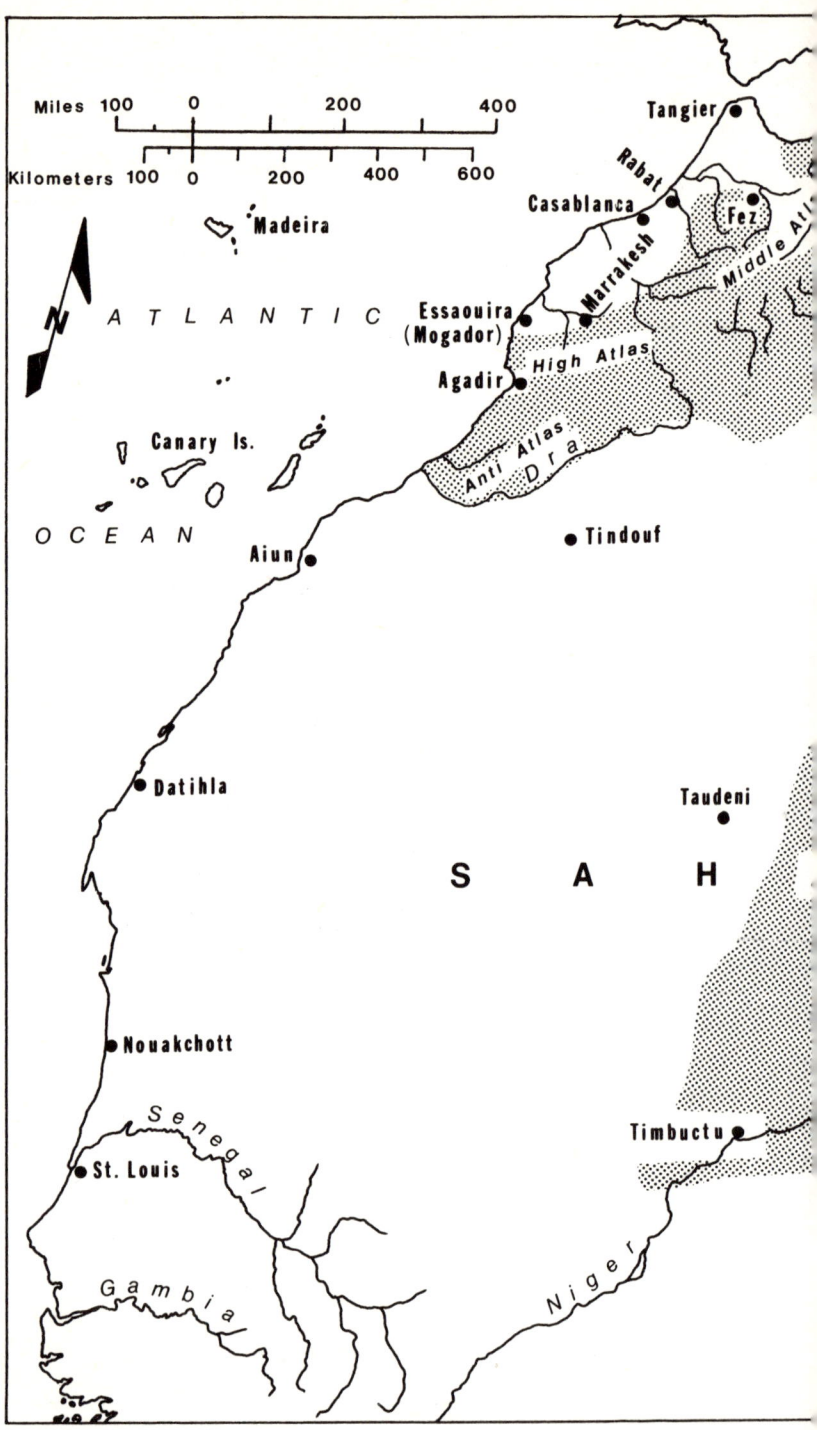

Map A: The Maghreb and North-West Africa, with regions of Berber speech shaded. Recent migrations and social changes have probably reduced the areas of Berber speech. Redrawn from Gellner and Micaud (1972: 16).

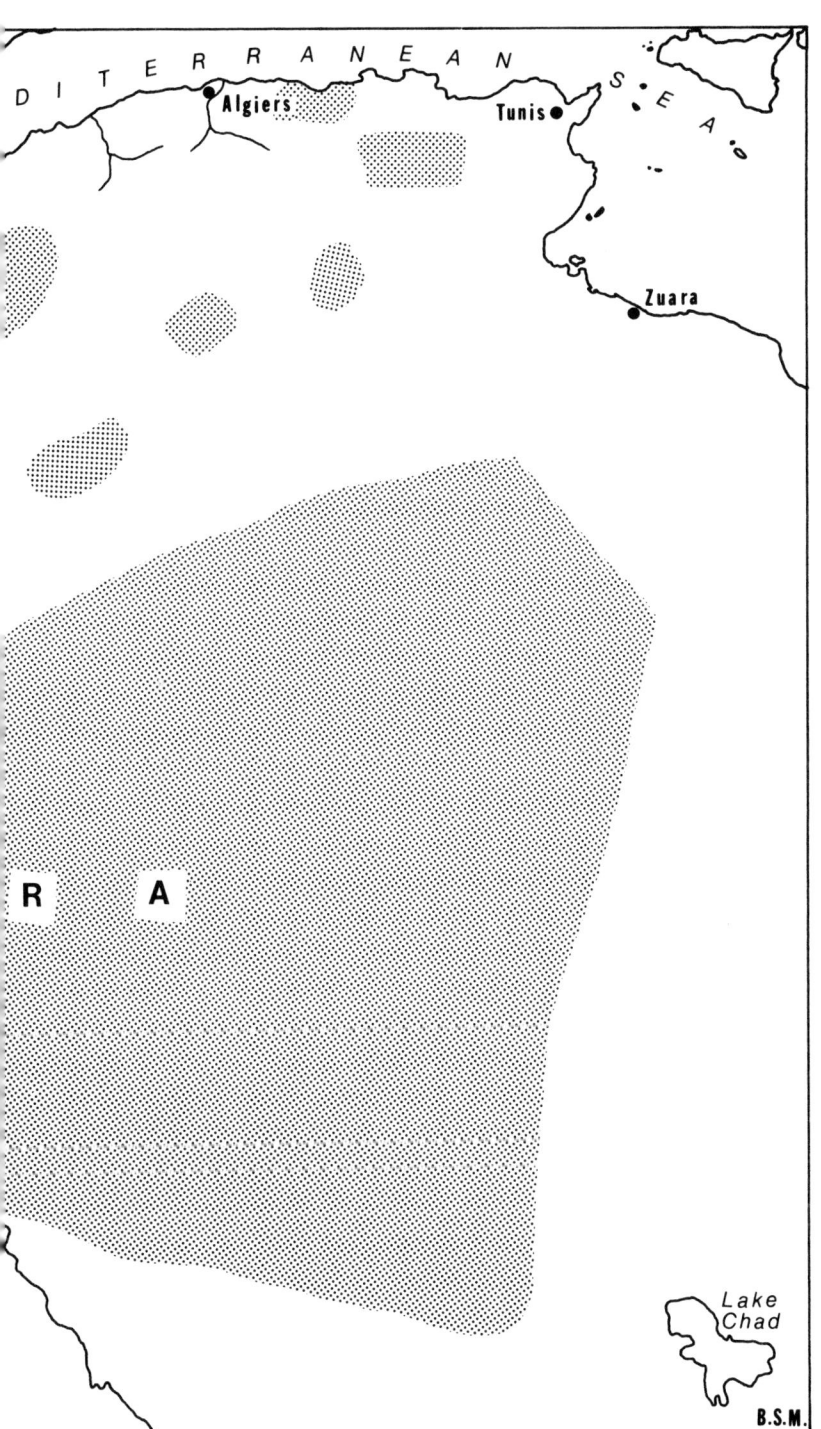

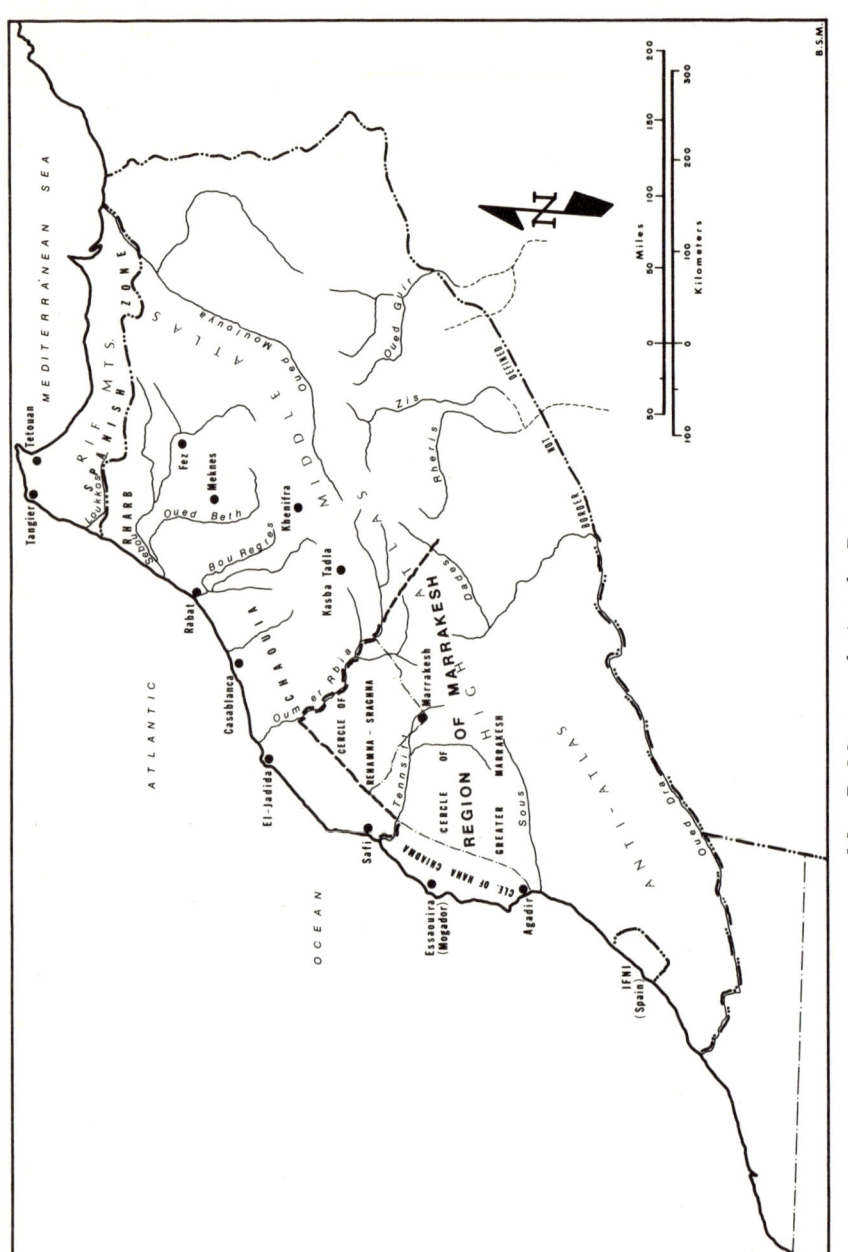

Map B. Morocco during the Protectorate.

the Arab countries, it is the westernmost country of the Maghreb — the countries of the west (see Map A).

Morocco's peculiar geography — the Rif Mountains surrounding the Gibraltar Straits and the Middle and High Atlas Mountains running from northeast to southwest — defines a broad coastal region of rolling hills and plains. To the south of the forbidding peaks of the High Atlas, the *Oued* (river) Sous runs from a pre-Saharan plain into the Atlantic; south of the Sous, the sprawling and rough Anti-Atlas range marks the absolute limit of any Mediterranean climate. Taken together, the Rif and the three Atlas ranges form a natural fortress which seals off the plains of Atlantic drainage basins from the less hospitable Sahara (see Map B).

Though the natural fortress of the Atlas and the Rif has made conquest from the outside difficult, the fortress itself is a worthy prize of conquest, all the more valuable for its strategic location between Europe and sub-Saharan Africa. Thus the nomadic, transhumant, and sedentary Berber tribal groups of the Sahara, the Atlas uplands, and the Moroccan plains — some of them inhabitants as early as 800 B.C.[14] — have been confronted with conquest at least since Roman times. The Romans were able to establish a military outpost on the Atlantic coast, as well as cities such as Volubilis. But they were not able to pacify tribes over the vast upland, mountain, and Sahara territory. With the decline of the Empire, Roman influence all but disappeared. Their conquest was followed by periods of influence of the Vandals and, subsequently, the Byzantines. Arab conquest was to prove more durable than any of these previous ones, though it too was plagued by resistance from indigenous Berber tribes. By 678 the Arabs had reached the Atlantic, and though subsequently they were more than once repelled, they ultimately prevailed. Arab invasion during the eleventh century, by Bedouin nomads who originally had been driven from Arabia into Egypt, finally actually settled the lowlands.[15] Perhaps the Arabs assimilated lowland Berber groups; perhaps some lowland Berbers sought refuge with upland and mountain Berber groups. In any case, today a cultural boundary exists between lowland Arabs and mountain Berber tribes.[16] The line is not a hard and fast one, in part because most Berbers have become Islamized. But Berbers are still able to maintain their distinct cultures and language, largely because they live in the highlands as a region of refuge.

The Berber and Arab tribal groups which became established in Morocco took many forms. Somehow these seemed keyed to the nature of subsistence and the degree of vulnerability to attack and domination by external groups. Sedentary groups were perhaps more vulnerable than pastoral ones, especially nomads. Under external threat, relatively free and autonomous tribal administration by elders or a colleagially selected *sheikh* (chief) could give way to a quasi-feudal situation, in which a caid would take tribute in kind or in exchange for protection. In some cases, caids actually usurped the more democratic power of tribal sheikhs; but they could also gain power as agents of domination from the outside; then their positions came to resemble patrimonial prebends dispensed by the dynastic ruler, the sultan, in exchange for a share of tribute.[17] But the persistence of tribal forms of organization and the great instability of vassalage makes feudalism a less than satisfactory model on which to base an understanding of pre-Protectorate Moroccan society.

As Ernest Gellner has observed, a special sort of society emerges when tribal relations are maintained, in whatever form, at the margins of a centralized monarchy.[18] This is the situation which developed in Morocco with the establishment of Islamic dynasties from the eleventh century onwards. The first of these dynasties — the Almoravids and the Almohads — were Berber in origin. By the fifteenth and sixteenth centuries, dynasties of *sherifs*, those individuals who traced their ancestries back to the Prophet, came to predominate in Morocco. The Saadien dynasty, and after it, the Alaouites, firmly established the Arab and Islamic hegemony which has persisted to the present day. The series of dynasties each contended with the persistence of marginal, but not autonomous, tribalism. The governmental administration and military force of the sultan — the *Makhzen* — operated out of urban strongholds. Its problem of rule was one of exacting tribute further and further outward from those strongholds.

Although all tribes, Berber and Arab alike, would give nominal recognition to the sultan as the spiritual leader of Islam, acquiescence to its political and taxation authority was another matter. The difficulty which the central Makhzen faced in controlling the tribes of the country has led to the classic French dichotomization of the *bled el Makhzen* territory and the *bled as Siba* (territories controlled by dissident tribal groups). This distinction, like overly concretized anthropological descriptions of Morocco's 'tribes', may have been a figment of French political imagination.[19] No one doubts the existence of dissidence, but the bled el Makhzen was perhaps more a nominal sovereignty than the French assumed. Alan Scham has countered the dichotomy by suggesting that three broad kinds of situations could be found.[20] In the bled el Makhzen, Arab tribes either paid taxes, or, as *guich* tribes, provided the Makhzen with military service in lieu of taxes. Even here, dissidence was not out of the question, as the case of the Rehamna tribe (discussed below) shows. Second, in the Djebala region — from the Oued Sebou up to the Mediterranean — Berber tribes recognized the sultan's religious authority and paid religious taxes, but retained their political autonomy and territorial sovereignty. Finally, the Berber peoples of the bled as Siba recognized the sultan as *imam*, or religious leader, but they paid few, if any taxes.

Similarly, Gellner describes the 'Inner Circle of tribes who extracted taxes, the Middle Circle of tribes who had taxes extracted from them, and the Outer Circle of tribes who did not allow taxes to be extracted from them'.[21] The point is that these conceptual boundaries are, in actuality, fluid. The conduct of affairs in Morocco prior to European penetration was based on a dynamic of long-standing antipathies between the Makhzen and its subjects, on shifting alliances and intrigues, and on the exercise of customary law in ways which did not always operate to the benefit of the Makhzen.

Nor was Islam itself a straightforward vehicle of centralized cultural domination. Although Islam certainly undercut tribalism as solidary social organization, it was itself permeated by a distinction between the authority of the imam and the independent charisma of *marabouts* ('saints') around which *zaouias* would form. The zaouias are important as arbiters of political and economic disputes between tribal groups; because they have come to hold significant agricultural lands in some cases, like many Catholic monasteries, they also have become significant economic actors in their own right.[22]

The multiple bases of solidarity and conflict, of authority and power in traditional Moroccan society undercut the power of the Makhzen in a way that makes prebendal patrimonialism (or 'oriental despotism', for that matter) just as inappropriate a model of pre-Protectorate Morocco as feudalism.[23] The sultan simply did not uniformly establish himself on the basis of granting prebends related to irrigation or any other state projects. He ruled from a fortified *kasba* on the basis of his ability to establish alliances with *pashas* (governors of cities) and caids, protect taxed tribes, and raise armies which could insure the stability of this fragile structure without turning on him in the process. As Max Weber noted, the distinctive *political* characteristic of the sultan is his attempt to rule totally by personal discretion. This is an extreme form of patrimonialism, one in which the administrative and military force as well as the treatment of the populace as personal subjects are less bounded by custom than is the case in traditional patrimonial rule.[24] The discretionary rule of sultanism, it should be noted in passing, cannot claim the same effective legitimacy as a patrimonial rulership more broadly based in tradition and custom. On the other hand, such customary limits of patrimonial rule would tend to constrain the flexibility of the sultan, and thereby impede his ability to deal effectively with autonomous powers such as independent caids and dissident tribes. Sultanism may be the logical outcome of patrimonial rule over territory with amorphous and shifting political boundaries.

If the Makhzen was not, strictly speaking, at the pinnacle of a feudalistic network of vassalage, not the orientalist state in an 'asiatic' mode of production, how did it survive economically? The answer lies in part in the Makhzen's ability to obtain tribute on the basis of its military capability, to be sure; second, the Makhzen derived wealth from its private domains, which in turn helped to feed the sultan's army. A third source, especially significant for Morocco's relations with other countries, rests in the ability of the Makhzen to control foreign trade by licencing and taxing it. From the eighth century, Morocco traded for sub-Saharan gold and slaves. As early as the twelfth century, it was involved with European trade for sub-Saharan gold, and gradually Moroccan crafts and commodities themselves became objects of European trade. For the most part, the Makhzen was successful in limiting foreign merchants to Atlantic port cities and controlling their activities to its own financial benefit. Thus to some degree the Makhzen 'floated' above the rural economy on the basis of its key location on trade routes. More accurately, the Makhzen survived (more or less) by cultivating its marginal relation to two separate modes of production — an indigenous pastoral and agrarian tribalism with feudalistic elements, and an international trade network tied to the emerging capital world-economy.[25]

This dual alignment of the Makhzen, more than its relations to the bled el Makhzen and the bled as Siba, helps us to understand its predicament when the colonial aspirations of the Great Powers reached imperialist proportions toward the close of the nineteenth century. European commercial interests were becoming increasingly dissatisfied with the limitations on trade within and through Morocco. The protégé system gradually emerged as a way of extending the network of European trade into the interior. Under this system, a European consulate or company could designate a specified number of indigenous Moroccans to act on its behalf in the interior. These Moroccans were to be 'protected' from the arbitrary exercise of local justice or taxation so that they could more effectively act for the interests they represented. In practice the system tended to amount to the exemption of the protégés from the obligations of Moroccan citizenship. They became de facto citizens of the countries by which they were protected. The tendencies of this system to undermine the Makhzen are well documented.[26] European companies sometimes informally or secretly sought protégés from among the ranks of caids, pashas, and other notables. The number of Moroccans protected ballooned, and the line between protection of a Moroccan's activities on behalf of a company and protection of purely personal activities and ventures became blurred. Under these conditions, conflict easily arose between local Moroccan judicial authorities and the protégés, and the European powers often then called upon the Makhzen to uphold the guarantees of protection it had extended. But the operation of the protégé system itself had undermined the authority of the Makhzen which had helped to create it. Thus the European powers were increasingly able to point to the inability of the Makhzen to govern its territories, and they began to threaten intervention if harm befell their commercial operatives and protégés. Such incidents were increasingly likely to occur, however, because local judicial authorities began to oppose the Makhzen's apparent support for expansion of European trade.

England alone among the Great Powers seems to have been convinced that its primacy in trade did not depend on political monopolization of trade in some form of protectorate; thus it was England which tried concertedly at the Conference of Madrid in 1880 to specify a commercially workable protégé system which nevertheless strengthened, rather than undermined the Makhzen.[27] But even the Act of Madrid hastened the disintegration of the Makhzen: the protégé provision only prevented abuses in theory, and other clauses set forth a procedure by which foreigners could petition to obtain land in Morocco. More significantly, the other Great Powers — France and Germany, and to a lesser degree, Spain and Italy — had weaker economies than England, and they thus could less easily endure the vagaries of free trade. They therefore were more interested in seeking imperialist monopolization. Thus Morocco, along with other parts of Africa and Asia, became caught up in the horse-trading of zones of influence among the European Powers.

At the same time that Morocco's political sovereignty was being undermined by the protégé system and the designs of the European states, it became economically dependent on European money for the financing of the sultan's court and the administration of the Makhzen. France took the lead in underwriting Makhzen finances, and it received considerable commercial and banking concessions in return. These concessions, like the protégé system, impeded the ability of a rapid succession of sultans to govern, and finally brought the Makhzen to accept the establishment of the French Protectorate in 1912.

The Protectorate provided an opportunity for French colonialist development of agriculture in a country where large, potentially arable regions were as yet uncultivated, and where previous agriculture had been marked by an almost complete absence of modern techniques, either of production or processing. This capitalist opportunity became a reality in large part because of changes in the political sphere. The initial French Protectorate administration of Resident General Louis-Hubert Lyautey brought to Morocco changes in administration and law, in property rights and land tenure policy, and in development of irrigation resources.[28] With the end of the French Protectorate in 1956, the colonial agricultural structures developed under the Protectorate began to be modified by the Moroccan king's new policies directed toward expropriation of colonial lands, development of state agricultural companies, and efforts at land reform.[19]

The Haouz of Marrakesh is an interesting region in which to consider how the play of world events sketched above came to be connected to Moroccan agriculture and the social and economic conditions in which it occurs. No argument can be made that the Haouz was *representative* of other regions, at least in any statistical sense. But the actors in the daily life of the Haouz — tribespeople and peasants, religious zaouias, caids and notables, the Makhzen and the colonial administration, European companies and private colons — are the principal actors all over Morocco. Thus to understand agriculture and capitalism in the Haouz is to understand a phenomenon which was replicated, albeit in somewhat different ways, in the rest of the country, and in other colonial 'protectorates' as well. The Haouz 'represents' nothing else, but it is a region where local events come to light so that it is possible to examine 'the thing itself', as it transpired.

The Haouz of Marrakesh is no exception to the rule that the boundaries of geographic space are defined in ways which evolve with their histories. In purely geographic terms the Haouz is delimited by the Atlas mountain range to the south; numerous streams run northward out of the mountain valleys down to Oued Tensift, the river which parallels the Atlas and drains westward to the Atlantic. Just beyond the Oued Tensift lie the rolling hills of the Jbilet which make up the northern boundary of the Haouz. The upper (eastern) end of the Haouz is naturally delimited by the drainage divide between the Oued Tensift and the Oued Tessaout, which itself joins with other streams emerging from the Middle Atlas and drains northward, and then to the west. The western limits of the Haouz are not so easily defined in strictly geographic terms, for the Oued Tensift continues westward to drain mountain streams practically to the Atlantic coast. The social boundaries of the central Haouz are therefore really defined by the city which dominates it — Marrakesh. Though the social limits slowly shift over time with the formation and withering of various political alliances, in the modern era the central Haouz can be said to end with the irrigation basin of the Oued Nfis, flowing out of the High Atlas. The Haouz, then, amounts to an inland plain centered on Marrakesh, some sixty miles in length, perhaps thirty miles wide at its lower end, and progressively narrower at its upper, or eastern, end (see Map C). The region is marked by a hot and arid Mediterranean climate. Rainfall is low and variable. It would not support much beyond pastoral transhumance were it not for the Atlas snows feeding mountain streams which can be used for irrigation.

Though the geographic features which define the Haouz generally run from east to west, the importance of irrigation results in an axis of ecological variation which runs generally from south to north. At the

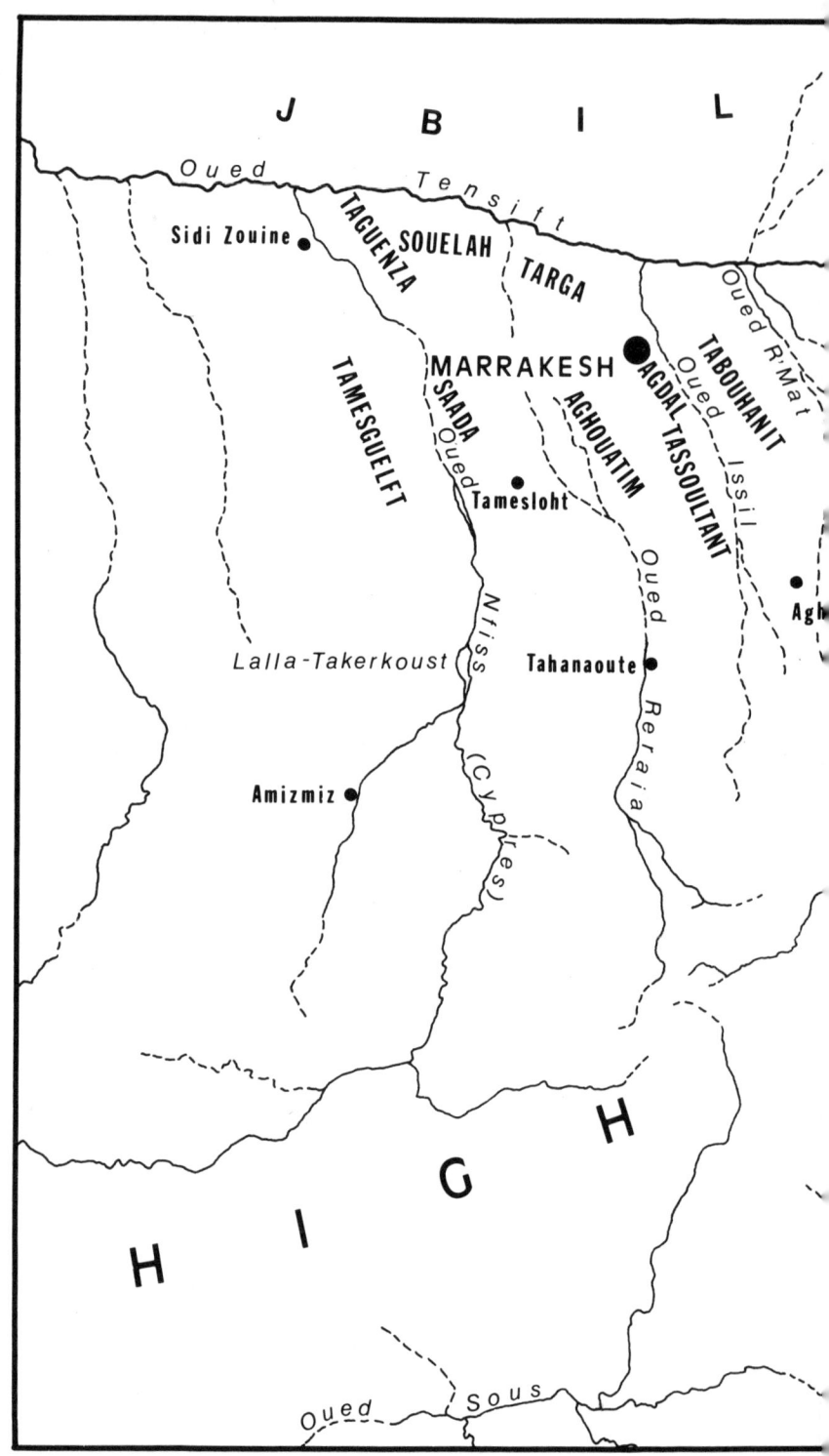

Map C: The Haouz of Marrakesh.

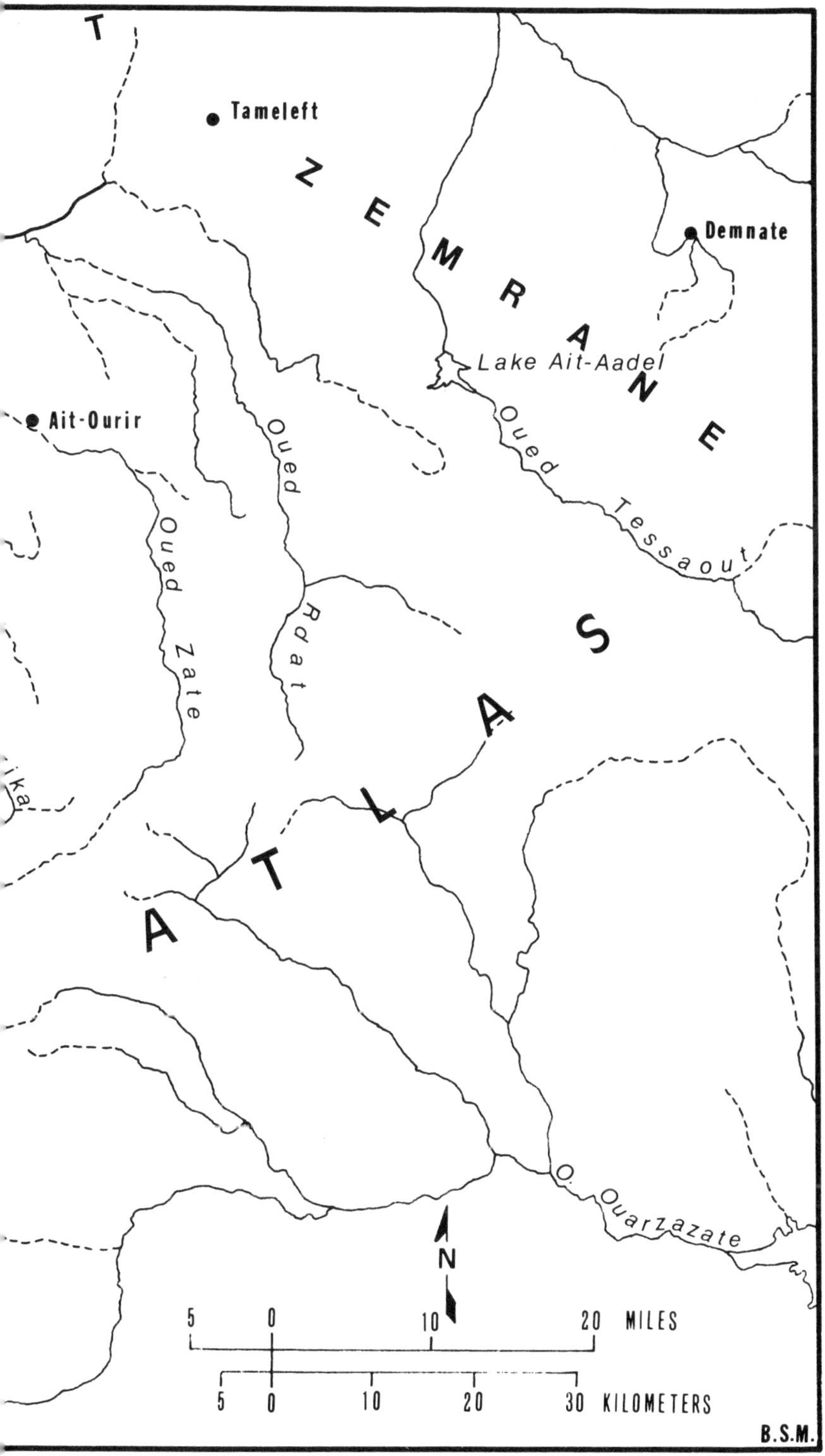

Tameleft
Demnate
Ait-Ourir
Lake Ait-Aadel
T
Z E M R A N E
A T L A S
Oued
Oued Tessaout
Oued Zate
Oued Rdat
O. Ouarzazate
N
5 0 10 20 MILES
5 0 10 20 30 KILOMETERS
B.S.M.

base of the Atlas Mountains, as one decends them from the south, lies the piedmont called the *Dir*. Streams come out of mountain valleys and the Dir, forming alluvial fans called *foums*, which have been intensely irrigated for centuries by tribal groups.[30] The displacement of surface water to the plains in the basins below the foums is more gradual. The broad basins of tributaries to the Oued Tensift have been irrigated more and more intensely over the centuries by networks of transverse *seguias*. These are channels which run from diversion points on the mountain streams to supply irrigation sectors with water, more abundantly in the upper end than in the lower, far end of the sector. Many seguias were built by Atlas tribes, which established usage through custom and the exercise of traditional justice.[31] Others, the grand seguias, were built at various times by corvée labor under the Makhzen or caids. Finally, below the basins of the Tensift tributaries lies the lower plain of the Oued Tensift itself. Here the source of water is more likely to be wells and *khettara* — manmade springs which tap groundwater and the subsurface runoff of seguia irrigation from the Tensift tributary basins.

Differences in agriculture in the Haouz stem from altitude and types of terrain, and most importantly, from the availability of water. The mountain valleys support almond trees and cereal cultivation, while the Dir serves mainly as grazing land. In the foums and the basins, irrigation makes possible the cultivation not only of cereals, but also of olive trees, oranges and other fruit and nut trees, as well as vegetables. Variations from tributary basin to basin in total water flow and ratio of maximum (winter-spring) to minimum (summer) flows affect the crops which can be raised, and thus, the agricultural value of land in the different river basins.

The lands of the Haouz are occupied largely by tribespeople; some land is also held by zaouias. These Islamic brotherhood lodges organized around local 'saints' obtain special political significance due to their abilities to arbitrate conflict, provide sanctuary, and otherwise intercede in secular political and economic affairs. Zaouias situated in the interstices of territories occupied by competing tribes are especially likely to play this role.

The form of tribal social organization itself provides a more fundamental basis that is called into play for resolution of conflict within any social unit to which all members trace a common ancestor. Peoples of rural Morocco participate in social life on the basis of their kinship relations along segmented patrilineal dimensions. In this arrangement, each individual exists within a series of ever-widening concentric circles of 'descent', the initial ones based on concrete and easily traceable kinship groups, the more remote ones involving real or putative ancestors whose importance for group solidarity does not hinge on strictly traceable genealogy. In sedentary groups like most of those in the Haouz, the more remote concentric circles typically also mark ever-widening circles of geographic territory and economic action — a family economy, common village lands, some division of craft labor between villages, tribal *fractions* on different irrigation sectors of a seguia, tribes on different seguias of a river, and the like.

The concentric circles of kinship extending outward from the individual take on a different character when viewed 'from the top down'. From this perspective a tribe appears as a series of segmented branches which theoretically counterbalance each other at each level by containing the potential to form into solidary groups should the occasion arise.[12] Thus, conflict between individuals nested in counterbalanced segments of the tribe (for example, members of different extended families in the same lineage, or different lineages in the same commune or *fraction*) is typically resolved by customary arbitration between the two solidary groups themselves. Individuals' identities are thus very much bound up in their positions in tribal groups, at the same time that the wider circles of tribal solidarity represent increasingly broad political interests (rather than any significant genealogical descent group). At least in theory, the counterbalanced nature of tribal segments permits a low-key, often ad hoc administration of disputes, except in the case of external threat.[33]

Description of the Haouz people in terms of a segmented patrilineal form of tribalism is most appropriate to the pre-colonial era, when the French had neither extended their administration into the nested levels of tribes (ultimately to the commune level), nor tried to substitute a modern 'legal-rational' framework for tribal arbitration and customary justice. And even in the pre-colonial era, it must be recognized that tribes existed in relation to the Makhzen and, sometimes, grand caids, who tried to treat territories as patrimonial prebends, as sources of tribute. Moreover, the theoretical model of segmented lineages should not obscure different concrete histories of tribal groups which came to occupy the Haouz, often in ways directly affected by the wider movements of events. The present life of the Haouz proceeds from the heterogeneous histories of Berbers, of Arab invaders, and groups awarded land by the Makhzen for one political purpose or another. Several concrete examples may indicate the range of these histories.

Numerous Berber tribes, including the Ourika, the Mesfioua, the Goundafa, and the Sektana, had practiced transhumance ranging across the Haouz and up into the High Atlas, beginning before Marrakesh itself was founded in the latter part of the eleventh century. They gradually moved into more sedentary patterns with the increasing settlement of Arab tribes throughout the sixteenth century. Some, like the Ourika, developed a sedentary tribal economic interdependence based on the holding of lands at different altitudes and of varying irrigation potentials. Different tribal members could thus specialize in the most suitable production activities and at the same time enhance the self-sufficiency of the tribe as a whole. Most Berber groups, however, did not control land down into the Haouz plain. The Dir and mountain valleys provided a region of refuge in the face of Arab conquest. Among Berber tribes of the Haouz, the Mesfioua alone were able to hold land in the plain itself up until modern times. Among tribes of the plain, the Mesfioua remained a dissident group: it was the only one effectively to resist producing a caid recognized as the Makhzen's effective power in the tribe's territory.

Beginning in the sixteenth century various Arab tribes, such as the Rehamna from just north of the Senegal River, invaded the plains around Marrakesh. They had been recruited as part of the *jihad* (holy war) against Spanish and Portuguese Christians. Arab victory in the war marked the founding of the Saadian dynasty. Presumably the victorious tribes were due some of the spoils. But the Rehamna did not simply receive a grant of land and settle into a sedentary way of life. Nor did they serve as a guich tribe, providing military service to the sultan in return for tax exempt status and a grant of lands. Instead, they held to their pastoral and nomadic way of life, coursing over the vast territory between Marrakesh and Safi, ninety miles west on the Atlantic coast. They combined the three intertwined vocations of camel raising, organizing transport convoys, and pillaging convoys! They remained a dissident tribe which operated independently of the Makhzen.

Other tribes came to the Haouz as deportées. The sequences are diverse and complicated. One group, the Ait Imour, had once served as a guich tribe, which in turn had rebelled against the Makhzen. After a round of dispersal, regrouping, and rebellion, in 1845 the Ait Imour were assigned Makhzen land in the Haouz 'in compensation' for their own lands which had previously been confiscated. The Makhzen's 'compensation' really seems to have been motivated by its own interests in displacing another group that was causing it trouble, and buffering Marrakesh from tribes which held land on the other side of the granted land. The Ait Imour became, in effect, sharecroppers on Makhzen land.

Another tribe, the Oudaya, was a true guich tribe which received Haouz lands from the Makhzen in compensation for long periods of service in military construction of kasbas and defense of frontiers.

The fate of another tribe was bound up in its dealings with the French. The Oulad Sidi Cheik were part of the Resistance movement against the French in Algeria during the nineteenth century. They came to Morocco after having been dispersed by the French in 1870. The Makhzen allowed them to settle on land in the Haouz, where they became a catchall tribe which took in numerous immigrants and fugitives. In the Haouz, the pre-colonial French managed to use them as intermediaries in real estate transactions.

These brief sketches show the diverse origins and conditions of existence of pre-Protectorate tribes in the Haouz. After the Protectorate was established in 1912, the French made continuing efforts to subdue all tribal groups, and to extend the state's administrative apparatus by appointing a caid to rule over each tribe. In some ways, this was an extension of the position of caid as it had developed in the pre-Protectorate Makhzen, when the Makhzen-appointed caid (or pasha in some cities) served as military governor and received the right to collect tribute in his territories. Usually, the Makhzen had tried to fragment tribes by appointing competing caids for different tribal fractions.

But in the pre-Protectorate period, there were also caids who ruled beyond the effective political boundaries of the Makhzen. Sometimes these were true tribal chiefs; the Makhzen might try to affirm such caids as allies, but it could not claim them as clients of its administration.

In certain cases chiefs were able to consolidate tribal and military advantages and establish themselves as autocratic rulers who subjugated additional territories and tribes. The most famous of these quasi-feudal lords were the 'grand caids' of the Atlas, the heads of three tribes — the M'Tougua, the Goundafa, and, most powerful, the Glaoua. Toward the end of the nineteenth century, the grand caids of these tribes capitalized on their tribes' control of Atlas mountain passes and a limited number of modern weapons to consolidate sizable lands around Marrakesh. With this de facto legitimacy, they were able to receive recognition and sometimes office within the Makhzen itself. They were able to exact vastly increased tribute from subjugated tribes, and though their own tribute to the Makhzen grew in turn, still the grand caids were able to live sumptuously and to play key roles in the political, military, and diplomatic life of the Haouz, and the whole of Morocco as well. Indeed, it is sometimes suggested that the grand caids prospered before the Protectorate because they received French support, and it is clear that they sometimes entered into common cause with the French. Others have argued that external threats to the Berber 'republics' opened up an opportunity for the grand caids by promoting the defensive mobilization of tribes under supposedly temporary war chiefs who were then able to establish themselves as autocrats. In any event, by 1907 the grand caids held as fiefs the vast majority of tribal territory in the Haouz. The rivalries between them ended with the ascendency of Madani el-Glaoui and his younger brother Thami el-Glaoui, who became allied with the French with the coming of the Protectorate in 1912. But even if another of the grand caids had prevailed, the result probably would have been the same: the grand caids upset the delicate balance of tribal segmented lineages, at the same time that they weakened the Makhzen by consolidating forces which stood outside it.

European capitalism was to exploit the power vacuums and intrigues which stemmed from the multiple and crosscutting institutions of power in Morocco — tribe, caid, zaouia, and Makhzen. But in more ways than one, the character of colonial capitalism itself was shaped by the climate, social relations of production, competing channels of expropriation, and culture of Morocco. The Haouz of Marrakesh is a region where the penetration of capitalism into an alien social setting can be charted as the interplay of these diverse forces.

John R. Hall

Chapter 1

The Penetration of Capitalism into the Haouz of Marrakesh

At the beginning of the nineteenth century, the Haouz, like the rest of Morocco, was almost totally indifferent to and little affected by the industrial, social, and political revolution that was having considerable social impact on the northern shore of the Mediterranean. Morocco was a durable and relatively coherent society, justifying its isolationism on the basis of the particular character of its religion.

One century later European capitalism had invaded Morocco; the country was no longer either isolated or in control of its own destiny. First, European capitalists confiscated the merchant economy of the caids and the Makhzen; next they dominated the monetary and paper currency markets; and finally they demanded the right to develop autonomously the natural resources of the country.

The best source concerning this entire process during the period preceding the establishment of the Protectorate in 1912 is the major work of Jean-Louis Miège.[1] This is an almost inexhaustible source of information and an excellent guide for researchers seeking documentation on the events of this period. Our objective, necessarily limited in scope, is to examine the situation in which capitalism developed in the Haouz. Thus we will focus on characteristic events that occurred in the region centered on Marrakesh.

1 Weakness of the Merchant and Manufacturing Economy in the Pre-colonial Haouz

Throughout the first three-quarters of the nineteenth century, commerce and technology in the Haouz retained a pronounced 'medieval' character. It might even be said that Marrakesh had experienced an actual decline compared to the opulence of the earlier Saadien period (1554–1569), perhaps due to the subsequent removal of the seat of the *Makhzen* (the traditional Moroccan governmental administration) from Marrakesh to Meknes and then Fez. The efforts of sovereigns interested in the introduction of more efficient production systems often failed because of the inability of the social structure to adjust to imported technology. For this reason, by the close of the nineteenth century European politicians had at hand a ready argument that the development of capitalism in the country could not proceed without colonial political domination. Briefly, let us consider the conditions that prevailed in the Haouz of pre-Protectorate days.

A   Scarcity of Mechanical Power
On the eve of the twentieth century, production depended on human labor, aided by animal power. Hydraulic power was confined to the operation of the caidal and Makhzen-owned grain mills located on the large *seguias* (irrigation canals) of the state. Energy produced by windmills and the steam engine was unknown.

Human and animal portage were by far the primary means of transportation. Carts and sleds were seldom used due to the absence of adequate routes. Perhaps a more important reason for the failure to use more efficient methods was the infrequency of long-distance trade. Prior to 1914, the caravans transporting pouches of oil, sacks of grain and bales of wool relied on camels on the plains and mules in the mountains, accompanied by armed escort in either case. Such portage was inefficient — on an average, one animal unit was needed for each 100 kilograms transported. It was also slow, and it required several men per ton of cargo in case of trouble.

THE PENETRATION OF CAPITALISM INTO MARRAKESH 43

Grain milling was carried out in a large part using the conventional double-stoned hand mill. Only a few caids, notables, and certain high officials of the Makhzen owned hydraulic mills located on the Tassoultant, Bashia, and Rha seguias.[2] There were less than ten animal-powered mills in Marrakesh.

The first power-driven flour mill, owned by the Mannesmann Company, was installed at My Yazid. This mill was well equipped for the large-scale production of semolina and flour. It was powered by a producer-gas engine. A pasta factory was also attempted, but it had to stop production both because of the unstable supplies of cereals and because of the general unrest which prevailed at harvest time.

Until 1914 human labor was the predominant method used to extract olive oil, though occasionally animal power was used in the few caidal mills. In the Haouz prior to 1912 there were nearly one million olive trees, which produced 25,000 tons of olives. A potential of approximately 5,000 tons of olive oil could have been extracted from this yield, but production by traditional methods resulted in only about 3,500 tons. Food consumption for the city of Marrakesh alone utilized 1,000 tons. Soap manufacturing required an additional 200 tons. As pointed out by Lagnel, a successful French businessman attempting to expand his business into Morocco, 'despite its large production of olives, the region of Marrakesh has no surplus for export. There is room for modern factories which could extract ten percent more oil.'

The sovereigns who were most preoccupied with the idea of progress initiated cautious attempts for technological change. These attempts deserve notice because they demonstrate one of the characteristics of the caidal Makhzen with regard to production; its nature is characterized more by acquisitiveness than by creativity. In the effort to utilize techniques from elsewhere, a fetishistic quest for machines often prevailed over the search for technology appropriate to an increase of production based on local conditions.

In 1851, Sidi Mohammed was *khalifa* (lieutenant) in Marrakesh of his father Moulay Ab der-Rahmane (Sultan of Morocco, 1822-1859). An inquisitive man attracted to science, Sidi Mohammed was concerned both with the introduction of new technology and with the opening of the Haouz to modernization. He ordered from Europe the first new plows to replace the swing-plows, as well as a new thresher pulled by four horses.[3] He even considered building a textile factory.

Amédée de Roscoat, who went before the sovereign to demonstrate the thresher's usefulness, added in a report concerning the proposed textile factory, 'the prince would have provided for the construction, furnished the wool, and *paid for the workers' food*'.[4] This plan would have perpetuated the caidal system, not to mention serfdom. This instance shows that Sidi Mohammed, 'the most advanced man of the country',[5] along with his advisor who had other vested interests, was little aware of the relationship between technology and social relations. Miège concludes, 'The measures of Sidi Mohammed entailed no reforms; they left everything of the former social situation untouched and were confined to the implementation, within the Moroccan milieu, of a few economic ventures of the European type.'[6] This is a somewhat harsh judgement of the man who first repaired the entire irrigation system of the Haouz and reestablished an agricultural prosperity that had disappeared long before. The incidents of the thresher and proposed textile factory and sugar mill (discussed below) should be seen as experiments, from which, moreover, lessons were quickly drawn.

B Barriers to Innovation

Cane sugar, silk and cotton had not been produced in the Haouz for a long time prior to the second half of the nineteenth century. Likewise the technique of producing gunpowder from saltpeter — for which Marrakesh had established a reputation in the sixteenth and seventeenth centuries — was later only utilized by a few dissident tribes cut off from foreign import sources.

As a part of his agricultural modernization program, Sidi Mohammed had as his first concern the reestablishment of sugar cane production. Sugar consumption had increased considerably with the increasing consumption of tea, which had spread to the entire urban elite. The sovereign undertook efforts of sugar cane production first in the Tassoultant irrigation sector, and then in other areas. The Makhzen was sufficiently impressed with the results to decide to install a sugar cane refinery. Schlumberger observed:

> They continue to work on setting up the refinery, but one of
> the engineers indicated that it was impossible to repair
> certain crucial pieces of equipment and that they would have
> to be shipped to Europe for repair, which would delay the

operation by three months. So the Sultan will have to give up all hope of seeing his processing plant in operation before he leaves Marrakesh.[7]

The refinery never produced a single grain of sugar!

In the opinion of Ibn Zidan, the failure of this attempt can be attributed to the negligence of Makhzen officials. From a broader perspective, Miège points to the social, economic and political problems encountered by such an advanced project in relation to the social structure of the Haouz in the middle of the nineteenth century:

> No doubt the Makhzen was responsible in part for these failures. There were several reasons — poorly conceived projects, lack of experience, and a tendency to try passing whims or fads without commitment to pursue them. Certain Europeans were another source of the problems; they were only concerned about the profits to be gained by this program... Vested interests played an important role in these failures.[8]

The same disappointing setbacks characterized both the efforts to improve cotton cultivation, which had to compete with imported cotton goods, and the attempts to resume production of gunpowder in the *Agdal* (royal park) somewhat later.

The experiments of Lagnel, which occurred twenty years afterwards, are particularly revealing. In 1891, after a visit to Marrakesh, he reported the low yield of traditional oil presses and the difficulty of organizing a large number of small olive oil producers to assure deliveries of a uniform quality. He succeeded in convincing the Makhzen to establish an oil refinery equipped with a producer-gas engine. For two years the processing plant experienced considerable operating difficulties because of inadequate supplies of both olives and wood for fuel. Lagnel finally gave up because of the incompetence of officials with whom he had to deal. Machines from Lagnel's plant were then sold by the government to Lhaj Meslohi, the largest producer of olives. Lagnel went into business with him, and then constructed a mechanized animal-powered olive oil press at Tamesloht. This machine, pompously referred to as a 'refinery', operated for two seasons, the winter of 1891 and the winter of 1892. Despite its success (or perhaps because of it), the operation was closed the following year due to widespread opposition to the innovation.[9] Lagnel was so effective that the more politically powerful, but inefficient producers of olive oil would not permit him to continue. This incident is significant because it involved only a minor technical improvement which could easily be employed in traditional oil presses. The real reasons for opposition were evidently quite different from technological backwardness; they arose from several sources — the political fight against economic supremacy by the Tamesloht *zaouia* (Muslim brotherhood lodge); condemnation of foreign penetration; the fear of losing taxable and marketable goods from the established channels of caidal extortion, and the loss of the new production from Makhzen taxation. The traditional politicians wanted to keep control of any increased production. Good reasons and bad reasons were fused into a single attitude — the condemnation of the ostentatious character of innovation.

The failure of this attempt, which must have been significant at the time since it is still alive in the memory of the Haouz people, convinced traditional powerholders of the effectiveness of their position. Those segments tempted by mercantilism, who could not yet seriously be called capitalists, realized from this incident that it was necessary to appeal even more strongly to foreign powers for their protection to insure that business and profits would be open to them.

2 Seizure of Domestic and Foreign Trade

The opening of Morocco to international commerce in the middle of the nineteenth century occurred only after many false starts and difficult negotiations. The fundamental position of the Makhzen at the beginning of the nineteenth century was that 'exports impoverish the State'[10] while strengthening the hand of foreign buyers; the practice of exporting merchandise was therefore limited to the minimum required to survive years of scarcity or to acquire arms and gunpowder.

In the face of impatient and aggressive speculation by European merchants, the Makhzen, which controlled trade and any large-scale economic opportunities, responded with heavy-handedness, rigidity, extreme caution, suspicion, and a stance of interference toward trade. Until 1860, prior to the double military defeat at Isly and Tetouan, the Makhzen was able to maintain its distance from the competition of foreign powers. Despite cautious efforts like those of Sidi Mohammed, isolationism, the status quo, and a certain nervousness were the rule in matters of foreign commerce. Politicians of the time exhibited shrewd and remarkable intuition and rational fears that Morocco would lose its independence through necessarily unequal exchanges with foreign countries. No doubt isolationism or, alternatively, restricted and controlled foreign trade, would have been politically wise at the time when the population and its needs were still minimal, if it had been accompanied by efforts at economic development within a favorable political and ideological climate. However, there were probably few leaders who could have thus prevailed over the situation of civil war to coalesce divergent forces toward development of Morocco's competitive economic position.

As a result of this weakness and fragmentation of the country's social structure in the face of foreign penetration, European commercial houses came to dominate trade.

A   Penetration of Moroccan Commerce and Protection of Foreign Trade

By 1840 the bulk of foreign trade was a state monopoly leased to the highest bidder, or granted in payment of debts or for services rendered. In particular, the exportation of wool, oil, animal skins, wax, saltpeter, sulfur, lead, and zinc were totally controlled by the Makhzen. Foreign trading of grain, cattle, and henna could be undertaken only with special authorization and by payment of unpredictable customs taxes that differed from port to port. Sometimes trade privileges were granted on a temporary basis. Foreign imports of tea, sugar, coffee, tobacco and cochineal were state monopolies, but this commerce certainly could not be considered nationalized by modern standards. In fact, commercial activities strictly defined — that is, the purchasing, packing and transporting of goods to ports of embarkation — were carried out by private individuals who had acquired temporary and revokable monopoly trade rights. Miège explains that this monopolization of commerce by the Makhzen rapidly filled the coffers of the state, but largely stifled commercial activity itself.[11] The mostly urban, privileged businessmen belonged to families of notables, or were operatives of the Makhzen who were temporarily out of political office. In Marrakesh the notables included Ghanjaoui, Touggani, Mansouri, and also some Jewish families such as the Corcos, Aferiat, and so on.

Little by little, the foreign commercial companies that had established agencies in the ports, especially Essaouira (then called Mogador), Safi, and El-Jadida, gradually acquired knowledge of the people, goods and culture of Morocco. Foreign demand rapidly exceeded the supply capabilities of the main Moroccan buyers who operated under Makhzen trade licenses. Political unrest, ethnic, or better, caidal, factionalism, the lack of currency, and fiscal exactions induced foreign businessmen to extend their purchasing networks by associating with Moroccans to whom they advanced working capital. At the beginning they entrusted Moroccan front men with small sums of money ranging from 50 to 400 duros so they could purchase cereals, olive oil, wool, skins, chick peas, etc.[12] The foreign businessmen then selected intermediaries at a higher level and progressively created alongside the trade administered by the Makhzen a private network that was strongly linked to foreign companies. Within twenty years, from 1880 to 1900, the bulk of trade passed into the hands of foreign businessmen.

The urban merchants who belonged to the nascent bourgeoisie of Marrakesh could not compete with these limited partnerships. It was in their own best interests to join with them and take on the role of intermediaries. Only the caids were somewhat able to seal off their territories from commerce by means of authoritarian decrees, threats and actual expulsion of merchants. El-Glaoui (caid of the Glaoua) and Goundafi (caid of the Goundafa) claimed for themselves the absolute monopoly of trade in almonds, oil, etc., in their fiefdoms.

At the beginning of the twentieth century, when the power of the grand caids was at its peak, competition was strong between merchant companies and the feudal lords. There are documents which show how Moroccan intermediaries, obtained commodities for foreign merchant companies, receiving as a result commissions based on a percentage of the value of the transaction.

In order to facilitate the activities of their intermediaries, commercial agents would ask their consulates to place Moroccan associates[13] on their list for protection and to defend them, not from the Makhzen as such, but from the interference of Makhzen functionaries:

The consular agent Lennox, in sending me the list of the proposed people requiring protection, pointed out that many among those for whom J.H. Fernau and Co. requested certificates have already been employed by Fernau and Andrews of Safi and Marrakesh, and that Fernau and Company have maintained that money can be entrusted to them for the purchasing of goods in the country.[14]

Undoubtedly, the progressive forfeiture to European trading houses of regional, and then local trade formerly controlled by the caids forced the caids to support the efforts of the sovereigns and various pretenders who expressed an interest in making the country more independent. Consequently, it seems inaccurate to view capitalist penetration as having its origins in purely economic and strictly commercial phenomena. To the contrary, colonial economic domination did not progress without a judicial and social adjustment — an extension of the capitalist social and legal arrangements that became progressively more rooted in Moroccan society.

In order to succeed, foreign businessmen had to obtain assurance of immunity, not only for themselves, but for their places of business, for the merchandise they purchased, and for their intermediaries. Since in Morocco power and wealth were based on belonging to a strong tribal lineage or on caidal service to the Makhzen, foreign businessmen could only obtain the needed assurances from their own government. Sociologically, it was the unavoidable conflict between the system of caidal spoils and the system of capitalist spoils that brought about foreign protection and the establishment of a foreign-dominated institutional enclave.[15]

The foreign merchants only preceded by a short time the consular officials and, in some cases, they themselves filled that role. A study of the establishment of German firms in Marrakesh demonstrates how the progressive European domination of commercial networks was closely followed by the establishment of foreign consulates in Morocco.[16] Weiss and Maur, a German firm founded in 1881 in Mogador, imported German textiles and exported skins, wax, dates, almonds and olive oil. The firm purchased grapes in the Haouz and even considered wine production. Maur established himself in Marrakesh in 1882 in order to open up another branch for the firm. He managed this branch until Weiss left Morocco in 1887, at which time he took over the entire business. In 1889 he went into partnership with some Moroccans on property in the Haouz which was to be farmed. In 1892 he was appointed the vice-consul of Germany in Mogador. He remained in office until 1914. In 1912 he was nominated by Mannesmann, a German consortium, to be its principal agent in the south of Morocco.

Weiss and Maur had dissolved their firm in 1906. The buildings and the networks of clientele in Marrakesh had already been taken over by Marx and Company in 1894. Within a relatively short period of time, the Marx firm became one of the most important German companies in Morocco, and by far the largest foreign firm in Marrakesh. The existence of such a large German firm in Marrakesh justified the presence of the German government to handle the affairs of its resident citizens. When German firms began to compete among themselves, it was no longer appropriate for them to perform consular duties. For a time, the German firms' interests were defended by members of the Moroccan royal family appointed by the sovereign. Occasionally Germans would appoint representatives of a third nationality to stand for their interests, and finally a professional consular arrangement was established. This arrangement was to prevent the consolidation of consular and commercial advantages in the hands of either Marx and Company, or any other German firm, for two large German companies were already keenly interested in the Moroccan South: Krupp and the Mannesmann Consortium. It would have been interesting to know the reactions of the indigenous bourgeois merchants of Marrakesh to the separation, as shown by the Germans, between business and politics, for it was a novel approach to Moroccan affairs.

The English colony followed a different pattern. It first organized itself around missionary and philanthropic activity. For example, an orphanage and a boarding school for young girls were opened. Then, in order to feed this colony, which was as much Moroccan as English in its composition, the missionaries felt the need to assure themselves of stable agricultural production protected against political insecurity. This is why they needed an established and fully accepted representative. The British consulate selected Boubker Rhanjaoui. He was an extraordinary character who owned an entire neighborhood of Marrakesh, a quarter complete with police and tax apparatus — a veritable state within a state. His wealth permitted every eccentricity.

In other respects, the provision of security for the English represented an effective arrangement for both parties involved; in these times of political uncertainty, it protected the property of large Moroccan landlords from the government confiscation that normally took place when they fell into disfavor.

But ultimately English interests never took on major importance in Morocco because France and England divided Morocco and Egypt as spheres of influence.

France focused at a very early date on purely political concerns at the highest levels; in the Marrakesh region, of course it focused on the family of el-Glaoui. Less known is the role played by the French Compagnie Marocaine and particularly its agent Lassallas in exploring the stance of the Glaoui toward French protection. A letter dated 24 April, 1904 from Mr Brun, general manager for the Compagnie Marocaine, to its headquarters in Fez illustrates how this arrangement developed.

> The caid Madani el-Glaoui, who is one of the wealthiest landowners in Morocco and who possesses immense riches, while passing through Fez during our stay in that city, asked us to loan him the sum of 35,000 francs (12,000 DH [Moroccan dirhams] in 1974). Because of the importance of commercial transactions that might result from a relationship with this distinguished Moroccan if we honored his loan request, we advanced him the above mentioned sum at the annual interest rate of eight percent. The monetary arrangements were described in a contract according to the terms of which the caid agreed to send to us goods in sufficient quantity to reimburse us before the end of the year. These goods will be sold by the company intermediary and the net profit thus obtained, after deductions for sales commissions, will be credited to the caid's account after the repayment of our loan has been completed. This same contract precludes the sale or purchase of goods by the caid other than through our intermediary for a period of three years.

The contract further provided that the company would receive a ten percent commission on exchanges completed. In addition, the intermediary between the company and el-Glaoui would receive a two percent commission. The intermediary was also responsible for arranging for the transport of the goods. The documents preserved by the company illustrate the calculated risks that the French consulate, in this case Mr Maigret in Marrakesh, permitted various businessmen to take.

There apparently was occasional ambiguity between the political interests of the French government and the interests of French companies. For example, a correspondent from the Tangier agency of the Compagnie Marocaine took information from a letter from Lassallas in Marrakesh, and sent it to the general management in Paris:

> We hear, although the rumors have not been officially confirmed as yet, that the caid Madani el-Glaoui may have recently become a French protégé... Last April we were informed by Mr Lassallas of the desire expressed by el-Glaoui to secure French protection. But the caid wanted to avoid at all cost having the consulate learn of his intentions. Under these circumstances we have been unable to reconcile rules concerning such matters. It is for that reason that we have not pushed the matter. But since the caid is still indebted to us for significant sums of money, and because the trade agreements he has entered into with us have remained, to date, a dead letter, we would like to know if he is in fact being protected by us. If so, he would come under French jurisdiction and we would have a certain hold over him should the question arise.

The general management of the company replied with a letter dated 15 February, 1907:

> Your message shows us that el-Glaoui is not a French protégé. From the information we have, there is no way of knowing whether negotiations had already been initiated in order for him to obtain protection and whether or not our Marrakesh agency was well-founded in suspecting that Mr Vaffier had been acting for that purpose. Should the circumstances permit we would be obliged if you would

sound out the consulate as to the probable reception that would be given to an official request by el-Glaoui. Should you be led to hope for a favorable response, we shall expect Mr Lassallas, before pressing the matter any further, to confirm to us the desire previously expressed by the caid. It should be noted that all steps and investigations in this matter, attempted by either the consulate or the consul of Mogador, should be performed with the greatest secrecy. This is the absolute wish expressed by the caid el-Glaoui. He would find himself in an awkward position with respect to the Makhzen should word about the negotiations be spread before the matter is concluded. Furthermore, he would be angry with the Compagnie Marocaine, which seeks the agreement as well as the caid's good graces.

B   Trade Prior to 1912 and During the First Years of the Protectorate
From the enormous mass of documents consisting of monthly reports of the consulates and military missions, it is possible to obtain an approximate idea, albeit qualitative and perhaps subjective, of the nature and importance of trade prior to and immediately after the beginning of the Protectorate in 1912. In order to study the subject in depth it would be necessary to inspect trading company archives. Such a detailed examination is not the purpose of this study. However, it is necessary to understand the origin and destination of agricultural goods. After reviewing principal exports and imports we will analyze the development of colonial commercial agriculture.

It is possible to provide the trade balance for the period 1911 to 1917 for Mogador, which was the port through which the bulk of the Haouz trade was handled (see Table 1.1). The information in Table 1.2 indicates the overall tendency and the effect of World War I on foreign trade imbalances.

These tables indicate that a relatively stable prewar period was followed by a strong upturn in exports during the initial years of the conflict, resulting from the increased demands of the French during World War I. A third period, characterized by a sharp reversal of the trade balance, probably resulted from the beginning of a process of mechanization in the Haouz.

In 1913, the first year for which anything close to adequate figures are available, the nature of the products traded are ranked in Table 1.3

Table 1.1: *Trade Balance for Mogador (Essaouira), 1911–1917*

Years	Imports		Exports	
	Tons	Francs	Tons	Francs
1911	10	8,117	7	8,872
1912	13	12,087	10	7,814
1913	40	16,495	5	8,454
1914	18	11,268	2	4,598
1915	14	13,465	3	6,521
1916	13	16,251	16	8,253
1917	11	19,388	16	7,436

Source: Bulletin de l'Afrique Française (corresponding years).

Table 1.2: *Trade Balances (value per ton)*

Years	Imports		Exports		Ratio of imports to exports
	in current francs	% of 1911 imports	in current francs	% of 1911 exports	
1911	789	100	1,200	100	.66
1912	917	116	800	67	1.15
1913	425	54	1,800	150	.24
1914	615	79	2,000	164	.31
1915	985	104	1,940	133	.51
1916	1,240	118	516	29	2.40
1917	1,850	147	460	24	4.02

in order of decreasing value. Let us first consider exports, and then turn our attention to imports.

Table 1.3: *Export and Import Products, 1913 (by percent of value)*

Exports		Imports	
Hemp	29.0	Sugar	43.7
Dried skins	24.5	Cotton fabric	12.5
Cumin	14.6	Candles	11.7
Almonds	13.2	Tea	10.1
Wool	9.8	Silks	6.3
Animal by-products	2.1	Cloth	3.9
Honey, wax	.8	Construction materials	3.1
Gum	.7	Coffee and spices	2.5
Miscellaneous	5.3	Miscellaneous	6.2
TOTAL	100.0		100.0

Hemp was cultivated on the lands of the Mesfioua, the Ourika and the Rhirhaia tribes, in the gorges of the *Oued* (river) Nfis and on the plain, on the banks of the Oued Tensift. Steeping or retting (to soak and loosen the fibers) was performed in small earthen basins along the rivers. Because hemp was manually stripped by means of a wooden tool, very low yields resulted. The coarse and broken fibers of hemp were brought to Marrakesh for braiding. During World War I, the demand was strong and the exports rose from 100 tons in 1913 to 500 tons in 1920; this was accomplished despite an increase in hemp production in two areas of France, i.e., the Sèvres and coastal Charente regions.

The second most important export, *dried skins*, came mainly from goats and sheep and secondarily from cattle. With the establishment of regular commerce between Marrakesh and Mogador, the region around Marrakesh supplemented the supply of skins from the hinterlands of Mogador. The salted skins, lightly treated with arsenic, were shipped mainly to Germany, and also to England and France, which in turn re-exported them to the United States. The demand dipped when the American public became more interested in box calf. Prior to this period, the Haouz imported cattle skins from Argentina; they were used for shoes, saddles, and in harness making. This tendency was reversed after 1914 due to the cessation of intertribal and caidal conflicts and the higher European demand during the war. For a time, the Haouz even exported large numbers of camel and hoofed animal skins.

At the beginning of the century, *cumin* was widely used for the distillation of kummel and as an aromatic. It was in great demand in central and northern Europe at the time when shipments from Asia Minor began to decrease. France served as the intermediary for exports of the spice to Tunisia, Egypt by way of England, Spain and the United States. Cumin production increased markedly in the Haouz between 1906 and 1918.

Almonds had long been a German export monopoly. This began to change with the arrival of two new companies on the scene, Braunschwig and the Compagnie Marocaine. Hamburg had been the primary export center for sweet almonds from Morocco, which were resold to Scandinavia, central Europe, and the United States. These almonds were mainly used in the production of *dragées* (sugar-coated almonds). The English purchased the small almonds of the Atlas valleys, which had a high proportion of bitters (around 20%); these were used in pastries, soaps, and perfumes. After 1914 the entire market passed into the hands of the Compagnie Marocaine, since all the other companies had been eliminated from the market because of the war.

The exportation of *wool* from Morocco was originally a monopoly of Manchester, England. Fleece was sold raw and was frequently criticized for inadequate preparation.

In addition, the following miscellaneous export goods can be listed: esparto (coarse grass used for cordage), eggs, henna, red dye made from madder plants, takaout dye, wax (widely sought after in Russia for candles and obtained via Hamburg), ostrich feathers for ornaments that were shipped to London and Paris, and Ouarzazate roses used for perfume.

Imports were led by *sugar*. It was especially widely used in Marrakesh for various beverages made of mint, verbena, absinthe, and citron water. Only much later, around 1925, did tea consumption supplant these beverages among the popular classes. Before the war Germany provided half the sugar, the remainder being supplied by France and Great Britain. Between 1908 and 1912 the Marx firm took over the entire sugar business in Marrakesh by glutting the market with its stocks. This was the period when the Germans were hoping to establish their monopoly strongly in southern Morocco, in order to impose a subsequent partitioning of Morocco in which the entire region of Morocco south of Oum-er-Rbia would fall within their control. However, beginning in 1912 with its own military occupation, France became the main supplier of sugar through Marseilles. According to the 1912-1919 financial economic yearbook, 'During the war France deprived herself of sugar in order to feed Morocco — for her "native policy".'

Cottons had always been an English monopoly. Several types of cottons from England had replaced the indigo-dyed cottons originally produced in the Haouz. Thick cloth, similar to felt, was in great demand for saddlemaking and the *burnoose* (a popular one-piece hooded cloak). Germany was the supplier of this thick cloth, and between 1910 and 1913 German firms increased their inventory to such an extent that Marrakesh was able to make do with the inventory on hand for the entire war. After the war, England, Italy, and France were in stiff competition for the sale of this thick cloth to Morocco.

Silk for scarves and brocades came from Lyon and Milan. The high prices for silk resulted in the resumption of silkworm farming in Aghmat and other regions. But the results were mediocre and costly, and the quality was below average. After the war the efforts to raise silkworms were abandoned.

Green tea from China became the national beverage of Morocco in the first quarter of the twentieth century. This tea was imported into Morocco through Great Britain except during the war when it was imported directly from China to Morocco.

Candles were made from paraffin of English origin. Until 1917 the Fournier firm of Marseilles strongly competed with the English brand by importing candles made of stearine.

Because transportation of construction materials was so costly, strong, durable materials were seldom used in Marrakesh until after the 1920s. This development awaited the building of good roads, and above all, the development of the railroad. Clay for bricks, stone for plaster, and limestone did exist in the Haouz, but neither wood nor other fuels was available in sufficient quantities to allow use of these materials on a large scale. In the brickmaking ovens, dried palms were used for fuel.

The primary products that were exported were of agricultural and animal origin. The quality of those obtained in Marrakesh responded less and less to the needs and requirements of European markets. If colonial businessmen needed a reason to justify extending the networks of exports toward the sources of production, in the problem of maintaining quality control they would have found a good one. However, it seems that foreign businessmen were prompted to contemplate colonizing the land more to assure greater regularity in supplies rather than to guarantee their quality.

3 Attempts at Development of Commercial Agriculture

In 1880 foreigners residing in Marrakesh were not at all interested in agriculture; by 1914, Europeans probably owned more than 4,000 hectares and they cultivated, directly or indirectly, close to 10,000 hectares in the Haouz region. Compared to the maximum foreign-controlled cultivation in the Haouz, which never exceeded 23,000 hectares, the pre-colonial land occupation seems particularly significant. During the colonial era, foreigners controlled up to 31,500 hectares, 11,414 of which fell under the law concerning 'official colonization' (acquisition and sale of land by the Protectorate administration). But of these 11,414 hectares, 3,572, or more than 31 percent, had already been appropriated by 1910. Some 53 percent of the lands ever privately colonized had been acquired before 1912, and an even greater proportion of land was in fact occupied by that date. These figures include two transactions taken in a very administrative context — 2,500 hectares acquired in 1922 by the Compagnie Fermière as a result of the confiscation of the Tassoultant property of the prince Moulay Kbir, and the 2,140 hectares acquired in 1923 by the Compagnie Agricole et Industrielle of Marrakesh in partnership with Thami el-Glaoui by illegally converting to private property *guich* lands (Makhzen lands, the usufruct rights to which were awarded to loyal tribes regularly available for Makhzen military service).

Thus, whatever opinions are held today, to be historically accurate it must be pointed out that the broad orientations toward land holdings had already taken hold well before the establishment of French political power in Marrakesh. When the French armies of Colonel Mangin entered Marrakesh, the capital of the South, the inventory of colonizable land had already been completed, and a considerable portion of that land was already occupied by foreign interests. It only remained to legalize the holdings and provide for the safety of capital investments.

However, as will be shown later, these land acquisitions were made by foreigners, contrary to the will of the Makhzen, of most of its civil servants, and of the population in general. In order to achieve so unpopular a goal, the agents of European business resorted to finding local intermediaries who were powerful enough and rich enough to act effectively on their behalf. On the strength of evidence derived from sources of oral history, from consular reports, and from private correspondence, it can be argued that the zaouias and the caids, past the zenith of their power and by then pushed aside during the frequent power struggles within the Moroccan State, were the most active partners in the process of foreign colonization.

And, as was shown above with regard to trading companies, these Moroccans, once cast aside, were forced to side with the Europeans if they were to avoid the vagaries of fortune and prosecution from whichever equally precarious and unstable regime was in power. They thus benefited from protection of both their lives and their property. On the other hand, indigenous Moroccan businessmen of the period were only weakly capable of asserting themselves in the face of caidal and Makhzen institutions.

It is difficult to obtain objective first-hand information and approximate quantification of emergent and shifting arrangements during the times of foreign agricultural partnerships with Moroccans, the subsequent foreign occupation of the land, and finally its legal acquisition. The sources include materials that are frequently anecdotal and at times quite subjective. It is probable that members of any given foreign diplomatic corps overstated the magnitude of land acquisitions made by competing powers in order to enhance their own struggle to acquire land in Morocco. Legally, authorization for foreigners to own real estate outside Moroccan cities was obtained only with great difficulty.[17] In 1880, Article 11 of the Acts of the Madrid

Conference specified that foreigners had the right to acquire real estate within a ten-kilometer perimeter of each of several coastal cities — subject to the authorization of the Makhzen. This clause did not apply to Marrakesh and, in practice, requests for authorization remained unanswered. Foreigners came to settle all the same, at their own risks and perils, ready to assume the political, social, and financial consequences of conflicts that could erupt over their land acquisitions. If difficulties could not be resolved, the foreigner could become *persona non grata* and the Makhzen had the right to expel him for want of the proper authorization. In the port cities, especially in the north, authorized acquisitions were notable although limited; for France they began in 1767, for Great Britain in 1856, and for Spain in 1861. Prior to these times it appears that no real estate was owned by non-Muslims.

It was the Act of Algeciras (April 7, 1906) that enabled foreigners to acquire land legally for agricultural use outside the ten-kilometer perimeters of coastal cities, and, by law, anywhere in the entire territory. But this legislation only put on a legal basis a large number of conflicts that had emerged from the former situation. If, after the Conference of Algeciras, the process of urban land acquisition by foreigners was greatly liberalized, the Makhzen still continued to exhibit the same reluctance to grant written authorization for foreigners to obtain rural real estate.

Generally speaking, the caids and the local agents of judicial authority (*adouls* and *cadis*) were totally opposed to the settlement of foreigners on agricultural lands of high production potential. Because of treaties it had been forced to sign, on account of its indebtedness and strong pressures brought to bear on it, the central Makhzen had to yield on the matter of principle, but it still gave its officials every opportunity to prevent foreigners from settling. It even took steps against those of its functionaries who were suspected of acting as intermediaries, or who failed to maintain vigilance against foreigners.

When it became apparent that a large proportion of notables were so in debt to the representatives of foreign powers that they regularly provided intermediaries for the foreigners, Moulay Hafid (Sultan of Morocco, 1907–1912) had a letter read in the mosques prohibiting the adouls from approving real estate transactions between Muslims and non-Muslims without express permission of the *pasha* (governor, who in Marrakesh controlled the *kasba* [governmental citadel], the guich tribes, and during the Protectorate, the *Cercle* [subregional government including the Haouz] of Greater Marrakesh). This prohibition encompassed all agreements including partnership contracts that were approved between Europeans and their *censaux* (agricultural intermediaries). The publication of this letter opened up a new diplomatic crisis between the sovereign and the European powers, for the formal attitude of the Makhzen was clearly aimed at discouraging the implementation of Article 60 of the Act of Algeciras. Consequently, various representatives of foreign powers entreated the Makhzen to recognize the Europeans' right to land acquisition, a move that some observers interpreted as an ultimatum!

In diplomatic conversations Moulay Hafid acknowledged the legitimacy of the requests of the powers which had signed the Act of Algeciras. But he let it be known that he could not realistically follow up with any immediate and practical course of action because he feared an uprising of the masses and the opposition of the *Ulama* (Muslim intellectual leaders).

Nevertheless, Europeans came increasingly into *de facto* possession of farms in the Haouz. But the colonization of land did not satisfy their full appetite until the collapse of the Makhzen's power in Marrakesh in October 1911 and the beginning of direct foreign military and political domination on 7 September, 1912. Until the Protectorate, land occupations were precarious, frequently contested, and hardly peaceful, and individual acquisitions by foreigners remained modest, especially in inland areas such as the Haouz. Only those companies financed by large banks or those individuals strongly supported by a consulate were able to establish direct farming operations without Moroccan partners.

Foreign nationals used various means to appropriate land — farming partnerships, joint companies with Moroccan protégés, and acquisitions through Algerian Muslims who acted as middlemen. Ranching partnerships preceded holdings involving annual crop production. Generally, in these partnerships the foreigners were in charge of the finances and marketing of goods as well as the political and legal arrangements of the operation. The Moroccans provided farmland, legal rights to the use of open range land, and physical labor. At first, Europeans and Moroccans shared the net profits equally. Frequently, however, Moroccan partners became financially obligated to foreign partners due to their previous indebtedness and their inability to free themselves from it. We know a good deal about examples of partnerships from consular reports undertaken with an eye to minimizing conflicts between foreigners and Moroccan partners who broke off relationships and disappeared. For example, the case of Jean B., a French businessman who apparently had little support from his consulate, can provide a clear enough idea of the context in which independent foreigners might settle in the Haouz of Marrakesh.

On January 7th and 8th, 1908, B. sent a series of letters and documents to Safi — where the consul Saint-Aulaire resided — and to Tangier. The bulk of this correspondence and the replies to it have been preserved at Tangier. After investigating, the legation recognized B.'s claims. We will let him speak for himself:

> Establishing myself in Marrakesh could only be accomplished after much time, difficulty, and costs. The assassination of Dr Mauchamp [discussed below] — for which the Makhzen has full responsibility — has obliged me to suspend all of my business, to which I had devoted the initial capital of approximately 80,000 francs (about 400,000 DH in 1974); the ransacking of my home, aside from the loss of objects having commercial value, succeeded in destroying all that which I had organized at the cost of great difficulties, and deprived me of all documents, information, and samples... that I had brought with me or been able to accumulate during the past two years. The Makhzen is all the more responsible for these thefts since, after my departure, it did nothing to protect my property in Marrakesh despite the precautions I had taken... In fact, no steps have been taken by the Makhzen and nothing can lessen its responsibility: my home has been plundered; my agricultural partners are nowhere to be found; and the native employee whom I sent to Marrakesh on two occasions [B. had sought refuge in Safi] to my creditors was unable to obtain anything and was given no assistance by the authorities of the city. As a result, since March 19, 1907 [the date of Dr Mauchamp's assassination], I have been unable to utilize the capital I had invested in Marrakesh. It is impossible for me to recover it in order to put it to work elsewhere.

B. provided a long list of individuals indebted to him through agricultural and pastoral partnerships, from whom he hoped to recover his lost capital. To all of this the consul at Mogador, whom B. had asked for assistance, responded on November 4, 1908:

> You realize that the political situation of this region and the prevailing state of anarchy represent almost insurmountable obstacles to such steps. The relationships of this consulate — by correspondence — with ... the pasha of Marrakesh have been, on account of this situation, completely interrupted for the past six months and I do not know whether it would be possible for him to take care of this matter efficiently.

A   Establishment of the Compagnie Marocaine in the Haouz
In contrast to the adventures of private individuals such as Mr B., which almost inevitably ended up in financial fiasco, the large companies, whose agents were strongly supported by their consulates, were able to establish themselves irreversibly in Morocco, even in the face of difficulties. The Compagnie Marocaine provides a remarkable example of this process.

This joint stock company was a creation of Schneider and Company, which became, at the beginning of the twentieth century, a foreign economic power in Morocco nearly the equal of the Banque de Paris et des Pays-Bas (Paribas) and the Société Immobilière. As early as 1899, Paquet and Schneider entrusted Gaston de Caqueray, a naval officer on leave, with the research mission of exploring the trade potential and possibilities for harbor development that Morocco offered. On the basis of his report, the first French joint stock company was established in Morocco on May 30, 1902. This company — the Compagnie Marocaine — acquired the quarters of the Gautsch firm at Tangier and also established itself at Fez at the end of 1902. It was Jean Denaut Lassallas (previously mentioned with regard to the company's dealings with the Glaoui) who was entrusted with the management of branch offices in the south.

The rapid expansion of the company, both into agricultural enterprises and geographically into the south, was the result of an agreement between the company and Paribas. It appears that on May 16, 1904, the then minister of finance of the French Third Republic,

Maurice Rouvier, had arbitrated a dispute that arose between the two firms in Morocco, which became known as the 'Lassallas affair'.[18] Both parties agreed that Paribas would only be involved in banking. The Compagnie Marocaine would be in charge of all other trade and industrial sectors, including the coining of money. To keep the origins of the Compagnie Marocaine's action in perspective, it must be recalled that it was backed by Schneider and Company. An additional impetus was the exaggerated French view of the threat of German competitiveness. The whole affair is revealed in a letter sent on May 17 from Paris to the Tangier agency. This letter stated that it was advisable not to circulate rumors about the agreement between the two companies.

Before 1906, in contrast to Paribas, the Compagnie Marocaine had fairly well adjusted to a legal situation that did not include a French protectorate, mainly because the company was no longer entirely satisfied with its relations with the consulate of France,[19] and because it had its petty and grand ways past the gate of the sultan's palace.[20] The company made the most of the fact that it was not trying to get Morocco into debt in order to keep it under control through subsequent intervention of naval forces. The company declared itself more virtuous in that it claimed to lead an operation for the establishment of a rational enterprise which would benefit Morocco itself.

Paribas was the outsider that had everything to gain by a reversal of existing conditions: thus it would not shun gunboat diplomacy. But within the Compagnie Marocaine, they would treat with a certain arrogance those newcomers who 'did not know the Makhzen and were incapable of working out a proper *modus vivendi* with it. The Compagnie Marocaine was proud of its victorious battle against the inherent difficulties involved in introducing capitalism into the Moroccan milieu. It was proud, too, of overcoming German competition within the areas of mining, public works, civil engineering, and the coining of money — all without support from Paris. The agreement of 1904 with Paribas involved a kind of honorable pretense which legitimized the predominant position of the Compagnie Marocaine. But in 1906 the Compagnie Marocaine was singing a different tune, itself hoping for gunboats and a protectorate. The Lassallas Affair was in no way decisive for this awareness that political domination was necessary for the protection of commerce, but it was a significant episode for the Compagnie Marocaine.

During the summer of 1906, Lassallas had made a series of contacts to try to establish some agricultural operations in the Haouz of Marrakesh. Four months earlier he had had a few successes in the South and in the vicinity of Mogador. In the Haouz, Moulay Lhaj Meslohi, son of the deceased saint of Tamesloht, had made some promises, and he recommended Lassallas to a local zaouia. This zaouia — bel Lahouel, which is in Tekna territory — is a very distant affiliate of an Algerian zaouia. Lassallas was negotiating with the zaouia's representative, Sidi El Mahjoub Ould Mekki, in order to lease or even purchase land. On September 19, after the business was seemingly concluded, he was attacked on his way home by an armed group which turned out to be composed of *mokhazni*, horsemen of the Makhzen in the service of the caid of the Tekna. Injured and detained for three days on a farm on the eastern border of Tekna territory, he was released upon the arrival of the caid. The latter allegedly declared to Lassallas that there had been a misunderstanding and that the ambush had not been intended for him, but had been organized against Mr Nier, a wholesale merchant and German consular agent from Marrakesh, who was known to want to purchase land from the zaouia. From then on the caid treated Lassallas with all due respect. But he did not release him until he had signed a declaration absolving the caid's men from any responsibility for the ambush.

Things are probably much less clear than the account agreed upon by those involved. For Sidi El Majhoub was detained at the same time as Lassallas. After vigorous intervention by the French legation with Moulay Hafid, then khalifa of the sovereign at Marrakesh, Mahjoub was freed and the caid of the Tekna himself was detained for several days. But Lassallas had to renounce providing protection to Sidi El Mahjoub. 'This was,' said Doutte, 'a humiliation for the very zaouia which our political interests were leading us to support.'[21] In fact Moulay Hafid himself tolerated (if he did not actually conduct) the actions in order to severely hinder increasing foreign influence on the zaouias and notables.

Lassallas' comeback when he was detained was skillful: he alone had a stake in suggesting to the caid that the ambush was actually aimed at the German Nier, Lassallas' only real competition in the Haouz. He thus let it be thought that the Compagnie Marocaine enjoyed the favor of the Makhzen over and against the German agents.

But upon his return to Mogador, Lassallas wrote a candid account back to his headquarters. He explained that he was nearly killed and that he was continuously risking his life, that European businessmen could no longer stay in Marrakesh, and that all these conditions resulted in great losses for the company, mainly because he was compelled to rely upon agricultural partners whom he could no longer control. The company answered that his life was more important than business; they assumed that for the time being his view should prevail: slow down business efforts, and await further notice. This decision, they said, would be reviewed at a later time.

It seems the corner had now been turned: the Compagnie Marocaine would work closely with the French government, using newspapers, dinners, and discreet ploys in the corridors of the French Assembly and at the Moroccan Board to accelerate French intervention. It is well known at Dr Mauchamp's assassination (discussed below) and the events in Casablanca were used by the French to justify military intervention.

The Compagnie Marocaine and Lassallas would return to the Haouz only after the landing of the military at Casablanca. It was then that the Compagnie Marocaine really established its holdings. The best bargain was undeniably the Argoub, a piece of appanage land of the caid of the Rehamna located on the eastern border of the Haouz. This vast area of land, more than two thousand hectares, although fertile and rich in humus, had reverted almost completely to jujube brush.

A letter between two British consular agents describes the situation under which this tract of land was obtained:

> The Mannesmann Company, the Compagnie Marocaine and other individuals are presently purchasing land in the most fertile region of the Rehamna. They are buying plots of land belonging to the tribe. Not too long ago the people of that tribe had been forced to cultivate this land for the benefit of their caid. But today they take advantage of the rebellion to sell the land to obtain money and rid themselves of forced labor.
>
> Competition is stiff for such land. The Compagnie Marocaine was negotiating for a plot at the price of 25,000 [?] and was on the verge of sending an agent to examine the

land, but one of the Mannesmann people [Nier] purchased the land at the same price quoted without even having seen it. It is said that the people of the tribe are happy to have money to buy horses and rifles.

But while Nier was negotiating directly with the people, Lassallas was settling matters with the caid of the Rehamna himself. The arrival of French troops in Marrakesh in September 1912 gave more weight to titles acquired through such a caid, who had done so much to serve France.

The surest method for land purchases consisted, after all, of bringing into indebtedness those caids capable of occupying entire territories through violence. The family archives of the caid of the Harbil reveal, for example, that El Haj Abbas al Harbili returned from Fez with a *dahir* (sovereign decree) appointing him caid of the Menabha. He replaced the caid Najem, who was ousted on January 29, 1912. He paid the Makhzen 4,000 duros for his post by means of a letter of credit provided by the Compagnie Marocaine. In 1913 the Compagnie Marocaine began developing a little more than 1,000 hectares of rocky and infertile land for grazing in the territory of the Menabha.

By 1914 the Compagnie Marocaine owned 2,430 hectares in the Haouz, but it controlled an additional 12,000 hectares in several areas around the region.

B Real Estate Acquisitions by Other Foreign Nationals

The agents of the British consulate, though numerous and enterprising in the commercial sphere, did not acquire significant agricultural holdings in the Haouz of Marrakesh. They were especially interested in obtaining suitable plots in the immediate outskirts of the city for building country homes.

By contrast, the Englishman C. Nairn and his Protestant missionaries had at their command the land of four or five Moroccan partners to assure the necessary supplies for their boarding school. The school housed orphaned Moroccan girls whom the missionaries intended to convert to Christianity.

Special mention must be made of the purchase of large tracts of land to the northeast of Marrakesh by the English branch of the Rothschild family, foremost among them parts of the Targa and

Souihla irrigation sectors of the Oued Nfis. Years earlier the Rehamna had been expelled from the lands, which had been claimed by the caid Ayyadi in 1902 after the disappearance of the previous caid. This same caid Ayyadi also occupied the entire *Ouidane* (flood plain of the Oued Tensift) and the Argoub without authority to take legal possession of it. Two thousand hectares were transferred in 1904 to an agent of the Rothschild Bank at the price of 5 francs (17 DH in 1974) per hectare. The bank did not follow up with agricultural development. It seems, in fact, that the Rothschilds, after having loaned a considerable amount of money to the caid, had taken the land as collateral. But subsequently, when Great Britain withdrew from Morocco, this collateral was transferred back to the French Protectorate according to procedures that have not yet been brought to light. Indeed, the lands that were once acquired by the Rothschilds became the main basis for the Private Domain of the State in the Targa irrigation sector. This sector was portioned off to the profit of the official French colonization in the years 1921 to 1923. Today there are no traces of the presence of the great English banking house in this region except for a well site bearing its name, marked on the 1936 map of the Corps of Rural Engineering.

Competing with the Compagnie Marocaine, there were mainly the various German interests — represented first by Marx, who had succeeded and taken over the interests and the censaux of Weiss and Maur in 1894; from 1904 onward, by the agents Brandt and Toel of the Emile Nier Company; finally, and especially, by the numerous agents of the Mannesmann Company.

Within ten years, despite enormous difficulties engendered by the opposition of the Makhzen and the local population, despite the lack of support from their consulate, which was the reverse of the situation of French businessmen, the representatives of the German companies, because of their activity and their keen sense of business, succeeded in bringing together more than 5,000 hectares of land which they regularly farmed. Moreover, they introduced new kinds of crops, such as cotton. Thus, unlike most other foreign operatives, they were not satisfied to gear their own channels of commerce into the more stable arrangements for traditional agricultural production. Instead, they were engaged in what could be viewed as preparation for colonization.

Some figures from the monthly consular reports enable us to trace the progression of German interests in the area of agriculture and animal husbandry in the Haouz. Table 1.4 illustrates the number of protégés and partners associated with German firms.

Table 1.4: *Number of Protégés and Partners Associated with German Firms, 1901-1910*

Patrons	Number of mochalat [a]		
	1901	1905	1910
Brand-Toel	1	19	25
W. Marx	2	14	20
M. Richter	–	10	10
C. Ficke	–	6	20
W. Jaap	–	4	–
Dannenberg	1	3	–
Weiss-Maur	1	2	–
Others	–	3	20
TOTALS	5	61	95

Source: Monthly consular reports.
[a] Term used in the consular reports (see note 13).

One French report indicated that the Germans may have been acquiring land for 'the past fifteen years', that is, since 1881. This statement seems extreme because the first purchases were probably not made until 1897, and in Haouz, only after 1902.[22] But despite their late beginning relative to other foreign powers, the Germans enjoyed a spectacular progression in land acquisition. According to one report:

> For some time already the German firms have been involved in agricultural pursuits; they are looking for protégés and native partners. They hand out protection cards very liberally and they appear to have strong support from their consulate. The Germans have numerous protégés in the

tribes of the Zemrane, Sgharna, Rehamna, and Mjat. The head of the zaouia of Mjat is a censal representing the Marx firm, and nearly all its members are German protégés. Despite the opposition of the Makhzen, they purchase property through their censaux (who act as intermediaries) and they endeavor to acquire and obtain mortgages for properties, gardens and plantations at the very gates of Marrakesh.

Through their agents, the German firms started using techniques similar to those of the Compagnie Marocaine. Although the case falls outside the Haouz, it is interesting to note the methods used by representatives of the Mannesmann brothers to buy land from the Oulad Said and the Oulad Gaid tribes in the Zemrane region of the Oued Tessaout. Tribal and family feuds were exploited, indebtedness was used to acquire leverage on individuals, and money and protection were made available to Moroccan partners whenever necessary to assure cooperation. Si Omar, a Moroccan well known for not owning anything himself, had established strong bonds with Nier. This relationship, as anyone could see, provided the only source of his wealth. After becoming a caid, a title he acquired at the expense of his father, he compelled the lineages of the Oulad Said and Oulad Gaid to sell a portion of their collectively owned tribal lands — approximately 2,000 hectares — to representatives of the Mannesmann firm.

The irony of history was that at the time of the sequestration of Austro-German property in 1914, an agreement between the Glaoui and Si Omar involved dividing up the Mannesmann land in the Zemrane between themselves before the French Protectorate could gain control of the situation. These former German lands were divided up into three portions: one was given to Si Omar, another to the Glaoui, and the third to a French agent who had intervened to help speed up the real estate arrangements. The Frenchman later sold his portion back to the Glaoui.

A similar situation existed twenty kilometers away. Due to the complacency of Si Omar Tazi, minister of the Private Domain of the Makhzen, the Compagnie Marocaine had acquired property rights on the collective lands of the Oulad Yacoub. The company resold these lands to the ministry around 1936, and it was not until 1963 that the lineage was able to return to its former land. A similar incident involved a Belgian joint stock company; it also acquired lands during the colonial period; these lands were finally returned to their former owners in 1969.

The approach used in the latter acquisitions can be summarized as follows: at the time of a caid's fall from favor, appanage lands that were more or less well defined were reoccupied by the tribe. Competition for this land ensued between the tribe and the new caid. The new caid, who could only have obtained his position by paying large sums to his counterparts, would be financed by foreign lenders who thereby obtained power over him. The debts of the caid would be secured by real estate collateral held by intermediaries of the lenders, who obtained title as a form of loan repayment. The intermediaries were paid for their personal influence and for their knowledge of the 'thousand and one office doors' in the labyrinth of governmental bureaucracy.

All the land acquisitions were only landmarks in the uncertain future of an extremely unstable political situation. What later came to be called the 'pioneer spirit' of colonization was actually the extension of attitudes and risks taken by out-and-out adventurers who bought and sold influence. These adventurers were betting on an unpredictable future in which each of their European consulates convinced them that their own flag would prevail. It is understandable that in the face of such hazards, these 'wild-West' adventurers could not be expected to pay very much for questionable legal rights: there was nothing less real than the foreign-held titles of real estate.

4 Resistance to Foreign Intervention

European penetration of Morocco was not easily endured by Moroccans. Foreign agents and adventurers easily persuaded themselves that the instability of business and the difficulty in establishing capitalism were due to the Makhzen's ineptness and the intrinsic inability of Moroccan society, by itself, to promote 'progress'. Adventurers frequently courted and obtained spectacular, though often ephemeral, personal successes they could never have achieved in their own countries. But it required great effort on their part to persuade Moroccan society, including that of the Haouz, to accept, much less embrace, foreign protection.

A reading of consular reports, private letters and correspondence of the *sherifs* ('descendants' of the Prophet) shows a striking ambiguity of unfolding attitudes toward foreign intervention among Moroccan protagonists. An easy way to explain the variation would be to posit that it reflects the divergent ideas of social classes having opposing interests. In this simplistic point of view, the 'collaborators' would be compradors who represented the ascending strata of a nascent bourgeoisie; resistance came from popular classes and those in power who were threatened by a changing world. Religious attitudes and xenophobia toward foreign culture were the ideological cloak which obscured everything.

These assertions concerning this fruitless phase of the resistance to colonization give an air of credence to everyday political discourse, but they explain very little in reality. The explanations are only ideological projections taken from elsewhere than the rich sources available from the intellectual and popular milieux of the times.[23] In fact the rejection of foreign settlement in Morocco was manifested at all levels — on an ideological level with religious foundations, from an institutional viewpoint concerned with fiscal reforms known to be dictated by the Europeans, by the stance of the young sovereign Moulay Abd el-Aziz, and finally, in the sphere of economic competition.

Fiscal reform, in particular that of 1903 inspired by Sir A. Nicholson, provoked an outbreak of indignation, not only because it resulted in stronger pressure on tax payers, but also because it economically favored foreigners and their protégés. No doubt the caidal exactions for a long time had represented a breach of holy fiscal Koranic law. But at least these caidal exactions never had been recognized officially; the principle of Koranic law was preserved; the beneficiaries of exactions could experience total reversals of fortune; and 'Heaven bore witness to their iniquity'. But a new law proclaimed by the 'Commander of the Faithful', i.e. the Moroccan sovereign, was something else altogther: it resulted in a new illegitimate fiscal system: a weighing of money no longer in accord with canons of Muslim law, carried out by foreign advisors behaving in an imperial manner, on resources and land becoming in effect 'extraterritorial', and on legal issues deriving from other than the traditional laws. All of this led to a widespread national rejection, even among conflicting classes, of the representatives of foreign powers and, subsequently, of the monarch who tolerated them.

This was not the first time in Moroccan history that pretenders rose against the reigning sovereign, whether in a rivalry or to promote personal interests. Nor was this the first time that political competitors called for a *jihad* (holy war) and for the defense of the territory against invaders. However, never before had the country been so weak in its resistance, under such strong financial domination, and at such a military disadvantage. Never before had there been such a pronounced penetration of Moroccan society. Never before had the resistance to it had such little credibility. It was not merely a matter of fighting against the straightforward domination of a foreign nation, but of postponing the collapse of caidalism in the face of a triumphant capitalism. The examination of a few episodes of this resistance in Marrakesh enables us to gauge its limits.

A The Shoemakers' Revolt
This revolt was named for the trade of the individual who led the revolt; he received broad support among artisans, shopkeepers and tradesmen in Marrakesh. On January 20, 1904, Marrakesh underwent a popular insurrection which ended in a riot. The causes of the uprising were economic. One of the basic events which fed popular dissatisfaction was the circulation of new copper coins just before the holiday Aid el Kbir (commemorating Abraham's sacrifice of a ram rather than his own son). These new coins modified the copper/silver exchange rate in a manner very unfavorable to small coins. Before the establishment of the French monetary system in Morocco, two metal-based currencies (silver and copper) were in separate circulation. Copper coins were held in abundance by the popular classes while silver was held by the elites and the wealthy merchants. Traditional laws established the weight of silver coins and the rate of exchange of copper for silver coins. Tax rates were established in terms of silver dirhams. The penetration into the system of foreign moneys, especially Spanish and French currency, added to the confusion. Exchange of currencies between private individuals was worked out through mutual understandings outside of any regulation, following the fluctuations in local needs for cash and the movements of various foreign-exchange rates.

The financial crisis of the Makhzen was such that all measures were utilized to observe the manifestations of allegiance by the caids, pashas and governors on the day of Aid el-Adha, in order to maximize tax collections. Toward the end of the month of *Choual*, a law was passed fixing the dirham at 560 *mouzanna* (units of copper money) instead of the previous 500. Taxes had to be paid in silver.

Neither the new currency nor the taxes were accepted readily by the people. The artisans and merchants decided to establish a new market outside the city, so that the government could not control it. Guards were sent to close this illegal market. They were jeered and driven back by a crowd. A certain shoemaker, Allal ben Ahsan, harangued the crowd, and the whole city, quarter by quarter, rose in revolt. People took to the street and merchants quickly closed their shops; the shops that were not closed were ransacked. The home of the *Mohtasseb* (the regional treasurer of the Makhzen) was robbed. Fires were started all over the city. According to one source, 'The Roman Catholic church was destroyed and the corpse of a missionary was exhumed and his head carried through the city. Jews were harassed.' Toward the afternoon of the same day, a crowd of young people marched with a black flag, rallying the entire population.

During the night, while the populace was barely held in check, Allal ben Ahsan, the shoemaker, was called to meet with Moulay Hafid. The shoemaker spoke of the high cost of food and the unfairness of the new currency, which neither the peasants coming to Marrakesh for supplies nor the local government wanted. He also spoke of the corruption of the Mohtasseb, and of the arrogance of foreign businessmen, and said the Jews were becoming too assertive again. Assurances were made to the shoemaker, who then returned to his supporters. New measures that had been agreed upon were promulgated by Moulay Hafid, and the city became quiet when the news was announced by town criers. The new coinage was recalled, and so was the Mohtasseb. The Pasha of Marrakesh also was deposed and Jews were only permitted to leave their quarter barefooted. A *meks* (extraordinary, non-Koranic gate tax) for the city of Marrakesh was abolished. Foreign consuls received apologies from the government but were asked to advise their nationals to behave unobtrusively. After the celebration was over and things had returned somewhat to normal, the leaders of various quarters were gathered together and strongly rebuked, many young people were arrested, and the shoemaker was arrested and incarcerated for several days in

Marrakesh and afterward sent to Fez. Nothing more was ever heard of him.

In the annals of Marrakesh, and probably of all Morocco, this was perhaps the first popular urban insurrection.

B The Mauchamp Affair[24]

On March 19, 1907, Dr Emile Mauchamp was stoned to death by a crowd while hastily returning from the outpatient clinic to his home to respond to the popular concern caused by a 'pole' erected on the terrace of his home. When accurate information reached Paris on March 23, warships were dispatched to Tangier. The French Chamber of Deputies convened hurriedly, and the animated debate that ensued inspired the final decision of a French military intervention in Morocco and the takeover of the city of Oujda as hostage until the French government obtained satisfaction with respect to a list of demands and sanctions.

At Tangier three newspapers did not support the action of the French government, but their reservations boiled down to a plea for purely economic domination of Morocco; in short, they followed the English position.

This was the crux of the debate which raged in the colonial world at the time. All of the colonial powers aimed at economic domination, but since they were in competition with each other, they could not agree whether this domination was possible on a strictly commercial basis, or whether, to the contrary, it required a political protectorate. Undoubtedly certain powers — France and Spain — were better situated geographically to derive economic advantages from political involvement in Morocco. This explains in part the cleavage between the colonial powers on this issue. However, the overall aims of the various protagonists in this colonial competition were still different. The French representatives argued that 'progress' (here meaning capitalism) could no longer occur without a full-scale reform of Moroccan society. And this reform could only occur if a European nation assumed responsibility for the transformation.

The Mauchamp affair provided France with strong arguments to defend this position. One point on which all commentators consistently agreed concerning the murder of the physician was that neither Dr Mauchamp nor his associate Louis Gentil had proceeded with the installation of a wireless telegraph antenna outside their home. This may be true, but such was still an objective of primary importance among European businessmen in Marrakesh.

As early as eleven years before, a first attempt at wireless transmission had been made. On May 27, 1896, an engineer of the French National Telegraph Company, on leave, was sent to Marrakesh by a group of French financiers. In 1902 the same group of financiers obtained permission from the Makhzen to install relay stations for wireless telegraphy between Mogador and Marrakesh. However, due to the hostility of merchants and certain notables of Marrakesh, the project was postponed and the antennas were dismantled. The next attempt was made in 1905, but according to Louis Gentil, Moroccan authorities were attaching great importance to the entire issue of wireless telegraphs. Artisans had even received orders not to participate in any installation work.

When Louis Gentil arrived in Marrakesh on March 12, returning with Dr Mauchamp from France with all his geodetic survey equipment, he wrote, 'I had the impression from the first day that something had changed. As we walked by, the people said, "here are the French who have come to take Morocco!"' Gentil assumed that these attitudes had been fostered by the followers of Ma el 'Ainin (a religious leader with political aspirations), but he also realized that people were keeping a close eye on foreigners' activities whenever they were transporting cumbersome and mysterious equipment. He also noted that the crowd had moved toward Mauchamp's home after the Pasha Abd as-Salem el-Warzazi encouraged them to tear down the French flag, which the Pasha had heard stood on Dr Mauchamp's terrace. Gentil claimed that he had set up no surveyor's pole, pointing out that the mosque minarets provided excellent landmarks. In his account, he mentioned only the presence of 'reeds' on the terraces; these were quite typical in Marrakesh and were, therefore, unlikely to arouse the population. (Such reeds were customarily set up on rooftops for the purpose of drying clothes and wool.)

Whether or not the establishment of a telegraphic connection was in process, the eventuality of such an occurrence apparently led to public arousal at the time the two Frenchmen arrived in Marrakesh; the ensuing popular action led to Dr Mauchamp's death. To keep things in perspective (and admitting a completely different context), it should be noted that a similar distrust still occurs whenever ITT routinely obtains contracts for the installation of new communication networks. It is the same reaction to a visible and decisive technological domination which monopolizes for a foreign power a means of communication and basis of economic and political action.

The thing feared most by artisans, merchants, and others affected by the flow of goods was that they would be the last informed of the prices of commodities and goods in Mogador, of quantities ordered, and of the arrivals of merchandise. Already, thanks to stronger financing, the European channels of trade were sweeping merchandise off the market, but at least their 'telephones' (i.e., communications in person and by messengers and mail) functioned as poorly as did those of Moroccan merchants. Whatever the nationalistic reactions and magico-religious fears about the mysterious, long distance transmission of words, it still can be argued that this was an episode of essentially economic resistance and competition.

This resistance was to gain momentum during the days following the murder of Dr Mauchamp. Four German merchants were attacked. As was discussed above, Lassallas was insulted and threatened. The Pasha, whose removal from office was requested by the French authorities, was supported by the people, and after numerous delays, when the central Makhzen was forced to proceed with the French demands, the Rehamna entered into a state of revolt and proceeded to attack European convoys of merchandise.

On April 25, 1907, there was a violent anti-European demonstration that swept Marrakesh, forcing the Europeans to seek protection from certain Jews. On May 8, the Europeans decided to leave Marrakesh for Safi. They left behind only official representatives — six Englishmen and three Frenchmen. Under the protection of an armed escort provided by Moulay Hafid, the European exodus reached Safi on May 14. On June 7, the idea of replacing Moulay Abd el Aziz with Moulay Hafid began to circulate in Marrakesh.

Until the arrival in 1912 of Mangin's armed French detachments rescuing European nationals detained by el Hiba and protected by Thami el-Glaoui, foreign economic activities and enterprises remained nonexistent in Marrakesh. Undoubtedly the development of foreign capitalism could not go on in the Haouz without the establishment of political institutions based on military support.

Chapter 2

Development of Capitalism Under the Protectorate

The main justification for foreign political domination of Morocco rested on the proposition that Moroccan institutions and customs were incapable, by themselves, of putting into practice the European concept of economic progress, i.e. capitalism. In Europe and the free-trade countries, economic and social growth required overseas expansion of markets to absorb the increased consumption necessitated by mass production. In their own interests, the European governments willingly assumed the mission and the duty of the taking under their trusteeship the countries bordering the southern shores of the Mediterranean, from Syria to Morocco. This trusteeship, while preserving the appearance of traditional sovereignties, was dedicated to implementing major reforms of the colonized societies. It was generally assumed that each colonized country would subsequently come of age internationally. The so-called Lyautey policy reasserted ceaselessly that Morocco would be the beneficiary of progress and the accompanying reforms that France would bring in order for Morocco subsequently to assume responsibility for her own affairs.

The question is, what became of these important ideas, that had been debated around conference tables and in official discourse, when they were put into practice, for example, in the Haouz of Marrakesh? By simplifying somewhat, it can be said that in the Haouz, land colonization and industrialization have been largely a French concern. With some exceptions, during the Protectorate, capitalist production developed primarily as an enclave, independent of traditional Moroccan economic activity. It thus relegated Moroccan agriculture and crafts to the museum and at times brought on noticeable regression in technology, knowhow, and traditional production.

In the following analysis, the general argument will be tempered a little by certain exceptions, but the deviations to be noted — such as the partnerships of a few Moroccans with the French in their efforts to establish a colonialist, capitalist society — were all too often tolerated purely for immediate and politically utilitarian goals.

It is not a question here of passing a moral judgment or political condemnation. Ultimately, the European spheres of business and their supporting governments, in a masterly fashion, schemed to weaken the Makhzen until it was forced to accept, support, and call for the Protectorate. The Makhzen ended up giving the Protectorate its own resources and legitimacy so that the power of the Protectorate could be used to suppress civil war and occupy the country, even though the disturbances themselves had been induced by the weakness of the Makhzen and the intrigues of the European powers.

The large foreign companies ultimately assumed the social and political costs, as well as the financial investments of the operation: they reclaimed the rewards and dividends of this enormous speculation.

Sociologically, however, we are most concerned with a different issue: did the forty-year episode of the Protectorate allow capitalism to establish itself? For example, in the Haouz, has it eliminated the 'old man', tribalism, caidalism? Has capitalism left durable, self-sustaining structures that are likely to continue to develop over a long period of time? Will these structures left behind after the Protectorate link up with large-scale foreign commerce and thus become woven into the international division of production and trade that were the aim and justification of the colonial adventure in the first place?

Admittedly, all philanthropy aside, the large European firms thought that western European technology and institutions were too advanced to be easily exported; at best, they argued that countries like Morocco could absorb only the most basic physical technologies and methods of production imported from Europe. This did not prevent these same major businesses and banking interests from wanting to locate in an area where climatic conditions, the cost of manpower, the security of capital, and fixed costs were the most favorable for large-scale production. In the end, what has been the outcome? Do the institutions and social structures — the entire social formation — that were established as a result still today assure a satisfactory framework for capitalist development? It is in these terms that the relative success or failure of the attempts to establish capitalism in the Haouz can be assessed. This thread seems to provide the most objective way to consider the matter. The actors involved have a shorter-term viewpoint; they pursue their own self-interests, partly the subjects and partly the objects of broader events. In our analysis, we will follow them occasionally for their own interest, and thereby explore a bit beyond the general movement sketched above. Given the importance of agricultural and para-agricultural production in the Haouz, and the weakness of mineral and industrial production in the plain itself and in Marrakesh, the analysis will mainly consider the structuring of agrarian space.

First the foreign settlers occupied and populated the land; then they became aware of the importance of the sources of water for the Haouz of Marrakesh; they saw the need for its regularization. These first two developments hardly had been played out when the world economic crisis and the problems posed by the fluctuation of prices of agricultural raw materials oriented capitalist investment toward agribusiness. We will examine these three overlapping periods; at the conclusion we will examine the effects of colonization in the Haouz.

1 The Occupation of the Land

The entry of French troops into Marrakesh did not immediately result in a land rush in the Haouz. It was first necessary to know and appraise the legal status of rural lands, a difficult task in a region that had known so many usurpers and political upheavals. In addition, the war in Europe made the economic future uncertain, and consequently the protagonists, both public and private, remained cautious in their commitments.

Thus, during the first period, stretching from 1912 to 1920, the foreign colony did not acquire more than 5,000 hectares in total; before 1921, this was primarily a matter of consolidation of previously appropriated or occupied lands by companies such as the Compagnie Marocaine. In addition, during these initial years, the administration actively explored the problems posed by future colonization and the politics of distributing opportunities for land acquisition that the administration envisioned.

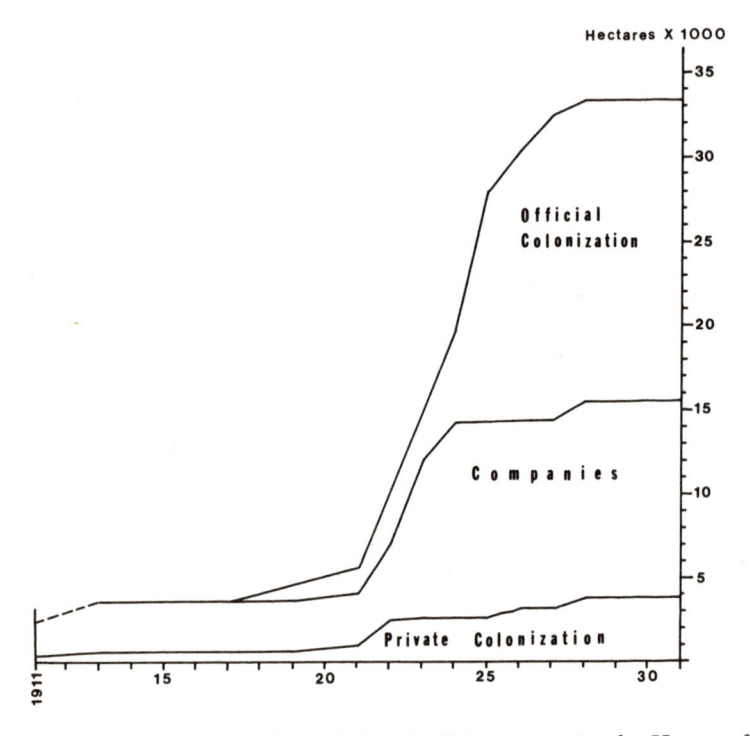

Figure 2.1: *Acquisition of Lands by the Colonization in the Haouz of Marrakesh, 1910–1930*
Source: Office of the Haouz.

It was within a period of seven years, from 1921 to 1927, that the lands of the Haouz were either allotted or appropriated. With almost 33,400 hectares, the colonizers occupied all the areas on which the native population were least able to prove their rights, and, compared to other regions of Morocco such as Beni Mtir and Gharb, they did so with the fewest immediate political and social difficulties. With few exceptions the land occupied in the Haouz remained remarkably stable. During the entire period of the Protectorate, the area was diminished by only 500 hectares (1.4%); this figure holds not just to the end of the Protectorate in 1956, but even up to 1961 when the formal repossession of colonial lands began. The land acquisition process began slowly, increased very rapidly, and leveled off.[1]

Figure 2.1 and Table 2.1 indicate the amount of land owned through official colonization, by private individuals, and by businesses: the diagram displays a typical S-shaped curve, indicating the leveling off of appropriation at the end of the period due to exhaustion of worthwhile lands.

A   The Search for Colonization Land

Nothing would be more erroneous than to assume that colonization was established on the best land in the Haouz and solely by means of violence. It would be equally erroneous to assume that the colonized lands were merely wastelands, lands with no other master than the state, or uncultivated lands, the occupation of which would inconvenience no one. Each extreme was championed at the time when the colonizers were trying to justify their occupation and Moroccans were seeking to defend themselves against it. These two extreme views can be juxtaposed today, distinguishing the concrete cases that were actually violent from those cases of amicable land transactions and peaceful agricultural development.

It is true that the Haouz, from this point of view, constituted a somewhat special case in Morocco. Difficulties and intertribal feuds between warlords at the close of the nineteenth century and waves of civil war never ceased to lash the walls of Marrakesh in the area contested by the Mesfioua and the Rehamna. On many occasions the actual farmers and the rightful landowners were swept aside. Fine cultivations and orchards were ruined. There were so many usurpers and masters that after 1908 it can be said that the Haouz belonged to whoever had the power to occupy the land by force.

Table 2.1: Acquisition of Land Through Colonization Before 1928 (hectares)

	Corporation Annual acquisitions	Corporation Cumulative area	Official colonization Annual distributions	Official colonization Cumulative area	Private colonization Annual acquisitions	Private colonization Cumulative area	Habous Annual occupations	Habous Cumulative area	Total foreign property Annual acquisitions	Total foreign property Cumulative area
Before 1914	—	2,974	—	—	—	597	—	—	—	3,571
1914–1920	1,647	2,975	1,637	1,637	427	1,024	—	—	2,064	5,636
1921	4,950	4,622	1,056	2,693	1,544	2,568	—	—	4,247	9,883
1922	2,126	9,572	—	2,693	26	2,594	8	8	4,984	14,867
1923	—	11,698	2,540	5,233	—	2,594	234	242	4,900	19,767
1924	—	11,698	8,178	13,411	—	2,594	—	242	8,178	27,945
1925	—	11,698	1,856	15,267	582	3,176	80	322	2,518	30,463
1926	—	11,698	1,957	17,224	—	3,176	—	322	1,957	32,420
1927	—	11,698	352	17,576	606	3,782	—	322	958	33,378
1928	—	11,698	—	17,576	—	3,782	—	322	—	33,378

The Protectorate itself did not have to resort to violence to obtain land: violent seizure of land had already been carried out by others; all that was needed was to negotiate with those who held these considerable territories. In other words the colonial administrators did not always have to confront the farmers who actually occupied the land. A large number had already cleared out, and those who had remained were subject to lords who themselves had already assumed the costs of violence to protect their own interests.

The first objective of the officials of the Protectorate in Marrakesh was to constitute a group of domanial (estate) lands, the disposition of which would be under the jurisdiction of the state. The confiscation of lands from various persons — discredited, disgraced, punished for their betrayal or their allegiance to an unlucky pretender or a fallen sovereign — had permitted the sovereign to amass large areas around Marrakesh, referred to locally as *bled Makhzen* (land of the Makhzen). The rotation of caids basically worked to increase the crown's holdings, for the wealth a caid had accumulated by virtue of his position could be confiscated at the time of his dismissal by the Makhzen.

If, on their arrival in Marrakesh, the French administrators had found a complete and relatively precise register of these successive acquisitions, the extent of state domanial land would have been easy to establish. But the French were confronted by immediate difficulties: the imprecision of property boundaries, the relative confusion between lands of the state and those belonging to the sovereign, and the abundance of anarchical concessions made since 1908.

Understanding the ambiguity of the land tenure system discovered by the colonial administration can provide much insight into the problem. The lack of clarity resulted from the foreigner's tendency to look with his own eyes and to measure in terms of his own standards. Inversely, the inhabitants of the Haouz some fifteen years later found the new land tenure statutes established by the colonizers to be no clearer. There were several categories of land rights: leases of tribal lands; renewed leases of *habous* lands (non-transferable ownership of which is held by a religious group or family as a collectivity) to Christians; state land preferentially distributed to colonial settlers; communal lands given for perpetual use, and so on. In all of these various forms of land use and land ownership, the people of the

Haouz could only see the transfer of their land to foreigners, nicely disguised in formal judicial phrases.

The imprecision of property boundaries only becomes apparent when outsiders became involved with farmland. Ordinarily each plot is known by its own name, by its boundaries, and by the names of its neighboring plots. The borders of such plots traditionally were determined by group consensus and this consensus was seldom challenged. When such challenges did occur, they were a consequence of a very significant transformation of power relationships within a group. These occasions gave rise to lengthy discussions and negotiations. When a local group was dissolved, dispersed, or when an outsider was involved, the entire issue of property boundaries became crucial. Then the question of land ownership and the relationship of the various political forces within the group became paramount. This is because the distribution of land and flocks was closely linked to the distribution of power and social relationships. The ancient regime of this region of Morocco witnessed intense social mobility and an active modification of power relationships as a result of successive occupations of land in the Haouz of Marrakesh. This was particularly true in the areas at the lower ends of irrigated sectors, in the middle of the plain, away from *foums* (alluvial fans where streams come out of the mountains). Thus it is necessary to distinguish these unstable areas from ecological zones of durable and relatively peaceful occupation; the latter types did not preclude usurpation but did not involve land abandonment either; they have been characterized by fairly permanent settlements. Politically unstable zones, on the other hand, have experienced a succession of lords who frequently forced local people to leave their lands in order subsequently to establish entirely new villages.

The confusion between the domain of the state and property owned by the sovereign had already been challenged by the European powers. When they wanted to establish collateral for loans and found custom revenues insufficient, the countries that participated in the Madrid conference had required that the Makhzen establish a register of urban and rural property. This register was established by Makhzen officials, but with contents judged to be very insufficient or vague by the foreign agents in charge of handling the national debt of the Moroccan government.

But the succession of the three sovereigns— Moulay Abd el-Aziz,

Moulay Hafid and Moulay Youssef (Sultan, 1912 to 1927) — within five years, and the subsequent rotation of personnel in positions of authority, had so profoundly modified the Makhzen's map of land tenure in the Haouz that one claim was as good as another. Quite often, in order to benefit newly appointed caids, land concessions were made by dahir, without prior annulment of former concessions of dahirs. In this manner, each claimant could have pride in thinking that he had title to property.

The French agents stationed in Marrakesh frequently brought to the attention of their legation the dissolution of Makhzen wealth:

> The decline of the Makhzen's property holdings in Marrakesh and in its surroundings has increased greatly these past months. The Sultan has given away full ownership of certain state domanial properties to members of his family or his friends. Among the beneficiaries one notes the following: Moulay Boubker, khalifa to the Sultan in Marrakesh, Haj Hmed El Krissi hajib, and Taieb el Mokri. The adouls have also been requested to sell Makhzen land from the tribes of the *Dir* (piedmont hills of the Atlas); the state dominal olive groves of Demnat have apparently been ceded to Germans... Moulay Hafid is incorporating a portion of Makhzen property into his own private estate, selling the rest, or giving it to his close friends... The sovereign and his courtiers are gorging themselves with private and public riches to such an extent that we will no longer find any state domanial land available when we need it. In order to control such abuses it is necessary that we take in hand without delay the entire administration of all the bled Makhzen. This is imperative, particularly in Fez and Marrakesh.

This letter was written in 1911 by General Moinier in Casablanca to the Minister of War in Paris. There was a similar plea early in 1912:

> Moulay Hafid has just given the order to have habous property deleted from the registers of land in order to incorporate it into his own personal estate... This extraordinary misappropriation of state domanial property at

Fez as well as at Marrakesh shows how urgent it is that the administration of the bled Makhzen be entrusted to officials who are capable of holding on to the land which is still available; should the need arise, they must also be prepared to reclaim property which has been given away in contempt of any law. The monopolizing of land with which the Sultan and his entourage have been proceeding with such haste for the past few weeks indicates clearly their intention not to leave any State domains at the disposal of the protecting power on the day when the protecting power shall wish to exercise its rights obtained on the basis of the latest agreements [the Algeciras Conference].

Consequently, with the arrival of the French troops in Marrakesh, a notice from Resident General Lyautey concerning real estate transactions called to public attention the system of regulations that was in force in the whole occupied zone. In order to prevent any fraudulent transfer of property reserved for public use (the future public domain), it prescribed strict measures of surveillance for the protection of habous lands, forests, mines, lands for collective tribal use, and the Private Domain of the State. Foreigners were able to obtain real estate according to the procedure derived from Article 60 of the Act of Algeciras.

The real estate question was surely one of the prime preoccupations of the authorities of the Protectorate, second only to military operations. As soon as Moulay Hafid was removed from office in 1912, an investigation entrusted to the *Vizir* (minister) el Mokri was begun in order to establish an inventory of the property that the ex-sovereign had obtained for his private estate through inheritance, gifts, or purchase. Since the property of the ex-sultan Moulay Hafid was sequestered* in 1922, we can compare the list of sequestered

*Sequestration was the legal framework within which the Protectorate came to requisition, hold, control and dispose of Moroccan real estate. Within this framework, lands were disposed of in a variety of ways: they could be returned to the original owners; redistributed to land tenants from land owners; confiscated for the Private Domain of the State; or expropriated by right of eminent domain, and then either held as part of the Official Colonization lands, or redistributed to native Moroccan allies or to the French colons [ed.].

properties to the one drawn up ten years before, so as to determine the significance of property that had been restored to the Makhzen by Moulay Hafid during those years.

This 'audit' to the profit of the domain of the state, apparently to satisfy the public, stood in stiff competition with the private land acquisitions of the colons themselves. Here is what the newspaper *Le Sud Marocain* tersely reported about the operation: 'The [Service of] Domains acted on the basis of the formula dear to Robert Macaire: "This land belongs to no one; therefore, it is mine."' The statistics certainly confirm the viewpoint of the colons: from 1914 to 1920, private foreigners acquired only 427 hectares. During that same period, the Service of Domains recorded and entered in its registry 85,214 hectares.

The search for land which qualified under the statutes of the Private Domain of the State even took an upturn during the years 1919-1921. As proof, witness the following letters written in Arabic and addressed to the caids by the Chief of the Intelligence Service in Marrakesh:

> It is absolutely necessary to extend the search for land for the French because the area around Marrakesh is no longer sufficient. The war is over; it is necessary to work toward the reconstruction of France. There are no longer troubles to be feared from foreigners.

More imperial in tone was the following letter:

> You are ordered to search for domanial and habous lands, of which a portion is likely to be put at the disposal of the Europeans for them to cultivate. It is necessary to establish precise boundaries between tribes. Have each tribe come forward with documents and agreements concerning the nature of land in their possession from which they presently benefit.

This is a strange procedure, for in the region of Marrakesh it is difficult to see what types of documents could have been produced by the tribes — except for the displaced ones (Ait Imour and Oudaya) — in order to establish their boundaries.

The following notice written by a French official to a caidal leader also had the tone of a lion:

> A new type of lease with respect to Makhzen land is hereby brought to your attention. On domanial lands, the Makhzen intends to prohibit the leasing of land to anyone alien to the tribe as well as to tribal members who are not up-to-date in their payments. Those who remain will be required from now on to provide the following: a deposit at the time of the request for leasing land, half the rent at the time of signing the agreement, half of the remainder within six months of the signing of the lease, and the balance three months later.

This 'new type of lease' meant that city dwellers were excluded from leasing Makhzen lands since they were alien to the tribe. It also eliminated from consideration those within the tribe who lacked adequate means to pay rent. In effect, in formal and official terms, and without saying so explicitly, the new procedures limited access to public lands to foreigners.

The quest for colonizable lands took three additional directions: 1) seizures; 2) liquidation of the debts of the grand caids through land transfers; and 3) audits of guich lands occupied by tribes traditionally conscripted for military service.

The seizure of property from Makhzen officials who had too openly opposed the French (most notably in the holding of agents of the consulate at Marrakesh during the occupation of the city by El Hiba) was the most direct and physical approach: the former pasha of the city was held by force until he relinquished the deeds of property in his possession. To be sure, it was perhaps forcing him to return lands that he had acquired solely on the basis of his post in the Makhzen, but the procedure was judged irregular enough to prompt an inquiry by the English consulate.

There were numerous other cases of land seizure. An example is the property of Haj Omar Tazi, a little more than three thousand hectares in irrigated sectors on both sides of the Oued Nfis. This land, which had been the property of the Makhzen under Moulay al-Hassan (Sultan from 1873 to 1894), had previously been acquired through confiscation from Homad al-'Abdi, who had rebelled against the central government. This parcel of land was seized and distributed to partisans and seized again by several successive sovereigns of the Makhzen. The final outcome of the dispute concerning this land was an agreement with the following provisions: the partisans surrendered the property located on the left bank to the Makhzen, and sold the property on the right bank to the Société Industrielle et Agricole de Marrakech (SIAM) at the price of 500 francs per hectare.

The property of the leaders of the Mesfioua rebellion was also seized. Although there is no proof, it would seem that the administration did this in part to help Thami el-Glaoui, then the Pasha of Marrakesh, pursue his revenge against the already much punished Mesfioua tribe. Before long a large portion of these lands became the property of Thami el-Glaoui. Obviously the zeal of the administration in pursuing domanial lands could only spur the Pasha on, so long as he too could hope to benefit from the acquisition and sale of the lands.

One final example of seizure: in 1914 the Franco-German conflict resulted in the authorization of the seizure of all Austro-German properties in Marrakesh. As a result the Private Domain of the State was increased by about 10,000 hectares.

Another major source of holdings was land owned by caids who fell too deeply in debt to the state. A typical example of this phenomenon is the case of the caid Al-Ayyadi. He entered into a temporary alliance with his traditional rival, Thami el-Glaouia, at the time of the arrival of the French troops, and occupied much of the territory of the Rehamna. To insure his gains, Al-Ayyadi recognized the frontiers of the Mesfioua to the east of Marrakesh as belonging to el-Glaoui. The extent of the indebtedness of Al-Ayyadi was legendary. At the beginning of the Protectorate he lived in the manner of an overlord, attempting to emulate Thami el-Glaoui but without adequate means. His 'empire' was less populated, smaller in size and provided a more narrow fiscal base. Above all, it could be more easily controlled by the administration than the territory of el-Glaoui. For a long time, the administration had tolerantly to ignore what was happening in the Atlas Mountains valleys and on the other side of the Atlas, toward the south. But it had been directed to restrict as much as possible the activities of the caids in the area between Casablanca and Marrakesh. The permanent deficit of Al-Ayyadi, as caid of the Rehamna, was largely paid off on the basis of mortgages, and subsequently by the sale of the collateral for the benefit of the Private Domain of the State. This procedure enabled the Service of Domains of the Makhzen to obtain discreetly properties in several areas — the Targa, Seggara and Souelah irrigation sectors, and a large part of the Argoub. Until his death in 1964 in Marrakesh, the caid Al-Ayyadi continued to sell his lands in order to maintain his lifestyle. The last sale was that of Mhamdia, an estate of 800 irrigated hectares.

There is a final category of land which the Service of Domains sought to obtain: guich lands, held by tribes willing to provide allegiance and military service to a sovereign. Jean Le Coz has described at length how lands in the western suburbs of Marrakesh became guich lands.[2] He has also analyzed the use of subtle judicial equivalences between the right of eminent domain and the right of usufruct, put forward to facilitate the State's appropriation of a portion of these lands. The State utilized the technique by first recognizing the two judicial categories of real estate ownership and of usage on guich lands, then assigning the first category to the State and the second category to the tribe involved. The final step was to declare the two rights of equal value in legal claims and to grant the tribe full ownership of half of the land while retaining the other half for domanial land. In practice the tribes involved in this process were faced with the confiscation of the use of one-half of their lands and gained on the other half purely formal rights that nobody could really dispute. Even so, they did not escape the supervision of the State, since the lands were more or less controlled as collective lands.

Colonel Voinot, who had been assigned to investigate the rights of tribes on these lands, dissuaded the administration from really considering the lands as guich lands. And in practice the process of acquisition of so-called guich lands in the region of Marrakesh was relatively limited. In particular, neither the Ait Immour nor the Oudaya relinquished one square inch of land. The two tribes asserted their rights, claiming that they were 'displaced' and thus were not subject, any more than others, to military service. Besides, it seemed unwise to consider these tribes as guich from the perspective of real estate transactions, since they were being taxed in the same way as the other peoples of the Haouz, under the pretext that the guich regime had disappeared.

In the final analysis, a census of domanial lands assembled during the first ten years of the Protectorate estimated that 85,214 hectares were available to colonization. This represented approximately forty-two percent of the arable land in the Haouz.

The acquisition and registration of Makhzen land was legally and formally indisputable and it thereby supposedly guaranteed the security of later investments. But the question remained: were these lands empty of people? The study of files of the Land Registration Service and the Service of Domains, and the minutes of the Committees of Colonization risk losing sight of an older occupation, more modest but also more persistent — that of the tillers of the soil who remained on the land through the succession of lords and colons. For generation after generation they were the ones who had insured the productivity of the estates.

A personal interview conducted August 23, 1962, on the estate of Haj Omar Tazi, summarizes very well the worldview of the tenant farmers who, veritable serfs tied to the land, had endured the succession of masters for generations:

> My father was a Rehamni and he was settled on the holdings by Moulay al-Hassan. Moreover, the lands of the Haj Omar Tazi estate once belonged to the Rehamna, as is proven by the names of local places such as Sellama and Oulad Zbir, which are parcels of land here and also the names of Rehamna lineages.
>
> We have been moved from one location to another by a succession of sultans. Toward the end of his reign, Moulay al-Hassan sent us to work at Tassoultant. The Abda and the Hmar had invaded our land. Upon the death of Moulay al-Hassan, we remained in Marrakesh during the unrest. At that time no one wanted to leave Marrakesh to attempt farming. During periodds of relative peace some of us cultivated land as sharecroppers.
>
> It is possible that the estate may once have been owned by Hmad ben Aissa l'Abdi, if one can call the land occupation practiced in former days ownership. I do not know who this man was; my father has mentioned his name to me. It remains the name of an orchard in the estate. Later the whole estate was seized by the Makhzen, which claimed that people there were rebelling against the crown. It was the sultan's palace which managed the land. Under Moulay 'Abd el-Aziz the land was managed by the sultan's cousin, Sidi Mohammed b. Rachid. I myself leased land from Sidi

Mohammed at the rate of two-thirds of the harvest for the lessee. The land did not used to be what it is today. At one time it was a forest of jujube trees. It used to be cultivated between the huge clusters of trees. You could earn as much money by cutting and selling the branches in Marrakesh as by farming the land. There were neither orange nor olive trees. The land then passed into the hands of Ben Dhima and then into the hands of Ben Dhan; was it in the form of sale of lease? We do not know anything about it, except that our relationships with the royal family vanished. Shortly before, the Protectorate the Sultan sold or gave, I do not know which, the entire estate to two of his vizirs, one of whom I already mentioned — Haj Omar Tazi, and Si Taieb el-Mokri. As far as we were concerned, this brought no significant change; we farmed just as before but in a more regular manner, except during the episode of the 'Sultan of the Sahara', Ma el-Ainin, when the entire Haouz rose in rebellion and the cannons were thundering in Marrakesh. Then the Sultan withdrew to the south, crossing over the mountains. We returned to our farming.

Shortly after the Protectorate, Tazi and Mokri sold out to a company, SIAM, which started to clear the land by removing the jujube trees. We were put to work breaking up the soil with pick axes. Then the company brought in a machine with two engines and a cable bearing blades which dug up the ground to a depth of more than one meter. They used every method.

They would give land in *khobza* (a form of sharecropping), only claiming in payment the seed required to continue cultivation. They also employed us as *khammes* (another form of sharecropping where the worker received one-fifth) on a large portion of the estate, to cultivate cereals. For three years they grew cotton, using wage labor. It went very well, but sales were bad and they had to give up this operation.

The company then dug six wells and equipped some of them with pumps. With water from a local seguia and the wells they were able to plant a fair number of trees: almonds, apricots, oranges, prunes, and cypresses. But after spending much money, the company did not succeed: there was no market!

The land was sold to el-Glaoui shortly before the construction of the dam. After the dam was built, el-Glaoui created a lake and planted olive trees using wage labor. He organized his estate in the following manner: first, olive trees kept and irrigated by the khammes, without pay; harvesting was done by corvée; second, direct cultivation on four plots with khammes (thirty-five farmers were involved). There was one khammes foreman for six khammes, and several cereal grains were grown; third, indirect cultivation in the khobza form, where sharecroppers had the right to cultivate anything they wished. At the beginning the khobza (share) was at one-third. There were so many sharecroppers with their own threshing sites that the Glaoui later used the *hars* (feudal tax) system, in which rent was estimated at the farmer's fields by one of six inspectors who came a little before harvest. The hars was somewhat lower than one-third of the gross returns.

Generally, in order to become a khobzataire sharecropper you had to belong to the family of a khammes or pay a gift to el-Glaoui before working any land. The khobzataires were exempted from corvée harvesting of olive trees. Around 1953 el-Glaoui leased his estate for six years to a neighbor wishing to grow *kif* (marijuana). The latter agreed to pay eight million in rent, but during the course of the first year kif cultivation was prohibited. The rent was reduced to five million francs per year. The new lessee drove away the khammes of el-Glaoui, who left to search for a living some place else. The new lessee obtained his own khammes and cultivated a large part of the land using tractors. The rest of the estate was given in khobza to relatives of some of the new khammes. But a good number of el-Glaoui's former khammes slipped in among the new khobzataires. The khobza paid by tenant farmers at that time was forty percent. The khammes always received one-fifth of the grain harvest, without counting chaff, plus food.

At the time of independence the land was seized by the Makhzen, but the lessee continued his operation by paying rent to the Service of Domains until 1959, the date of the land redistribution.

Almost all of the former khammes, as well as the former khobzataires, have been taken on again. Also some people came who had never cultivated the land before. Finally, we are still here ... It is our land.

B Land Allotments for Colonization

Although during its first ten years the administration of the Protectorate had strongly limited spontaneous private land acquisition in the region around Marrakesh, it did tolerate a few minor purchases. In addition, a large number of transactions arranged by private agreements must have been completed before 1921. These dealings became public knowledge only after the relaxation of restrictions that resulted from the pressure of French public opinion in Marrakesh.

Relations between the French colony and the administration of the Protectorate were far from perfectly harmonious. The press regularly revealed secret and sometimes violent disputes of colons who had come to Morocco as though it were the frontier of the American West. These colons were indignant about the way the colonial administration tempered their aggressive enterprise. The French press of Morocco from 1918 to 1930 bore an extraordinary resemblance to the news sheets published in the hastily erected small frontier towns during the great western expansion in the United States. In the Moroccan newspapers one finds denunciations of the corruption of public servants, reports of 'heroic' crossings of the Atlas by a few 'daring' colons, advice for improving land, business offers, claims about the advantages of one region over another, as well as reflections on the benefits of replacing private militias with a state police force. But the strongest arguments dealt with the difficulties caused by an administration that reserved for itself the main portion of available land in the Haouz:

> The French colons, divided into the old [before 1912] and newer residents of Marrakesh, are both equally undesirable in the eyes of the military and civil authorities ... Little by little, by all possible means, the colons were prevented from touring their properties in the areas of the Mesfioua, Goundafa and Glaoua. The indigenous chiefs, who had until then

found buyers and lenders among the colons, no longer dared receive them for fear of retaliation. We remember a friend of General Brulard who had come with the intention of creating a farming operation and, finding himself unable to obtain anything other than rocky ground, left with his money for greener pastures. The French colonists were just vegetating. They had to be given compensation; thus, the inspired idea of giving them an allotment in the Guéliz.[3]

The Protectorate officials were following a political line outlined by Resident General Lyautey. This policy had been formulated to serve the State, French political power, and the large companies rather than allowing land speculations and the anarchic competition of adventurers. Without falling into the imagery which portrays the first colons as brigands and freed convicts who had found in the African colonies a territory for developing their talents, we still can have no doubt that the lands of the Haouz have been traversed by lively and rather colorful characters who were both obstreperous and lazy. Such individuals, from the perspective of the 'civilizing' mission of the French Resident General in Morocco, could only be viewed as marginal. Upon being informed of the escapades of some of his fellow countrymen, Resident General Lyautey remarked, 'One does not build an Empire with rose maidens.' He did, however, deem it necessary to squeeze the colons' voracious appetites for land into the narrow corsets of the French mission. With regard to the land issue, the French aimed at the development of capitalistic undertakings using advanced technology. This was primarily the domain of the large companies which had sufficient capital and tested technology at their command. In addition, there were a few 'honest and upstanding French small farmers' who received support from the French administration through contractual agreements concerning agricultural production

In other words, the French intended to colonize, but by strictly controlling the development to prevent the repetition in the Haouz of events that had occurred in the Rharb and the Meknes region. This attitude is revealed in the following statistics of land occupation: in 1928, the official colonization comprised 53.3 percent of foreign land holdings; companies held 35.1 percent and the remaining 11.4 percent involved private colonization. The private holdings were actually

1,540 hectares (almost five percent) less than the statistics indicate. Fondère acquired that amount from the sequestration of Moulay Hafid, in close partnership with Thami el-Glaoui, on the land of the Mesfioua tribe. This land was later organized into companies. Almost 600 hectares had already been appropriated by private individuals prior to 1912.

In actuality, the colonial administration allowed private individuals to settle on only five percent of the land colonized after 1912. On the other lands the Protectorate established fairly good control of the subsequent development by controlling the credit of the large banks which dealt with the corporations and large companies. These large companies were in any event eager to implement modern capitalistic technology. Control was also exercised by the Agricultural Service on the basis of specifications that went into effect beginning in 1920 with regard to lands of the official colonization.

Land Acquisitions Contingent Upon Improvements
It seems evident that the Protectorate officials did not have perfect confidence in the capacity of liberal capitalist competition rapidly to bring about development of land distributed to the colons, because the main objective of the specifications and contracts aimed precisely at insuring such a quick development. A study of the regulations brings to light the precise characteristics of the envisioned land improvement model and the economic preoccupations of the government. This study also reveals, through the detailed accounts of prohibitions and the seriousness of sanctions, the 'spontaneous' behavior of French farmers thought to be incompatible with the orientation of the State.

One of the requirements was that the owner of a plot of land had to reside on that land and build his principal residence on the site. The objective of this requirement was not so much to settle Frenchmen in the Haouz countryside as it was to assure direct 'modern' farming of the land, which included the regular supervision by Frenchmen of hired labor.

A Frenchman was specifically forbidden from becoming partner with or leasing his land to anyone he wished, particularly Moroccans. The pre-Protectorate procedure of forming partnerships with *mokhalats* (intermediaries) by now could have encouraged bold speculators. These practices were condemned and individuals who undertook joint efforts with Moroccans were summoned to the local commandant: there they were strongly reprimanded and threatened with being officially declared undesirable. The development of estates was built around four- or five-year plans which specified certain improvements (clearing land of stones, breaking up the soil, and planting hedges) as well as the system of cultivation to be practiced. Finally, colons were obligated to use salaried manpower, a policy that reinforced even more the requirement of direct cultivation of the land. Lots put up for lease-purchase were subject to the various regulations. Periodically, officials came to the sites to draw up progress reports, which were validated by joint meetings between officials of the administration and representatives of the colons (colonization committees).

Thus, the model of capitalist agriculture was strictly defined, assuring the land base for agriculture, programming investments, orienting speculations toward commercial production, forecasting markets, and establishing the social framework for both a permanent wage-earning class and seasonal wage earners employed during the peak work periods at harvest time. The discontinuity between this mode of production and the former mode of production in the Haouz was clear-cut and decisive. Within seven years, on 30,000 hectares (i.e., nearly one-third of the land that had actually been cultivated in 1912) intense activity of land clearing, construction, and cultivation had taken place. This phenomenon could not have failed to capture the imagination of the people. The question is whether all this activity did not also strike the native onlookers with apathy and despondency in the face of so much assistance, financing, information, and public support given to a foreign population that had in one sweep confiscated the entire available area of large plots for agriculture. The Moroccan population soon became disturbed with the display of so much arrogance and indifference on the part of the authorities of the Protectorate, even toward people allied to their cause. In several places, city dwellers who were former leasers of Makhzen property showed latent resistance; opposition even surfaced among rural notables.

Size of Colonization Tracts

The theoretical and practical justification for determining the size of colonization tracts was never given by the Protectorate. The expressions used — 'viable tracts', 'sufficient areas', 'decent means of living' — are obviously very subjective and approximate. Equally, the notion of a 'populating' colonization was more a slogan than an actual intention: the Compagnie Fermière shows that agribusiness populates more than the large family farm. The policy emanating from Marrakesh from the beginning was oriented toward development of relatively large farms with dry land cultivation of almond trees, sheep raising, and cereals. Small irrigated areas around the main dwelling might be used for orchards and a kitchen garden. The policy was clearly geared toward production for market of wool, meat, almonds, cereals, and even legumes.

The size of tracts took into account the quality of land so that colonists would have different amounts capable of similar levels of production. The law was based on specifications for the quality and depth of soil, and other characteristics such as soil density. There was much discussion concerning the means of recovering waste land and how to deal with rocky soil and dense concentrations of jujube trees. In general the tracts distributed in the Haouz covered areas ranging between 60 and 250 hectares.

Land Improvement
The period when colons cleared the land belongs to classical colonial imagery. In the main meeting room of the Chamber of Agriculture in Marrakesh, there are two large paintings designed to display the merits of European colonization. The Moroccan landowning notables who sit on the same benches today look at these images of the past in an amused and untroubled manner: in one painting a plowman dressed in a *jellaba* is equipped with a wooden swing-plow pulled by a camel and donkey who are attempting to avoid the clusters of jujube. On the opposite canvas is a colon standing in a military manner with his boots and his riding trousers. With a straw hat on his head and a riding crop in his hands, he supervises Moroccan workers who are leading a team of strong horses pulling a Belgian plow. In the background a woman carrying a water jar slowly vanishes between two rows of orange trees. The alpha and the omega of the doctrine of land colonization are contained in these two paintings. One must pay tribute to the succeeding presidents of the Chamber of Agriculture in Marrakesh for having enough humor to allow such historic documents to remain on the walls.

The memory of the clearing of the central region of the Haouz is not only preserved by these images and the archives of colonization; it is also preserved in the memories of the people. Any person over sixty years of age remembers these episodes, which themselves parallel similar efforts of a few Moroccan landowners powerful enough to use corvée labor to clear their land in the same manner; Thami el-Glaoui and caid Al-Ayyadi are among them.

The open competition for manpower, which occurred throughout Morocco in the early stages of land colonization, led to a rapid inflation of salaries and consolidated the position of tenants who already occupied the land. The latter were the first hired, and when their position stabilized, they themselves became recruiting agents.

Local newspapers objected to the recruiting of Moroccan workers from the Haouz of Marrakesh to work in other regions of Morocco or abroad:

> Fears have been expressed in the Council of Government at the fact that this recruitment is depriving the region and Morocco as a whole of a substantial proportion of its industrial and agricultural manpower. In order to mitigate the manpower shortage which threatens the workyards and the companies, it would be desirable for these companies to send agents to the south to recruit workers on the basis of labor contracts...
>
> The systematic effort at the depletion of the region around Marrakesh is proceeding. We lack manpower! The manpower problem is greater here than in the Chaouia region where the harvester is paid five francs per day, even though in the Haouz he is paid between eight and twelve francs per day and fed too.

The district chief of public works indicated in 1928 that 'the development of public works projects in building seguias is hampered by the difficulties of recruiting manpower'.

A quick calculation based upon reports of the agricultural service shows that the clearing of 30,000 hectares in five years at the rate of 50 working days per hectare required 300,000 working days per year, which would have implied the presence of 1,000 workers. The population at that time in the Haouz was approximately 30,000 people, of whom only about 4,000 could have been mobilized for heavy manual labor like land clearing. These figures suggest the size of the drain on manpower at relatively high wages which land development caused.

Undoubtedly the impact of such massive employment of workers in such a short time was taken as a favorable sign about the establishment of capitalist social relations in the region. Employers were not able to introduce a supply of unemployed workers in order to maintain lower wages and make personal considerations more significant in work relationships. The siphoning off from the traditional feudal channels of manpower for colonial development compelled the caids to discipline their tenants more strictly, adding to the unpopularity of their own regimes. If all of the change had not been the work of foreigners who had brought their own customs, it would have been described as revolution, obviously capitalist, but revolution all the same, after decades of economic and social instability. Even the most disadvantaged stratum of peasants could not help perceiving immediately that the new masters paid better and more regularly than the former ones.

There is a need for historical honesty. Colonialism can be seen as much as a check as an inducement to general progress. But whatever judgements can be made about the system of colonialism and its ends, it must be said that in all the interviews of workers and peasants alike in the Marrakesh region, regrets were never expressed about the period immediately preceding the Protectorate. To the contrary, although the seizures of land and water have always been denounced, the peasantry, which had been in a state of quasi-bondage, still remembers its liberation from the corvée and gaining access to disposable income. That is not to say that the peasantry did not suffer in numerous regions as a direct result of colonial settlement, or that they willingly wanted the colons to spread further. Far from it! Just as in other regions of Morocco and the Maghreb, people of the Haouz have often been driven from their lands and forcibly relocated; their land was seized under the guise of tailor-made legislation full of legal formalities which were totally obscure and unacceptable to the occupants.

C *The Compagnie Fermière in the Tassoultant Sector*

The story of the origin and development of the Compagnie Fermière merits a detailed account because it illustrates the interlocking of the interests of the large companies, the colons, and the administration. It is an excellent example of the competition and alliance between three types of socio-political actors, in agreement concerning overall direction, competing over terms and conditions, divided by their own interests, and facing a peasantry which could only offer passive resistance to the entire process.

On June 22, 1920, a fairly unusual agreement was reached between Eugène Regnault and Moulay 'abd er-Rahmane b. al-Hassan al-Alaoui (who was called Moulay al-Kbir). Regnault, representing a company in formation, leased for forty years 'all of the lands which are determined to be a part of the latter's property' in order to farm them.

These two individuals are worth describing in order better to understand the scope of this contract. The lessor was the brother of Moulay Abd el-'Aziz and Moulay Hafid. He resided in Marrakesh and possessed substantial areas of land in the Rharb, the Loukkos and around Fez, as well as in the Haouz.

For some as yet unclarified reasons, Moulay al-Kbir's brother, Moulay Hafid, perhaps on account of Moulay al-Kbir's effort to pose as a pretender in Taza in 1909, declared the sequestration of his brother's property in the course of the year 1910. Moulay al-Kbir formally appealed to the French consulate at Tangier, affirming the loyalty and legality of his own behavior. Eugène Regnault, at that time the French Minister at Tangier, succeeded in convincing Moulay Hafid to sign two dahirs giving his brother back his rights. In fact the confiscation of Moulay al-Kbir's land lasted until Regnault, no longer having an official position, felt capable of restoring the prince's estates. An agreement in 1920 was the first step in a long undertaking by which Regnault, as lessee, could benefit from the lands of the lessor only after having obtained the property for the latter.

Eugène Regnault had been a well-known diplomat before the Protectorate. He became the comptroller of the Public Debt in 1904 and principal financial advisor to the Makhzen prior to 1906.[4] He appears to have had connections with the Banque de Paris et des Pays-Bas (Paribas). Confident because of information gathered 'in the field and at the palace', he found himself on the other side of the table as 'technical delegate' at the Algeciras Conference that opened 16 February, 1906. From 1909 to 1912 he was the French Minister at Tangier. It was in that capacity that he intervened with Moulay Hafid to restore the sovereign's brother Moulay al-Kbir to his rights. In 1925 Regnault, along with Saint-René Tallandier — both private citizens by then — created the Compagnie Fermière Marocaine d'Exploitation Agricole to develop the lands of Moulay al-Kbir.

The first question Regnault had to deal with was the determination of the scope and content of the rights that the dahirs of reinstatement entailed; next he had to have Moulay al-Kbir's patrimony consolidated and titled. Simultaneously he took a contradictory course by having the Service of Domains and the representatives of his lessor draw up a statement stipulating three categories of property claimed by Moulay al-Kbir in 1920: a) those lands occupied by third parties that the State agreed to 'free' (4,730 hectares); b) those lands the State intended to keep in order to allot within the framework of colonization programs (1,488 hectares); c) those lands Regnault would immediately restore to Moulay al-Kbir (460 hectares).

Urged to do so by Regnault, Resident General Marshal Lyautey accepted the principle of compensation to be granted to Moulay al-Kbir in order to indemnify him for the properties kept by the State:

> This compensation shall consist of giving the full ownership to Moulay al-Kbir of colonization lands which are to be set aside from the available domanial land within the Marrakesh region. The amount of compensation must be determined not only from the appraisal on the basis of property lost, but also from the loss of usage starting from the time when this property should have been restored to him ... For his part, Moulay al-Kbir acknowledges that he will not at some later date exercise any further claim whatsoever.

The diligence shown by the administration from the beginning of this affair encountered serious obstacles on the actual lands. The lands which were to have been granted as compensation, those of the Tassoultant sector, had all been leased by the Pasha until October 1922, and the Pasha wished to remain on the land. The highest notables in the administration were dispatched to Marrakesh to see how the matter might be resolved. It seems that there was a patient but clear intention to work at taking back these lands for the benefit of the colonization. This maneuver was made possible through interposing agents, thanks to a prince, Moulay al-Kbir, who had ceded all rights of management for the next forty years. It seems that heavy pressure was exercised on the Pasha of Marrakesh. The Crédit Foncier D'Algérie et de Tunisie set the pace by sending Edmond Doutte to the properties, supposedly 'to gather agricultural data', in fact to negotiate with 'old friends'.

Finally a solution was agreed upon and an area of 1,280 hectares in the Tassoultant sector was freed up by the former leaseholder. A minor reservation still was posed by political authorities in Marrakesh who intended to see that the rights of natives already established on the land be safeguarded. The mention of people residing on the property is very discreet. One gets the impression that the existence of 'a few *fractions*' (groups of tribal lineages based on geographic districts) was discovered almost by accident in the inventory of lands, waters and trees. On 1 May, 1922, Regnault went to inspect the land, accompanied by the Director General of Agriculture and all the notables who had to understand the transaction. But during the entire visit the main subject of debate concerned the water rights to the land situated on the Tassoultant seguia. This issue gave rise to animated debates which are inscribed in the minutes of the expedition. About the inhabitants? Not a word! Indeed, they had not been seen.

The first struggle to follow was not with the inhabitants of the lands, but with the colons of Marrakesh. As was observed in a colonialist newspaper:

> Thousands of well-watered hectares are being given to Mr Regnault and Mr Lebon. The former used to be the ambassador to Japan after having nearly become the Resident General of Morocco; the latter is one of those men who are on so many boards of directors that they have difficulty in keeping track of all the vouchers they receive. The simple colons have the right to at least as much administrative benevolence as the large companies.

Regnault, who wished to expand the Tassoultant estate to 4,000 hectares to create 'a large modern colonial plantation', pleaded with the colonization committee concerning their mutual interests in the improvement of the land. The colonization committee tried to get

Regnault to spell out the maximum area of land he wished to obtain. In June 1922, Regnault ended up only claiming 2,700 hectares, and the colons demanded that the administration rapidly allot the remaining land in the Tassoultant sector for the exclusive benefit of medium-sized colonization farms.

Increasingly Regnault became preoccupied with the existence of peasant villages on the land he was to occupy. In October 1922, he pressed the commandant for the Region of Marrakesh to get the Pasha to move the occupants. The response from the commandant is a classic:

> It is in the interest of the Pasha, who presently is the leaseholder of the property, to come to an understanding with the people he governs to cultivate these lands in partnership. He will not seek to oust them. It is clearly a fact that one could not, without encountering serious inconveniences, sweep away the rights of occupants. Comparable situations have already provoked incidents between Europeans and natives in Tabouhanit. I had to intervene because the owner had, in a fashion, monopolized a village and chased off those among the occupants of the village who wanted to retain their freedom ... On reflection, one understands that this type of conflict cannot be avoided in the long run. These enclaves constitute rather awkward burdens for the European owners, especially because the natives are surrounded on all sides and are often tempted to trespass on the land of the owner.
>
> In order to avoid dangerous frictions, it would be best prior to any concessions to arrange for the creation of a sort of native canton in order to completely eliminate these enclaves. This would not prevent Europeans from finding manpower. They would only have to establish wage workers on their property. This is how the colons usually proceed.

After having acknowledged the existence of four village enclaves and nine peripheral villages which were thriving on the Tassoultant land, in total 600 families, the commandant, Voinot, evoked their forced removal:

I asked verbally for the Pasha's opinion concerning the advisability of these measures. He, too, thinks that the allotment proposed by the Service of Domains will inevitably give rise to difficulties. In order to ensure himself that the expropriation of the holdings will trigger no opposition from those concerned, he has conducted a discreet survey of the natives, so as to leave higher authorities completely free to take their decision. The information he obtained establishes that the natives in question would welcome the opportunity to be relocated in another area of the Tassoultant provided they received an indemnity, the amount of which would be determined by a commission entrusted with estimating the value of their property (trees and homes).

One can imagine the situation: Pasha Thami el-Glaoui, following obscure negotiations, is compelled to give up the Tassoultant estate that he had occupied since 1908, leased since 1912, and that he wished to keep as a true sign of his sovereignty in Marrakesh. The Pasha has been asked what he thinks about the resettlement of his tenant farmers and of the relationships the latter are going to have with the company that will succeed him. Of course the Pasha is to be 'kingpin' of the evaluation commission. Sums will be given to him to buy out the tenant farmers, who will themselves never resettle, for they will never receive any indemnity. They are still on their lands today and they are still claiming their rights. Four of their descendants were thrown in prison in 1974 for illegal occupation, leasing, and water diversion on lands of the Tassoultant.

Competition became more intense on the Tassoultant lands with the approaching retreat of the Pasha. The Pasha requested the allotment, for his benefit, of a farm 'in the area furthest from Marrakesh'. Some of Moulay Abbas's heirs also wanted to receive allotments and to benefit from the advantages given to the colons. Finally, there were the colons, who mounted a vigorous campaign both against the large companies and against the covert intentions of the administration.

The political authority continually equivocated and attempted to satisfy all parties involved. The commandant of the Region of Marrakesh commented:

I am in agreement with the district head of the Service of Domains of Marrakesh with regard to the principle of a forty-year lease to Mr Regnault for a 1,200 hectare parcel of the Tassoultant lands, but at the same time I am proposing the creation of an allotment reserved for the small- and medium-size colonizations on an area at least equal in size. I propose as well to reserve a certain number of plots for the natives. It is in our greatest interest to favor the creation of a sort of native rural bourgeoisie; this does not now exist in the Region of Marrakesh and it would provide substantial political support for us. As far as the villages are concerned, they should be relocated on the periphery.

These proposals indeed seem to reflect the characteristic and perhaps precarious state of relationships between the different social forces that the administration was confronting. The administration appears to have had no guiding light. It seems to have been swept along by events while giving partial satisfaction to everyone, except of course, to those who were unable to express their interests at that time — the tenant farmers and *soukkanes* (non-tribal immigrant peasants).

Regnault then decided to strike hard. He revealed grandiose projects he had in mind for the Tassoultant: the cultivation of sugar beets, the installation of a factory, the raising of cattle to provide Marrakesh with dairy products. In 1922 he wrote to Lyautey:

> It is now a matter of our group obtaining the necessary area for farming sugar beets in order to supply a sugar factory and refinery in Marrakesh. The establishment of this industry, with the Pasha Thami el-Glaoui as partner, would bring genuine prosperity to the region in the form of work and wages... It is necessary that your benevolent influence be exercised in favor of this undertaking so intimately linked to the general interest.

From Regnault's point of view time was an important factor. Two years had already been lost since the signing of the agreement with Moulay al-Kbir.

In order to 'revolutionize' agriculture in Marrakesh, Regnault asked for guarantees: an expansion of his land up to 4,000 hectares, and all of the waters that remained available on the Tassoultant. If he was reproached for removing lands that otherwise would have been available to small- and medium-range colonial farmers, he responded that he, personally, was ready to allot land to colons. He would develop their plans for cultivation and restore to them after forty years the lands that they had improved within the larger framework of a modern industrial farm. Otherwise, he would abandon the entire project and break the agreement with Moulay al-Kbir; then nothing would stop the latter from cultivating the land according to the old tradition.

This was genuine blackmail for the sake of land development! Because of Regnault and the exclusive contract that Regnault had with Moulay al-Kbir, the administration saw to it that Moulay al-Kbir's compensation would be located in the Tassoultant. If Regnault withdrew, extraordinarily well-situated lands would be removed from the colonization.

But what was really intolerable for the administration was Regnault's proposal that he would look after the interest of the small- and medium-size colons on the Tassoultant lands. As the Director General of Agriculture told the Committee of Colonization in 1922, 'The small colonization does not need the intervention of a third party between the administration and the colons.'

After looking at all points of view, highly placed officials of the Protectorate agreed on the plausibility of Regnault's proposals, as much from the economic as from the political point of view. The improvements of the Tassoultant by the Compagnie Fermière would populate the land as much as the small- or medium-range colonization efforts, would be more profitable, and would be without effective competition from other metropolitan financial circles.

The only objection that seems to justify the administration's reservations concerned the sociopolitical framework of colonization around Marrakesh. The Protectorate did not wish to abandon the idea of establishing French farmers under the direction of the administration, a plan aimed at settling the Moroccan countryside with individuals who intended to remain established. For the French government it was not politically wise to withhold lands at the gates of Marrakesh for any length of time while the colons were consistently pleading for their allotment. Small colonization homestead farms on the outskirts of cities were being encouraged by Pointcarre, the President of the Council, supporting Lyautey's point of view.

This entire controversy illustrates the administration's hesitancy in the face of the choice of capitalist formula to introduce and the variations to be made in response to regional variations of Morocco. Thus, the Protectorate decided in other regions — the Rharb, Chaouia — to favor the Compagnie Marocaine, for example. On the Spanish-occupied zone at the same time, in 1925, the Company of the Loukkos was creating an agribusiness complex of nearly 7,000 hectares on domanial lands.

But in the Haouz, in the end, Regnault did not obtain what he wanted and abandoned the broad proposals he had outlined. In 1924 he gave up the entire affair and handed the local operations over to Cruchet, who represented the company from then on. Cruchet was then exposed to all of the problems with the resident population and with the rightful claimants to the Tassoultant seguia. They were all pursuing their own interests, while being discreetly supported by the Pasha of Marrakesh and his relative, Caid al-Ouriki, who retained control over the diversion point where the seguia took water from the river.

To assess the collapse of Regnault's dreams, let us consider the following request addressed by Cruchet to the Service of Domains on February 5, 1925:

> I ask your permission to establish partnerships with the natives until 1928. My goal is to be fair to the inhabitants of the Tassoultant sector, to only remove them gradually from any piece of land they are accustomed to tilling, and to win them over to our methods of cultivation by absorbing them as workers. We are already so short of manpower that we have to agree to lease plots to the villagers in order to obtain workers. Three years are, therefore, a minimum for us to proceed in the direction indicated.

The Service of Domains found unacceptable this serious infraction of the rules of modern agricultural development. On January 30, 1926, it initiated a procedure for forced resettlement, the first action being an appraisal to estimate the sums to be paid to the inhabitants. Seven villages were affected. The commission agreed to pay 73,000 francs in 1926 (48,000 DH 1974). Cruchet thought the appraisals quite exaggerated:

Moreover the empty dwellings which remain after the natives' departure and the orchards will have to be cleaned up and will represent an expense and not a profit for the company. The Compagnie Fermière cannot possibly assume the charges for forced relocation.

The various protagonists kept putting the ball back into the other party's court. No one wanted to pay, and the tenant farmers continued to occupy the estate. In 1927 it was proposed that the inhabitants leave the enclaves for some plots of land situated on the edge of the estate. The peasants accepted on the condition that they first receive indemnities for resettlement, which they evaluated at 79,000 francs in 1927 (51,000 DH 1974). The general commanding the Region of Marrakesh strongly rebuked the administration for its doubts:

> ... the tranquility of several native families is well worth the 79,000 francs, and if the operation is not justifiable from the domanial point of view, it is defensible from the political point of view.

Finally, the sums were handed over to the Pasha el-Glaoui, who distributed them among his sheikhs and some of the inhabitants. A fuzzy situation then developed. There was neither genuine resettlement nor a stable habitation within the enclaves, nor was there any definite relocation on the tracts of land bordering the estate.

In a letter from the subregional government district which included the entire Haouz, the *Cercle* of Greater Marrakesh, an administrator made the following candid comment:

> Ultimately one does not know who received indemnities nor why the question of the cemeteries was not brought up during the negotiations. There is absolutely no doubt that those responsible for natives show no enthusiasm for resolving the question of resettlement in a suitable and final manner. For the time being the natives of Tassoultant have increased their presence; they still occupy the enclaves and they already occupy the new lands which have been offered to them in compensation.

A final attempt toward large colonial plantation agriculture was initiated by Phillippar, the general manager of the Compagnie Fermière in Paris, at the Office for Moroccan Affairs: he sought to 'transform the handling by virtue of provisional title into a holding by virtue of definitive title, as a large colonial farm, in order to obtain long-term loans and intensify agricultural development'. The Director General of Agriculture again refused.:

> ... because the managers of the Compagnie Fermière are transients, while the goals of the colonization are precisely to bind individuals more permanently to the soil. It would be necessary for the Compagnie Fermière to establish tenant farmers — French, of course — with leases and promises of future right of purchase.

For the sake of resolution, the Compagnie Fermière finally agreed to commit to this plan the 1,617 hectares that it really had at its command, that is to say 1,213 hectares based on the agreement with Moulay al-Kbir (1920 to 1960) and 404 hectares leased from the Service of Domains for a twenty-four year period (1924 to 1948).

In fact the Compagnie Fermière succeeded neither in excluding the inhabitants from the lands nor in developing the estate. In 1967 at the time of an administrative inquiry, it was determined that the arable land had been given in partnership for a gross return of 50 percent of the harvest to forty-odd lessees who lived in the neighboring villages and enclaves. Furthermore these inhabitants had always been permitted to allow their flocks to graze on the Compagnie Fermière's lands so long as they paid the company six dirhams per head of cattle and three dirhams per sheep each year. In short, the most traditional methods of agriculture were applied on 1,549 hectares, more than 95 percent of the estate; only 68 hectares were planted and cultivated directly by the company.

The main reason for the failure of this effort by the Compagnie Fermière to develop the Tassoultant lands was the company's lack of ability to secure sufficient water flow. To obtain it, the Compagnie Fermière would have had to obtain a monopoly for the exploitation of the Tassoultant sector. The Department of Agriculture did not wish to displease the official colonization. The politicians of the Protectorate did not want to reinforce the power of Pasha el-Glaoui through the emergence of a large company with ties to him, that would end up dominating the Haouz economically. It was acceptable for the Pasha to make law in the traditional sector and in matters concerning the population of the valleys and mountains in the south, but not for him to expand his influence in the advanced capitalistic sector of the country.

D   The Failure of Efforts to Expand Official Colonization Lands After 1930

After the irrigation problems encountered by the colonization efforts in the Haouz were partially resolved through the construction of a dam on the Nfis River, Mr Trintignac, the chief engineer of the Corps of Rural Engineers in Marrakesh, attempted to launch a new program of colonization. He developed a detailed description concerning the status of colonized land in the Haouz and decided that it was possible to extend this program into three other regions — the Mrabtine, Askejjour, and the Oudaia. (Mr Trintignac had just returned from a study mission in California and was committed to encouraging a spirit of initiative and free enterprise among the colonists.)[5] The importance of his report, which was submitted in April, 1936, and widely circulated among the various regional government services in Marrakesh, was that it triggered unanimous opposition of the administration toward any new efforts at land colonization. The colons themselves only supported the recommendations of Trintignac concerning the possibility of a supplementary source of water for European farmers who already possessed lots but had received inadequate water allotments.

The main arguments repeatedly put forth by Trintignac's detractors were that there was no longer available land, and that any new land that might be allotted at the time or in the future would have to be confiscated from Moroccans who would surely oppose any such efforts. Some responses in 1937 were as follows:

> The guich of Askejjour is the most depleted: the natives have been almost completely stripped and there is hardly any land left which is not already being cultivated.
>
> Moreover, the native population of the Haouz is in a process of growth: in the past ten years it has increased by 41,500 natives. [Undoubtedly these figures must include the

entire Marrakesh region and not just the Haouz.] What will happen to this excess population if we do not set aside land with water in sufficient quantity to help these new people establish themselves? The surplus population will be forced to emigrate, and by so doing, will probably increase the floating population of the northern cities and add to the growing proletariat at the risk of serious social and political consequences...

I am registering a few reservations [to the Trintignac report] about the possible expansion of colonization into the territory of the Oudaia. The Bour al Ghaf lands can be made available only after settlement of the Cazes affair, and outside these boundaries, promises have been made to the Oudaia on several occasions, with reference to preventing the establishment of colonial areas on their lands... Adding new European farmers in the plain may cause discontent among native farmers that might lead to serious political repercussions.

Another colonial official noted:

Not only did we not do anything to help the natives of this [Mesfioua] region, but what is more, for the benefit of the Tassoultant colons, we have dispossessed them of the water which once enabled them to have fine crops and orchards. The result is that more than 150,000 olive trees have been cut down by their owners either because they were dead or had become unproductive for several years, due to the lack of irrigation water... It is my duty to call to your attention the frame of mind which is characteristic of the Mesfioua of the plains... Each time our public officials from, say, Public Works or the Corps of Rural Engineers visit the countryside, our natives ask themselves anxiously, 'What more are they going to take away from us now?' It is necessary for the natives to realize that the protecting power is not solely interested in Europeans. But efforts on behalf of the natives have only been made in those areas where the interests of the natives were connected with the interests of the European colons.

DEVELOPMENT OF CAPITALISM UNDER THE PROTECTORATE   115

After 1930, almost no lands could be obtained without considerable social and political costs unless Moroccans themselves were partners in the development. More precisely, it was necessary to find new water, not currently appropriated, in order to intensify the productivity of the lands that had already been distributed.

New attempts were made in 1945. At the same time that the Section for Modernization of the Peasantry was launched to modernize native agriculture, the administration of the Protectorate attempted to encourage a vigorous revival of colonization efforts.[6] At this time the French rural population was barely over 30,000, compared to more than 6 million rural Moroccans in the country.[7] The colonization objectives simultaneously included pursuing government policies for settling the territory with colons, resettling those who had been discharged from the military, and also 'providing work for certain elements of the mother country who had been forced to leave their devastated country'.[8] Frequently this method was used to deal with the cases of French farmers and villagers who had collaborated too openly during the German occupation, and for whom life in their own villages had become impossible.

In Marrakesh, 'two domanial regions were likely targets for this new effort at allotment — those of the Tamesguelft sector and of *Bour* (non-irrigated lands of) El Raf, of which the available land surfaces comprise 10,000 and 2,000 hectares, respectively'.[9]

In fact the colonial administration did not take the risk of resettling the people who had occupied Tamesguelft after the deportation of the Cherarda. These lands had been occupied for a while. Then, the Makhzen, little by little, had let neighboring populations from the western part of the country settle the region. On these cultivated lands the State levied the *hars* tax [one-tenth to one-third of the harvest on irrigated lands] and the *usur*, a tithe tax on non-irrigated lands. The large irrigated region, because of all its histories of resettlements and conflicting land claims of the zaouia at Tamesloht, the Crown, and others, had become a practically inextricable mosaic of customs, traditions and overlapping real estate claims (see Table 2.2). A 1946 study (see Table 2.3) concerning the occupation of domanial lands noted the establishment of a large population.

The administration assumed that these lands, because they were leased on a short-term basis to city residents, were readily available and sparsely populated. An initial survey made them aware that,

Table 2.2: *Distribution of Land and Water in the Tamesguelft*

Landholder	Area		Water		
	Hectares	Percent	Liters per second	Percent	Liters per hectare
State Domain	7,855	87	151	83	0.019
Glaoui	588	6	7	4	0.013
Meslohi	245	3	5	3	0.02
El Biaz	111	1	2	a	0.02
Tebaa	110	1	1	a	0.01
Cadi	108	1	9	5	0.083
Habous	18	a	—	—	—
Z^a Sidi Zouine	0	—	4	2	—
Driss Oulad Mennou	0	—	3	a	—
TOTALS	9,035	100	182	100	

Sources: State Land Register, 1927, Survey; Bulletin Officiel No. 1415 (1939); Hydrological Gauging 1927; Bulletin Officiel No. 1219 (1936).

a Less than 1%.

in fact, these lands were dotted with illegal settlements. Whenever one of the city tenants took a lease, he actually leased only the right to raise a land tax on people who gradually laid claim to the land. The distribution of the Tamesguelft for colonization proved unfeasible. The colons would not be able to find employment for 1,196 Moroccan households on 7,855 hectares, or one homestead for every six or seven hectares, and especially not one household for every 0.13 liters of water per second. In these poorly controlled parts of the Haouz, by 1946, demography had already become the foremost constraint.

Consequently, the administration gave up the idea of dividing

Table 2.3: *Population of Domanial Lands by Groups, 1946*

Group	Douars (villages)	Families	Population
Oulad Brahim	9	219	1,244
Oulad Hamadi	10	215	1,157
Tekna	7	164	858
Mjatt	18	218	1,354
Oulad Abdeslam	12	92	676
Oulad Hussan	14	239	1,493
Oulad Si Ahmed	4	49	307
TOTALS	74	1,196	7,089

Source: Rural Military Engineers' Report, Tamesguelft file, June 6, 1946.

Tamesguelft into plots. But, behind the scenes, it tolerated private initiatives that led to some transformations — the expansion of the Pasha's holdings, the settlement of a man named Cazes who had rendered some services to the Oudaia, allotments to Moroccan war veterans on 200 hectares at the extreme ends of seguias (on lands so poorly irrigated that they were soon abandoned by their new owners, who then moved back to the cities and left partners to herd a few sheep).

With respect to the Bour el Raf, the Ait Immour and the Oudaia successfully opposed a formal proposition for allotting the land for colonization efforts, but they agreed to lease some poorly irrigated plots to private foreign individuals. In fact the administration undertook no additional deliberate allotment activities, and if private colonialists acquired some additional land after World War II, it was through private purchases from Moroccans.

Since the colonization effort was concerned about the sale of lands of colons to Moroccans, an inquiry was launched in 1951 by the Secretary General of the Protectorate:

The opinion has been expressed that, due to the political

situation, the French landholdings in Morocco are diminishing... Such a diminution, if it does exist, might indicate two distinct tendencies of individuals: the French are becoming sellers of land in greater and greater numbers, while there are few in the buying market.

In Marrakesh, between 1942 and 1950 the registered transactions show an increase in favor of Europeans. Table 2.4 illustrates for each year the number of transactions of various types. As the table indicates, the craze created in 1948 was an overeaction. It was really the result of the exceptional sale of four parcels of land. The

Table 2.4: *Land Transactions Between Moroccans and Europeans, 1942–1950*

	Transactions		
Year	Moroccans to Europeans	Europeans to Moroccans	Europeans to Europeans[a]
1942	12	—	6
1943	6	30	68
1944	37	—	—
1945	354	150	—
1946	649	72	9
1947	469	2	200
1948	104	589	—
1949	47	—	190
1950	67	105	1,166
TOTALS	1,745	948	1,639

Source: Regional Agricultural Services. Survey of the Protectorate Secretary General on Changes in European Landholding.

[a] Includes both sales and inheritances.

administration concluded that in fact colonial landholdings were increasing, and that no special actions were needed.

A new study, conducted in 1955 on the entire territory, dealt both with the land surfaces and the value of the European holdings in Morocco. It also demonstrated that the increase of foreign land acquisitions was gradually leveling off (see Table 2.5).

Table 2.5: *European Acquisitions and Sales of Moroccan Land, 1952-1954*

Year	Acquisitions		Sales	
	Number	Area (in hectares)	Number	Area (in hectares)
1952	175	1570	120	1520
1953	141	1578	106	1272
1954	97	1303	71	1339
TOTALS	413	4451	297	4131

The study included all European landholdings. Unfortunately, it does not show in detail the situation of the Haouz, and documentation has not been found which relates specifically to the Haouz. As the table indicates, the net diminution of European holdings began in 1954. This marks exactly the beginning of the colonial retreat from occupation of the land. But the volume of investments in equipment for the farms had regressed sooner and more quickly than the landholdings themselves. Figures for the years up to 1954 therefore indicate a rather precipitous drop in the number of requests for loans and the amount of money borrowed by the colons. In the two-year period from 1952 to 1954, the number of requests decreased by almost half and the amount of money borrowed decreased by nearly two thirds.

The 1955 report of the Secretary General of the Protectorate concluded:

With respect to real estate, the event that is more important than a slight deficit balance of French holdings is that these holdings — which in the course of thirty or forty years have grown to more than one million hectares — are no longer increasing. The growth curve has leveled off and there is uncertainty with regard to its future direction. It seems unlikely that it will go higher. The decade of the 1950s is likely to be characterized by a slight decline.

History was to confirm this observation!

2 The Problems

Around the 1930s a series of circumstances dampened the enthusiasm of the colons, and the stark reality of the Haouz revealed itself to them in all of its severity. The three major reasons for this situation were the technical ignorance of the colons, the lack of water, and the economic slump.

In a 1929 official report on the water resources available for the land allotted to the colons, the administration acknowledged:

> At the time the development projects were worked out, the hydraulic question failed to assume the importance that the peculiar climate of the Marrakesh region demanded. The colons themselves did not realize this initially.

In fact the areas of the plots of each allotment had been determined much more by the characteristics of soil quality than by the available irrigation resources. The Chief Engineer for Public Works at Marrakesh commented: 'The result was that the majority of the colons encountered difficulties in developing their lands due to the insufficiency of water.'

The following proposal from a representative of the Irrigation Service to the Committee of Colonization indicates the administration's lack of preparation and the ignorance of those receiving allotments: 'We concede that it is necessary for each plot, whatever its surface may be, to have a minimum of twenty-five liters of water per second in winter, and that water in the summer is not absolutely essential.'

No one recorded an objection to this suggestion when it was presented to the Regional Administrative Commission. When it was submitted to the Directors General of Public Works and of Agriculture, it received their approval in principle. It even became the basis for the demands extended by the Joint Chamber of Agriculture to the Resident General when he visited Marrakesh.

The unreasonable character of such a proposal's water requirements is revealed by its specifications for the rotation of crops, for plantations, and for 'victory gardens'. The actual water endowment in this region could only ensure a winter cereal crop and the raising of sheep. What then was the meaning of all of these land clearance and improvement efforts, these quickset hedges, and this considerable indebtedness, the final outcome of which was only wheat cultivation?

We will not follow the oratorical jousts that were so scrupulously reported in the minutes of the Committees of Colonization at the point when those receiving land allotments finally had their eyes opened at the end of the sixth agricultural season! But this episode suffices to illustrate the low level of experience and technical expertise of these men who found themselves located in a region totally new to them.

For the colon arriving in Marrakesh after World War I, appearances seemed inviting: an agreeable climate, vegetation growing effortlessly with minimal irrigation, wheat prices that permitted fantastic profits even with the smallest yields. But one of the major factors contributing to these conditions was the very low cost of manpower during the twenties. The Protectorate at that time was concerned only with the social aspects of its intervention and with furthering its colonial policy of territorial settlement by Frenchmen. In its policy of land distribution, it favored individuals who were entitled to 'the nation's gratitude': war veterans, the disabled, the 'pioneers' of Morocco, and the fathers of large families. To the speculative adventurers of the preceding phase were added the social casualties. 'The genuine farmers aware of the difficulties of land development were a tiny minority,' according to Trintignac.

Those who had experience in North African agriculture were even more rare. Even if they had an agricultural background, they would most likely not have succeeded any better because the unique conditions of the Haouz were poorly understood by even the best-qualified specialists of the day.[10] While the colons in Marrakesh, in contrast to the rest of the colonization in Morocco, were better prepared and initially more financially affluent, ironically it was in this very region that the 'failures', i.e. the abandonment of land plots, were the most pronounced.

These difficulties and failures were well known by the whole official colonization at least, thanks to the commissions of development. The commissions visited the holdings at regular intervals to appraise the development efforts that had been undertaken, to give advice, to assess the extensions to be granted, and to deliver documents discharging individuals from completed obligations. These visits resulted in the recording of minutes that enable us to trace in detail the progress of development, the difficulties, and the attitude of the administration.

On December 28, 1931, upon the formal request of the Joint Chamber of Marrakesh, a turbulent meeting took place during which the colons accused the administration of the Protectorate of not having kept its promises, of having distributed uncultivable lands, and of failing to provide for absolutely necessary hydraulic equipment. A 'Commission for Reform' was appointed to travel to the Haouz in order to receive the colons' grievances, allotment by allotment, before making a general disposition of the problem. As the minutes indicate, in the course of these visits (in February 1932), lack of water was always first among the complaints and accusations. A large number of colons also quite explicitly expressed their demand to abandon their plots or asked to be relocated in other regions of Morocco. Table 2.6 indicates the course of land abandonment during the period. Because they were less indebted, most of the colons who remained were able to hold out in the hope of taking over the land, and especially the water rights, of the farmers who were leaving. The colons discovered that their lands, located at the extremities of irrigation sectors, were relatively unpopulated because they lacked water. In fact, the objective of the drive to expand farms was not to increase land surface itself, but primarily to obtain water rights of the acquired lands. These water resources would then be concentrated on only a small section of the land, leaving the remainder uncultivated.

Table 2.7 illustrates the progression in the acquisition of water in various irrigation sectors. The increase of water available for farm

Table 2.6: Evolution of the Surface Area of Farms Following Abandonments

Sector	Total hectares owned by colons	Hectares per colon acquired through allotment	Number of colons at time of allotment	Number of colons in 1932	Number of colons in 1935	Hectares per colon in 1935	Per cent decline of colons holding land through allotments
Tabouhanit	1,056	106	10	5	4	264	60
Tassoultant	2,657	221	12	11	11	241	8
Aghouatim	5,521	240	23	12	10	552	57
Targa	2,540	110	23	18	17	150	26
Saada	1,920	192	10	4	4	480	60
TOTALS	13,694	170	78	50	46	300	41

Source: Archives of the Marrakesh Office of Colonization.

Table 2.7: *Irrigation Allotment per Farm by Sector, Over Time*

Sector	Total liters	Irrigation allotment per farm		
	at the date of the allotment		1932	1935
Tabouhanit	100	10	20	25
Tassoultant	120	10	11	15
Aghouatim	70	3	6	20
Targa	160	7	9	25
Saada	0	0	0	30

Source: Office of Agriculture and Corps of Rural Engineers Regional Office Archives at Marrakesh.

lands from the date of allotment to 1932 was made possible by the abandonment by some colons of farm lands which were then acquired by others. In 1935 various efforts at increasing access to available water were responsible for the increase in the flow of water. More than the desire for lands, it was the quest to appropriate water for the benefit of the colonizers that gave rise in the Haouz to the most iniquitous plundering. It was those Moroccans situated midway in the irrigation sector who suffered the most from the colonizers' search for water.

A The Hydraulic Question[11]

We shall not dwell on the system of distribution for the waters of the oueds among the seguias and for waters of the seguias among individual farms. When the colons occupied the lands that the administration had put at their disposal they found themselves in a situation of variable, complex and shifting customs. While devoid of legislation, these customs invariably resulted from definite rights directly connected to power relationships, the occupation of the riverbanks, the establishment of dominant (upstream) positions, and the taxing of water usage on transverse seguias.

It is contrary to the nature of capitalism to invest in too hazardous a situation. The profit from an investment must have a reasonably high probability of being realized or the investment will go elsewhere. Capitalism can compete with other modes of production only if the factors of production are reasonably assured and at well-defined costs. Within this framework it is impossible to maintain production if, at every moment, one has to fight for rights, resort to force, and appeal to political powers. This is all the more so when investments are rooted in real estate based on precarious ownership; such a situation is bound to scare capital away.

Thus the program of real estate registration aimed at clearing the land plots of all former rights in order to make them inviolable properties. Similarly, if the objective of colonization was the establishment of a capitalist formula of production, it was essential in a region where irrigation was of such importance to fix water rights on a legal-rational basis.

Colonial action concerning the hydraulic question sought to achieve several parallel objectives at the same time: to establish water legislation appropriate to capitalism, to increase the water endowment for the benefit of foreign properties, to improve the distribution of water (by cementing seguia walls), and to regularize the flow of the oueds (by dam construction) — all while seeking to retain the imperial supervision of the state over such an important resource.

Legislation Aimed at Establishing Water Rights
The first effort in this direction was to establish the principle that all water rights fall under the public domain. This was immediately tempered by establishing a 'grandfather clause' for those traditional rights predating 1914. It was a radical sharing of two different models: freezing the rights existing prior to the promulgation of the decree, and putting at the state's disposal all of the remaining water, both existing and yet to be discovered. All waters placed in the public domain could, without appeal, be put at the disposal of 'users' instead of owners, within a well-defined procedure based on granting of formal authorization to draw on public water supplies. The goals were the same as those of dahirs concerning collective lands and inventories of domanial lands: everything which is not claimed belongs to the state; everything that is claimed is immobilized; usage is frozen at the level of custom![12] By recognizing the practices that

predated 1914, 'just as they were', the legislators checked their evolution, while virtuously claiming to have respected the rights of the people, albeit at a very small cost. Their rights would have amounted to something if they could have participated in the general evolution by giving their water rights over to expropriation by the public domain in return for access to the benefits which could be derived from agricultural development (e.g., increased supplies of irrigation water derived from building of dams, improvement of seguias, etc.).[13] But under those conditions the 'colonial party' would have been too powerful, and the groups expropriated by the right of public domain would have been expropriated only, without receiving any benefits, and thus left in total ruins.

Although they benefited from the whole operation, the colons did not readily accept the state's restrictions and consequent curb on their appetites for more water. Upon their return from a study mission in California, some colons pointed out that public ownership of water there was unknown, and property owners could draw on sources of water directly, without requesting authorization. The Moroccan administration, in response, stressed the scarcity of water in Morocco relative to California. In addition, they emphasized the importance of the rights of natives in Morocco, which were unknown on the west coast of the U.S.

These events show that the model of society pursued by the administrative 'class' was not exactly comparable to the one envisioned by the colons. The image of an administration of the Protectorate as a mere instrument of colonization and the mere executor of an imperial project determined at the highest levels would be a rough caricature, and even erroneous.

Establishing Colonial Priority on the Seguias
The main principle for the distribution of water from rivers to water channels resides in the domination of those upstream over those downstream. This is not exactly a right, but an unavoidable fact based upon the simple practice of direct action. It is the recognition of rights of those downstream on the part of those upstream which is difficult to obtain. This requires constant vigilance and repeated recourse to force. On the other hand, the establishment of an upstream diversion water control gate also requires violent action, but the action needs to be taken only once for all time, and it can only be reversed, as far as the

DEVELOPMENT OF CAPITALISM UNDER THE PROTECTORATE   127

downstream is concerned, by an action of the same magnitude.

The administration of the Protectorate pushed upstream as far as possible the diversion points of seguias that irrigated colonial lands. The best examples of this phenomenon are the Tassoultant seguia on the Oued Ourika and the Oued Nfis–Tassoultant connector seguia. In these and similar cases the canals feeding the colonial lands had very good access to available waters. On the Nfis, on the right bank, the four seguias that provided water for colonization lands were the third, fourth, and sixth out of a total of twenty-nine diversion points. On the Ourika, the Tassoultant-Etat seguia was the fourth after the *foum* — the alluvial fan where the stream comes down from the mountain — this out of a total of 38 taps.

Regulation of Seguia Flow

Positive rights flowed from previous practices: each seguia took as much water as possible, on the basis of the industry, effort and vigilance of its users. Procedures for water diversion had, until then, been rudimentary. The water distribution system had spread quite evenly its inability to handle floods and periods of high water. It was to the advantage of the administration of the Protectorate to recognize rights based on a failing and mediocre old technology in order to draw off for its own benefit the increased water resources of a new system based on modern irrigation technology.

If the regulation of the flow of the seguias had been aimed at a fairer distribution of water in the name of social equity, it would have fixed the rights of seguias on rivers in proportion to the land areas covered by each irrigation sector.[14] In fact it can be demonstrated that the water flow was arranged to benefit those with power, first the colons and then the allied caids. The procedure that was followed was to figure out the relative flow of the river and each seguia by means of direct measurement over an extended period of time, in order to establish the amount of water being removed relative to the water level of the river. The administration was well aware of the swindle and deceit that resulted from this procedure.

> It is advisable to make frequent measurements of the river and the various seguias *while preventing the users from knowing the goals of this operation*. At the end of the two years at most, the interpretation of curves thus established enables

one to ascertain *approximately* the relative flow of each
seguia in relationship to the flow of the river.[15]

Continuing to recognize water rights established prior to 1914 at least guaranteed the flows that had been established by these measurements. Once the levels of water withdrawal had been established, the next step was to legislate water distribution, by means of 'decrees of water distribution'. It might be pointed out that these decrees often used the word 'provisional' for rivers without irrigation supply dams. The regulations specified the water appropriation for each seguia when the river flow reached certain levels. Any increase to the benefit of one seguia was almost always at the expense of another.

One stream, the Nfis, was largely diverted during the summer to benefit directly the colons in the Targa irrigation sector. Colonizers owned seventy-nine percent of the surface of the Targa sector and the remainder was divided between the Pasha Thami el-Glaoui, al-Meslohi, and various domanial properties.

In order to insure the execution of the regulations and decrees, a corps of official water regulators was constituted.

A European watchman shall insure the operation of the
padlocked water control gates which are placed at the head
of each seguia; ... he shall insure distribution prescribed by
decrees; ... he shall make sure that no clandestine use
patterns are established.

Favoring the Colons in the Allotment of Seguia Water
European farmers, established on upstream seguias where water endowments had been increased, also benefited from a privileged allotment when they were co-users with Moroccans. Only Thami el-Glaoui and al-Meslohi had at their command water endowments that were comparable in their proportions to the Europeans. The favored position of colons is illustrated by a letter written in 1926 by the chief of the Cercle of Greater Marrakesh to the Director of Indigenous Affairs:

The distribution of the water of the Tassoultant, i.e. two-
thirds for the colonists and one-third for the Ourika during
the dry season, was imposed by the Administration on native

users on May 31, 1924 following the decision made at the meeting of the Committee of Colonization held at Marrakesh on the third of May. This decision was justified as follows: 'The Secretary General has decided not to take any notice of the claim of the Ourika.'

Decreasing Water Losses on Seguias Controlled by Colons
Land occupation by foreigners at the far ends of irrigation sectors was justified by 1) the fact that they were only slightly populated, 2) the fact that the Moroccan notables did not covet this land, and 3) the relatively low cost. These conditions can all be explained by the fact that these lands were either scarcely irrigated or not irrigated at all. The skillfulness, unconscious though it was, of colonization in the Haouz lay squarely on these factors: first abandoned areas were acquired at very low prices; then the water supply was placed in the public domain at an inconsequential cost. The waters from the general region were then to be focused on these inexpensive lands through irrigation.

The problem that remained was how to transport water to these lands over long distances while minimizing substantial losses by seepage into the beds of seguias. In his study of the hydraulic question, Martin pondered whether it would not be desirable to 'create masonry summer seguias or even enclosed ducts, especially where the canals involved are long or where the slope is steep'. In 1929, after a visit to Marrakesh by Saint, the Resident General of Morocco, it was decided that the work on the *khettara* (wells from underground drainage used to develop water for surface irrigation) would be begun immediately by the administration of the Public Works Department, 'for the khettara are not exposed to the open air, and thus will minimize evaporation and the theft of water'. In 1931, at the time of the debate over the 1932-1939 loan, Trintignac judged the technique for using 'modern khettara' to be:

> ... slow and costly in its realization, and ... other means may be necessary to salvage the situation. Experiments attempted at Tabouhanit conclude that the general cementing of seguias for water conveyance and distribution will greatly reduce the losses, which have been established at four liters per second per kilometer.[16]

Trintignac took pride in having cemented two hundred kilometers of seguias for the colons.

The effective solution was indeed the cementing of the seguias — work that was done at the expense of the state and only on the canals which served colonization lands. The losses on a seguia such as the Tassoultant dropped from thirty percent to six percent.

Efforts at Regularizing Stream Flows
The radical solution to the precariousness and variability of water resources was found, of course, in constructing dams to capture winter flood waters to permit their use in the summer. An even better solution was to find dam sites where reservoirs could be established for several years' storage. Although the technology of dams for diversion of water had been known and widely used in the Haouz since the Almohad dynasty in the twelfth century, it was not until 1929 that the first small dam for storing water for future use was built at Lalla Takerkoust. It regularized less than thirty percent of the flow of the Oued Nfis.

The selection of the Nfis as the first stream to be controlled and regulated was based as much on hydrogeographic considerations as on sociopolitical ones. In a recent study on the development of the greater Haouz region which only considered natural site conditions and the costs of construction, and assumed the complete utilization of water on all Haouz lands, the Nfis ranked third after the al-Akhdar and the Tessaout.

Other than cost, socio-political considerations made the Nfis preferable to other rivers: the water flow of the Nfis from year to year was the most irregular of any river in the Haouz, and before the construction of the dam, its waters were the most poorly distributed by the system of seguias. The progress made from regularizing the water flow on the Nfis would be the most substantial, and thus the greatest amount of 'new' resources could be added to the public domain. As Martin suggested in his report:

> Generally speaking, the natives had made the best use of all the surface waters which were not too difficult to divert, that is, of all of the water except flood water.
>
> But with the reservoir dam, when high waters occur it will be possible to store the entire flow... and when the dam is opened, the water will be distributed through the old seguias

based on the flow of the river *measured upstream from the old dam*.[17]

The decision to 'stop history' for the Moroccan users of this river and to preclude them from any participation in progess — in this case based on the hydraulic regulation of the Oued Nfis — took a turn which was both comic and tragic, because the logic of this formulistic montage located the rights of Moroccans 'upstream from the dam'. This amounts to saying that the dam did not really exist for the Moroccans: there were two realities, irreducible and geographically separated.

Martin showed a dim awareness that there was something invalid in this attempt at obfuscation based on segregating perceptions of reality:

From the political point of view, this system, although it is in perfect compliance with our acquired rights, is likely not to be accepted without some difficulty by the native users who, being unable to see what happens upstream, will harbor fears of being ill-treated.[18]

Despite the construction of this dam, the Haouz did not enter the era of rational irrigation. It was once thought that it would be useful to create a large new land allotment in order to use the newly available Nfis waters immediately downstream from the dam in a regular distribution system with the minimum of transportation. But the serious problems of existing farms obliged the irrigation system manager to 'shuffle' the distribution network and set up some branch distribution lines to transport water for land parcels that had been distributed randomly from previous acquisitions spread all over the whole plain. If the technical services had been aware, before the 1920 land distribution of the official colonization, of the absolute primacy of water availability, there is no doubt that the colonization lands would have been laid out within the first irrigation sectors of the Nfis.

A few indicators illustrate the incoherence of the colonial irrigation system which was superimposed on the traditional one. In the Haouz there were 130 precolonial seguias totaling 140 kilometers in combined length (a little more than one kilometer per seguia) for the annual distribution of four hundred and eighty million cubic meters of water (around 3.3 million cubic meters per seguia kilometer). The cemented irrigation network of the colonialists was one hundred and twelve kilometers long and distributed one hundred million cubic meters of water (around 800,000 cubic meters per kilometer of seguia).

The step by step outfitting of this irrigation system, without any overall plan and with no true economic justification, shows the grip of politics in the strategy of water distribution managers of the 1930s. It will make it difficult, for a long time, to think about optimal water management for the plain.

The Effort to Secure Groundwater Sources

The 1925 dahir placed all waters in the public domain, including underground waters. Rights prior to 1914 concerning the water table were gauged at the points where water was removed from the khettara, as the quantity of water drawn up (by means of animal power) had always been almost negligible. In 1972, the net yield distributed from the khettara was estimated at forty-four percent of the usable flow from the water table, but this was after a long rebuilding campaign; it is likely that in 1930 it was no more than thirty percent. Furthermore, these khettara were located in areas sparsely or not at all occupied by the colonials. In short, a significant portion of underground water, in certain areas almost all of it, was placed in the public domain devoid of any competing claims. The colonials waged the same battle to acquire access and rights to the use of underground water as they had over the right to control seguias. They wanted to eliminate from the dahir of 1925 those clauses which made authorization of water allotment both uncertain and revocable without compensation for loss. A subcommittee of the colonization in Marrakesh pleaded:

> Given the importance that khettara are assuming in the region, this legislation needs revision ... The costs required for development of a khettara are already considerable; furthermore, this water frequently will be used for the cultivation of orchards. The revocability, without compensation for losses, of water authorizations thus would be doubly detrimental to private individuals, since they would simultaneously lose both the cost invested in the construction and their plantations.

In fact the colons did not privately undertake the digging of khettara. It was done by the administration.

The colons were particularly interested in irrigation pumping; they used pumps with small producer gas engines for their individual needs and electric pumps for collective projects with state assistance. It was particularly in the Targa sector that this movement was begun. In 1935 five pumps with electric motors were installed by the Corps of Rural Engineers. Each provided a flow of thirty liters per second. In 1941 the number of pumps had increased to 35, and by 1968 there were approximately 100. The development of the Targa could not have been achieved without these pumps.

The monopolization by the colonialists of irrigation resources led to the drying up of Moroccan family farms and their confinement in a survivor economy. Though the administration reports of political authorities attached little importance to the colonial occupation of land, by contrast they did underscore the serious political and social consequences which the seizure of irrigation resources entailed.

When the Trintignac Report was released, the various government services were asked to give their reactions to the possible expansion of colonization. Their unanimous response was to warn about the dangers of any new water restrictions that would adversely affect native Moroccans. The chief of the Cercle of Greater Marrakesh argued:

> In most tribes a very small minority actually receive sufficient water supply. It is among these disinherited people that most new resources should be distributed when they become available.

Another commentator noted:

> With regard to the Bachia seguia ... It has been impossible to reach an agreement. The natives lack water not only for the irrigation of their trees and crops, but for their flocks as well. Political reasons stand in the way of granting the colons' request of one hundred liters feeding the seguia of Talougart and Tagouramt, upon which, as the investigation has established, the natives have rights.

Yet another pointed out:

> To add new colons in a heavy proportion would be tantamount to moving towards a catastrophe in dry years and especially to cause native users discontent and resentment which could have grave repercussions.

Finally, the Vaughan-Russell report expressed a still stronger point of view:

> At the present moment the state colonists have reason to be fairly satisfied as far as the hydraulic question is concerned; but, on the other hand, many private owners of land, having lost all or part of their water supplies, are very dissatisfied and feel, not without justification, that the old established laws with respect to water rights have been violated. Great dissatisfaction is also felt in some districts at the redistribution of river water effected by the Protectorate authorities. In one case, in order to satisfy ambitious schemes for the colonization, and therefore for the irrigation of a large district near Marrakesh, river water has been diverted almost entirely from the district which it formerly irrigated with the result that the latter district, which used to be renowned for its fertility, is now notoriously barren.[19]

On the basis of Table 2.8, one can see comparable acquisitions of land and water by the colons. The figures reflect only sixty-eight percent of the land occupied by the colons, but the proportions they indicate would be substantially modified if they were calculated for all irrigated lands.

These water allotments should probably be reported by individual households. Each foreign family had at its command 190 hectares and 700,000 cubic meters of water per year. The Moroccan families averaged 5.5 hectares and 11,500 cubic meters per year. These averages, different in magnitude as they are, conceal many other differences which will be examined later.

The disparity of water usage is even more conspicuous when surface water is compared to underground water resources. In the latter case, the institutional and judicial advantage of the colons was

Table 2.8: Irrigated Land and Irrigation Allotments in Selected Tributary Basins of the Haouz

Basin	Total irrigated hectares	Total irrigated hectares owned by colons	Percent of irrigated land owned by colons	Total cubic meters distributed per year (x 1,000,000)	Total cubic meters distributed per year to colons (x 1,000,000)	Percent of water distributed to colons	Moroccans	Europeans	Total
Nfis	50,000	8,380	16.8	100.6	49	49	1,240	5,847	2,012
Rhirhaia Ourika	59,000	9,600	16.25	150.3	30.7	20	2,421	3,198	2,547
Zat	26,600	5,800	21.8	67.8	9.4	14	2,808	1,621	2,549
TOTALS	135,600	23,780	17.5	318.7	89.1	28	2,050	3,740	2,350

(Land / Water / Water per hectare in cubic metres per hectare per year)

magnified by their financial advantage, especially in the zones where pumps were employed. Table 2.9 illustrates the distribution of water by seguias, khettara and pumping. By 1956, colonials were the beneficiaries of ninety-eight percent of the pumped water in the Nfis and sixty-one percent in the basins of the Rhirhaia and the Ourika.

Table 2.9: *Distribution of Water by Seguia, Khettara, and Pumping*

Basin	By seguia — Total volume distributed[a]	By seguia — Colons' Volume	By seguia — Colons' %	By khettara and pumping — Total volume distributed[a]	By khettara and pumping — Colons' volume	By khettara and pumping — Colons' %
Nfis	62	13	21	38.6	36	93
Rhirhaia Ourika	106.4	23.7	22.3	43.9	7	16
TOTALS	168.4	36.7	22	82.5	43	52

[a] Millions of cubic meters per year.

B The Economic Slump and the Debt Problem

The economic depression of the 1930s obviously went far beyond the Haouz. But, with less than three thousand cubic meters of water per hectare per year, the colons could base their agriculture only on production of cereals, the prices of which were remunerative at the close of World War I. In the long run the colons were more vulnerable than native Moroccans in the face of the depression because they had few alternatives. Monoculture farming is fragile in a market economy. For his part, the Moroccan farmer had to contend with hazards of climate that his system of production and reduced water supply did not allow him to master. The Moroccan cultivator suffered less from the drop in prices: having sought refuge in self-sufficiency, he ate his own grain!

Unable to sell at a good price, the colon had to go into debt; in any case he could not pay his debts. The administration of the Protectorate had made credit widely available to him. The colon now had to pay for the hazards of the market, against which the capitalist system offered him no protection.

It is difficult to establish the exact level of indebtedness of the colons. The administration itself lost track: there had been so many subsistence loans, subsidies, credit funds, time extensions for postponed compensations... After having examined a large number of files and having spent hundreds of hours trying to close in on reality, we still are not certain of having obtained even an approximate idea of the extent of this indebtedness. For example, having finished these calculations in 1973, we discovered a file concerning twelve colons of the Saada and Targa sectors, each of them the beneficiary of a loan of twenty-five thousand (1929) francs (13,000 DH in 1974) without interest or any reimbursement for ten years. We are still not sure that we have exhausted all the sources of information.

The analysis of debts is made more difficult because of the many varying sources of information. It is possible to distinguish eighteen different categories of credit and loans and eleven different approaches to analyzing the tax base. In order to have been completely thorough it would have been necessary to study the financial records of each colon; the information exists in the archives of the Department of Finance, but the task was too enormous for us. The following figures, which indicate the extent of debt, are available from a 1935 analysis of these records and from the Trintignac report.

Apparently in 1935 those foreigners involved in the colonization effort in the region around Marrakesh were indebted for a minimum of 25 million francs. That is approximately 1,000 DH (1974) per hectare and approximately 250,000 DH per colon, on the average. These debts were largely concentrated in the initial costs of settlement of the colons. Trintignac, in our opinion, gives a somewhat exaggerated figure:

> The investment can easily exceed 5,000 F per hectare
> [approximately 3,300 DH per hectare in 1974]. The initial
> colons did not lack credit; it was widely distributed, albeit at
> a high rate for agricultural enterprises. The credit rested
> upon collateral which was frequently fictitious (buildings,

clearing of land, plantations), while the only real wealth resided in water. Consequently today in a period of general devaluation, the colon on his estate, even if the estate is suitably equipped, is hard pressed to make enough money to earn a net income above the interest on his debt.

Jacques Berque recalls the episode of the 'shorn colons' who, on February 6, 1934, marched in ranks to the residency to request an extension of their debts and, more important a reorganization of the economic conditions of the colonization, and indeed, of the Protectorate.[20] The shaved heads tell a great deal; they symbolized the colons' feeling that they were being treated like 'natives' — that they were not being protected by their own government, that their own enclave of prosperity was suffering like the rest of the country from the casual indifference of an impotent colonial administration.

The Federation of the Chambers of Agriculture proposed that the interest on loans be decreased to two percent and that loans be refinanced for fifty year terms. However, the Subcommission of Finance adopted a decrease to three percent and had repayment extended to thirty year terms only. In addition to these arrangements there were provisions for making up for additional costs which were to be carried by state finances. Various financial steps were taken to lighten the financial burden the state took on by managing the extension of the debts. For example, one of these steps was the elimination of a credit of 400,000 francs that had served as a subsidy on phosphates. This resulted in an increase of the price of phosphates abroad, which increased its price for farmers in Europe.

More than a mere revision and a simple 'reform of the colonization', a major reorganization of the State's finances, of the equilibrium of its resources, and even of its economic principles was involved. For example, on 12 April, 1932, the Cherifian Office of Exports (OCE) was created to support the development of speculative crops for export. In 1937 the Cherifian Interprofessional Cereals Office (OCIC) was created to stabilize the price of these commodities. These were politically wise policies that moved the economy away from the liberalism and open competiton which had been advocated previously.

The measures designed to benefit the colons, combined with a few good farm years, and then the closing of the country as a result of World War II, oriented regional production toward the internal

Moroccan and North African markets. During the postwar period these developments resulted in a remarkable resumption of colonial agriculture.

3 The Results

A   The System of Colonial Cultivation
The first steps in the development of an industrial agriculture in the Haouz preceded even colonization. To mention only the nineteenth century, since the vice-royalty of Moulay Abd er-Rahamane, the large-scale cultivation of cotton and sugar cane had been one of the aims of foreign merchants. All European travelers optimistically praised the exceptional conditions of the Haouz, the richness of its lands, and the advantages of its climate.[21] These visitors were thinking about the use of the most advanced developments in agricultural technology, developments which could not easily be applied in Europe. Finally, well before 1912, the Germans, and particularly the agents of the Mannesmann Company, in numerous places undertook cotton cultivation which 'thrived very well'.

In contrast, the specifications for development that were imposed on colonial farmers by the administration of the Protectorate from 1919 on seemed fairly timorous and mediocre. For example, in the Tassoultant sector, it was required that colons plant 'five hundred fruit trees within five years' on two hundred hectares of land, that is, using less than five hectares for the trees. On the remainder they could sow wheat and graze sheep; all that was necessary was to clear the land. In the Aghouatim sector, policies required one hundred and fifty fruit trees. In the Targa sector, the recommended crops were cereals as well as 'some forage and a few olive and apricot trees'. But the lease-purchase notices for these farms indicated that water was not available and cattle raising not advisable because forage could not be grown. Market crops and summer crops were not recommended due to a lack of water. Sheep could be raised only if a sufficient food supplement was available.

The Compagnie Fermière reacted to this lack of initiative by opening new vistas for agribusiness in the Haouz. In 1933, Regnault submitted to the Director General of Agriculture, Commerce and Colonization a particularly ambitious project for development of the

Tassoultant sector. Undoubtedly behind this recommendation the agent was aiming at obtaining more surface area with longer lease times. However, the people and interests that he associated with this project and the care given to his calculations indicate that the prophetic project was intended to go beyond mere negotiations.

For example, he wanted to concentrate the waters from March to September on only one-third of the 12,000 hectares of the Tassoultant. He hoped to thus concentrate the winter waters on the eight thousand remaining hectares for the production of cereals, legumes, and sheep.

The advocated solution was to reserve the low summer and autumn water for market commerce operations that would be carried out only on one-third of the twelve thousand hectares of the Tassoultant. The more abundant winter and spring waters would be utilized as follows: on the remaining 8,000 hectares there would be cereals, legumes, and fallow lands for sheep; well-watered lands would be used to raise sugar beets to supply a refinery 'capable of providing sugar for all the south and southwest of Morocco'; alfalfa would serve as forage for a large animal husbandry industry that would supply Marrakesh with dairy products as well as improved grades of beef; hemp, flax and cotton would be produced in order to compete against foreign (at least non-French foreign) imports and supply fibers to Marrakesh workshops; and finally, there would be orchards of citrus trees and apricots. As for the 'cultivation of cereals', Regnault argued, 'it must progressively give way to a position of secondary importance.'

These projects obviously implied considerable capital investment, the construction of factories, the availability of mechanical power and qualified manpower. But these were all issues to which the administration reacted with extreme caution, checking calculations, and questioning even the possibility of 'transporting sugar beets under the sun of Marrakesh'.

Although the Compagnie Fermière ultimately failed, it did increase the awareness some ten years later of the need to diversify crops and orient speculation toward an industrial transformation. The new orientations which agronomic research would take on experimental farms in the Menara and Souelah beginning in 1924 are significant in this regard. Research on the growing of alfalfa, hemp, cotton, beets and apricot trees until then had been minimal, but it soon surpassed the studies that were already underway on citrus fruits, olive trees and cereals. Trintignac's report observed:

> Debt amortization and the payment of interest can only be assured from revenues from high-income crops. At the normal selling price and with average yields, wheat is too weak a commodity. What will pay off is arboriculture based on citrus fruits, animal husbandry based on the fattening of cattle, and certain special crops (seeds, plants for pharmaceutical and dyeing purposes) — all crops which might cost as much as ten thousand francs (13,000 DH in 1974) per hectare for the initial planting investment.[22]

We will not follow in detail the attempts and errors that gradually modified the colonial cultivation system and adjusted it to the ecological conditions and to a general economic framework largely oriented towards exports. Such research would have to take into account agronomic conditions as well as complex and detailed economic competition, which would exceed the scope of this work. A general description will be sufficient to establish a relationship between farm production and the developing para-agricultural industry in Marrakesh. Table 2.10 describes the cultivation system on a few farms that benefited from land allotments through the official colonization. Because private colonial farms were scattered and accounted for a smaller amount of land area, the private farmers had established a system of cultivation of the Tassoultant type which favored the cultivation of apricots. Of the land utilized for arboriculture, two-fifths was for apricot trees, two-fifths for citrus fruit, and one-fifth for olive trees.

But the indices which measure land productivity by the hectare do not really mean much; the more accurate way of comparing farms to one another is based on amounts of water allotments. A practical formula using water as the prime variable shows that development efforts were approximately the same for all farms. Table 2.11 illustrates the relationship between water and land surface.

The farms of Aghouatim were not sufficiently irrigated, with only two thousand cubic meters per hectare per year on the average. Except for them, the gross product per cubic meter of irrigation water was almost constant. By comparison, the surface area of the land was only a formal means of determining how much water was appropriate for a

Table 2.10: *Agricultural Production Characteristics for Official Colonization Farms in Selected Irrigation Sectors*

Sector Characteristics	Saada %	Saada ha	Targa %	Targa ha	Tabouhanit %	Tabouhanit ha	Tassoultant %	Tassoultant ha	Taguenza %	Taguenza ha	Aghouatim %	Aghouatim ha
Area of sector (in hectares)		940		4,822		1,114		2,288		355		3,600
Area of land being farmed		230		150		200		200		355		450
Number of farms		4		32		56		11		1		8
Land use	%	ha	%	ha	%	ha	%	ha	%	ha	%	ha
Aboriculture	61	140	40	60	47	94	26	52	23.6	84	14	63
Olives	13	30	14.8	22.2	23	46	12	24.4	4.7	17	2	9
Citrus fruits	40	92	18	27	9.4	18.8	8.6	17.2	16	57	—	—
Apricots	6.5	15	5.2	7.8	3.8	7.6	3.9	7.8	2.4	8	—	—
Almonds	—	—	—	—	7.5	15	1.3	2.1	—	—	10	45
Miscellaneous	1.5	3	2	3	3.3	6.6	0.2	0.5	0.5	2	2	9
Cereals	15	34.5	7	10.5	13	26	15	30	13.5	48	27	121
Legumes	—	—	—	—	—	—	2	4	—	—	2	9
Gardening	—	—	3	4.5	—	—	2	4	—	—	—	—
Forage crops	10	23	15	22.5	—	—	5	10	—	—	3	13.5
Fallow	—	—	7	10.5	13	26	15	30	13.5	48	27	122
Pasture	4	9.2	18	27	17	34	25	50	39.4	140	17	76
Other[a]	10	23	10	15	10	20	10	20	10	35	10	45
Land use totals	100	230	100	150	100	200	100	200	100	355	100	450

	\multicolumn{7}{c}{Sector Name}
Sector Characteristics	Saada	Targa	Tabouhanit	Tassoultant	Taguenza	Aghouatim
Livestock						
Cattle	47	80	7	23	—	10
Sheep and goats	230	—	90	114	200	230
Days worked	14,000	6,000	5,000	5,000	8,000	6,000
Permanent workers	24	11	30	8	13	10
Value of inputs × 1,000 DH	130	75	400	500	180	35
Gross product × 1,000 DH	771	374	302	267	433	262
Irrigation × 1,000 m^3/ha	6	5	3	3	2.3	3

Source: Declared inventories of June 1965 corrected by contradictory inventories of September 1966. Office of the Haouz.

[a] Includes seguias, roads, buildings, etc.

Table 2.11: Selected Farm Characteristics and Indices of Productivity by Irrigation Sector

Sector	Annual allotment of water in cubic meters (x 1000)	Surface area in hectares	Annual number of workdays (x 1000)	Annual gross product in dirhams (x 1000)	Cubic meters of water per hectare	Annual gross product, dirhams per hectare (x 1000)	Annual gross product, dirhams per cubic meter of water	Annual number of workdays per hectare	Annual number of workdays per cubic meter of water
Aghouatim	900	450	6	262	2	.58	.29	13	6.7
Taguenza	825	355	8	433	2.3	1.22	.526	44	10
Tassoultant	600	200	5	267	3	1.33	.44	25	12
Tabouhanit	600	200	5	302	3	1.50	.50	25	12
Targa	750	150	6	374	5	2.50	.50	40	12.5
Saada	1,380	230	14	771	6	3.36	.56	60	10

certain balance of agricultural production. This proves, as is repeatedly said in the Haouz, that land is worth nothing save for the water available to it by its being situated in this or that irrigation sector.

In any event, the major importance of arboriculture on official colonization lands in the Haouz is apparent: eighty-one percent of the financial returns were derived from fruit, nut and olive production; only nine percent from dairy products; and the remainder from cereals and legumes. But the value added in orchard production accrues less to the plantation than to the factory.

B Agribusiness

During a twenty-year period, the colonial system of agriculture was reoriented toward arboriculture and industrial agriculture.[23] Around 1955 it had reached the stage of development that characterizes it today. With the entry into the era of production on a plantation scale, the inadequacy of industrial equipment in Marrakesh became widely apparent. Before the Lalla Takerkoust dam reservoir came into use, the sale of fresh and perishable goods on the European (particularly the French) market was more or less met by the OCE (Cherifian Office of Exports). But after 1935 the facilities for preparation, preservation and storage of fresh foods were so inadequate that the producers were at the mercy of a few industrialists.

The producers responded to this monopolistic situation by grouping themselves into cooperatives: the agricultural cooperative company, Le Bon Lait, dates from 1930; the Coopérative de Fruits et Primeurs de Marrakech dates from 1942. They also created industrial establishments to process their own production. It was especially the companies with adequate production land which proceeded in this way, notably the Société Oléicole de Marrakech, SOM (1929), the Compagnie Marocaine d'Arboriculture et d'Elevage (1937) and the Société Fruitière d'Emballage (1939).

Following World War II, agribusiness developed rapidly up to a processing capacity greatly exceeding the tonnage produced in the Haouz. This situation produced a crisis that was the reverse of the crisis of 1930 and 1935. If in 1932 the colons were justified in complaining about the low prices their olives and apricots brought at the processing factory loading docks, after 1950 the industrialists found the prices of the same products too high. These two opposite phenomena had the same effect: more advanced accommodation and integration of industrial and agricultural capital so as to shift the location of economic profit-taking either to the farm or to the wholesale market according to fiscal advantages or current prices.

Three variables — ownership of plantations, and of processing factories, and the (traditional or modern) sector by which the factories were supplied — enable us to describe four categories of systems.[24]

Cooperatives. These associations ('Fruits et Primeurs', 'Le Bon Lait') processed all the production of their members which measured up to quality standards established in advance. The processing capacity of these cooperatives was proportional to the production capability of their members.

Industrialists who supplied their own agricultural products. There were industrialists who provided all or most of the agricultural produce processed by their factories. They occasionally resorted to third parties to supplement their needs with production which measured up to their quality standards. This was the case of the SOM (with respect to oil, olives, and apricots). the Fruitière d'Emballage, the SFCI Dar Glaoui, and Benhamou of Saada. Such industrialists also tried to establish their production capability proportionately to the amount of agricultural land at their disposal. The proportion of supplemental production required decreased from thirty-five percent in 1950, for instance, to fifteen percent in 1960, and its utilization was always considered provisional.

Contractual processing. The processor did not possess plantations; he custom processed products for certain contracting producers. These were generally colons who owned large areas of land which were insufficient to support industrial facilities by themselves and who did not wish to belong to cooperatives. This model foreshadows the solution that the OCE was to adopt.

The autonomous industrialist. The classic industrialist organization developed late in the Haouz, only after 1946. Such firms developed anarchically, in full competition, practicing 'dumping' and greatly increasing the capacity for processing agricultural products in the industrial quarter of Marrakesh. This type of agribusiness was strongly criticized; it received threats from colons and the administration alike. But because it lacked sufficient agricultural inputs, it had two benefits: first, it gave impetus to the concept of comprehensive land management in the Grand Haouz region; second, it fostered

Table 2.12: *The Volume, Capacity and Supply Sources of Companies Engaged in Apricot Processing, 1960 (in metric tons)*

			Suppliers of apricots		
Companies engaged in apricot processing	Volume processed	Processing capacity	The processing company itself	Colons	Moroccans
Comar	600	1,200		400	200
Sudexport	600	800		600	
Cartier	500	500		500	
Hego	150	200		100	50
Sélection	350	500		350	
Vallier	450	900		350	
SOM	3,000	3,500	2,200		800
Coop. Fruits and Prim.	1,600	2,000	1,600		
Benhamou	2,200	3,000	1,000	700	500
Sicom	200	400			200
Galera	300	450		150	150
Olifruits	300	400		150	150
TOTALS	10,250	13,850		3,300	2,150
PERCENT			50	28	21

Source: Charles Lachkar (1964).

Table 2.13: *The Volume, Capacity and Supply Sources of Companies Engaged in Olive Processing, 1960 (in metric tons)*

Companies engaged in olive processing	Oils – Volume processed	Oils – Processing capacity	Oils – Suppliers: Processing company	Oils – Suppliers: Colons	Oils – Suppliers: Moroccans	Canning – Volume processed	Canning – Processing capacity	Canning – Suppliers: Processing company	Canning – Suppliers: Colons	Canning – Suppliers: Moroccans
Ganemoil	3,000	5,000			3,000	100	1,000		100	
Gomar						2,800	2,800			2,800
Zemrani	1,000	1,500			1,000					
Sudexport	2,500	4,000			2,500					
Cartier	1,200	2,000			1,200	1,000	1,200		700	300
Hego						1,000	1,500		700	300
Sélection						700	2,100	200		500
Vallier						1,000	1,500		350	650
SOM	7,000	10,000	2,000		5,000	1,000	2,000	1,000		
Coop. Fruit & Prim.	1,800	3,000	1,800							
Benhamou	3,000	8,000	750	750	1,500	500	1,000	500		
Sicom	2,500	6,000			2,500					
Solma						900	1,400			900
Oli-Fruits	1,000	1,500			1,000					
TOTALS	23,000	41,000	4,550	750	17,700	9,000	14,500	1,700	1,850	5,450
PERCENT	100	180	20	3	77	100	160	19	21	60

Source: Charles Lachkar (1964).

Table 2.14: *The Volume, Capacity and Supply Sources of Companies Engaged in Citrus Processing, 1960 (in metric tons).*

	Companies engaged in citrus fruit processing	Volume processed 1960	Processing capacity	Suppliers of citrus fruit		
				Processing company	Colons	Moroccans
Coop. Fruit and Prim.		4,000	6,500	4,000		
SOM		3,500	5,000	2,000	1,500	
TOTALS		7,500	11,500	6,000	1,500	0
PERCENT		100	153	80	20	0

Source: Charles Lachkar (1964).

exploration of the market possibilities of Moroccan producers who, until then, had been separate from and largely ignored by the capitalist sector of agriculture.

Tables 2.12 to 2.14 illustrate the relationship between the production of various agricultural products and the way they were processed by agribusiness. The tables also illustrate the relationship between production and the excess capacity of agribusiness industries. They show the overdevelopment of the agribusiness industry in Marrakesh relative to the production capability of the region. The limitations of agricultural production were determined with respect to colons by the availability of water, and for the Moroccans, by their poor integration into the marketing system. This latter limitation involved processors who reacted against Moroccan farmers, claiming they only brought to the loading docks small lots of uneven quality. It was a vicious circle of causes and effects: because the Moroccan farmer was marginal and supplied only supplemental produce, he had to bear the brunt of demand fluctuations. But he was unaware of market fluctuations because he worked through intermediaries. Since the Moroccan farmer was not a regular partner, he did not really appreciate the requirements of quality (the caliber, color, and neatness of the fruit) and the implications of the pursuit of quality for the upkeep of his orchards. Thus the Moroccan farmer's position remained marginal. After 1956, experience demonstrated that the capacity of the factories could be fully utilized only by including the produce of Moroccan farmers.

The other solution to revitalizing an agribusiness which had leveled off in 1950 was to launch the project for comprehensive land management of the Grand Haouz. Proposed as early as 1927, the project involved storing the Tessaout and el-Akhdar waters and transferring them by means of the Rocade Canal as far as the central Haouz. The water supply available to the colonization land would have doubled, from 4,000 to 8,000 cubic meters per hectare per year, permitting a tripling of orchard production. The Moroccans would have been the partial beneficiaries of the newly available water. Some considerations external to the Haouz — notably the orientation of investments toward the Tadla and 'administrative difficulties' — held the project up. Finally, when the project had become the least of its worries, the Protectorate administration abandoned it in the face of political uncertainties concerning its own existence.

C The Relegation of Moroccan Agriculture to the Museum

Without monopolizing the best lands, the colonists benefited from privileged allotments of water; they were also aided substantially by agricultural loans. The products of the colonials were therefore superior for processing and canning, and thus found better markets. It took exactly forty years for the colonization to succeed in establishing a system of capitalist production in the Haouz. Armed occupation, political domination, and the protection of property rights were required, and these could not be established prior to 1920. The idea of developing the region really had been the aim of the first adventurers and then of Lambert, Lassallas, Nier, the agents of Mannesmann, and Regnault. They claimed that if the establishment of a capitalist mode of production was good for them, it would be equally good for the Moroccans. Forty years later, their heirs had simply consolidated an enclave and relegated the Moroccan farmers to the museum.

Jacques Berque has described the fascination of the Protectorate

Table 2.15: *Surface Areas of Cultivations of Selected Crops by Moroccans and Europeans, 1915.*

	Surface area in hectares			Percent of surface area		
Crop	Moroccan	European	Total Moroccans and Europeans combined	Moroccan	European	Total Moroccans and Europeans combined
Wheat	4,628	2,200	6,828	24.5	63	30.5
Barley	11,468	770	12,238	61	22	55
Sorghum	938	286	1,224	5	8.2	5.5
Legumes	816	140	956	4.3	4	4.3
Truck farming	184	58	242	.9	1.7	1.1
Olives	800	6	806	4.2	a	3.6
Oranges	9	37	46	a	1	a
Other	26	3	29	a	a	a
TOTALS	18,869	3,500	22,369	100	100	100

Sources: Tertib (tax) of 1915 and 'Rapport sur les emblavures européenes à Marrakech'. N.B. The absolute figures in this table are not reliable, as the information was provided for tax assessment. More important are the relative proportions of the crops.

[a] Less than 1%

for the 'noble savage': 'its polity was inspired quite simply by a "national reservation" image'.[25] This observation is supported by the figures given in Table 2.15. In 1915 the systems of foreign and Moroccan cultivation closely resembled each other. The differences that existed revolved around distribution of the types of cereals. The proportions of barley and wheat are reversed for the colons; more detailed figures would probably illustrate the predominance of soft wheat over hard wheat in the foreign-owned farms, exactly the opposite of the Moroccan practice. It is obvious that the Europeans cultivated, absolutely and proportionately, many legumes. They supplied the troops! But these are nuances: for both Europeans and Moroccans, cereal and grain crops made up more than ninety-five percent of land cultivated, industrial agricultural products (hemp, dyes, etc.), less than two percent.

Forty-five years later the picture had changed considerably (see Table 2.16). For the Moroccans the picture was as follows: the production of secondary cereals (sorghum, oats, rye, millet) was stopped completely, and was replaced by soft wheat, and the production of industrial crops (hemp, flax, cumin, and plants for making dyes) was reduced. Moroccan cultivation of the three cereals was expanded substantially, by maintaining the approximate proportion of hard wheat to barley and expanding production of soft wheat. A noticeable development occurred as well in arboriculture: the percentage of surface it occupied doubled.

For the foreigners, cereal cultivation was reduced markedly. There was a very noticeable increase in the industrial crops, truck farming crops, and forage crops, and there was a massive development of arboriculture both in land area and as a source of profit. Table 2.17 shows the differences in profitability per hectare which had developed by 1960.

The distinction between traditional and modern agriculture for Moroccan taxpayers was introduced within the *tertib* (regular tax) region [north of the Atlas] in the last years of the Protectorate: we disregarded it in the presentation of these figures because in 1960 in the Haouz, this category of farming involved only one and a half percent of the total declared area and two percent of the gross agricultural production of the region. Essentially this involved a few grand notables like Thami el-Glaoui, who had modernized some of their farming enterprises, and those like al-Ayyadi and Mansouri,

Table 2.16: *Percent Cultivations of Types of Crops by Moroccans and Foreigners, 1960*

Crops	Moroccan		Foreign		Total Moroccan and European combined	
	hectares	gross product	hectares	gross product	hectares	gross product
Cereals Total	88	—	29	—	83	—
Annuals	92	51	38	7	89	45
Arboriculture	8	12	62	86	11	24
Livestock	—	37	—	7	—	31
	100	100	100	100	100	100

Source: General Report of the Haouz Management Planning Project.

Table 2.17: *Comparison of the Gross Product of Moroccan and Foreign Agriculture, According to Type of Crops (in Dirhams per Hectare)*

Crops	Moroccan	Foreign
Annuals	183	192
Arboriculture	494	1,411
TOTAL	122	1,021

who had received help similar to the colons. If there were a few attempts at modernizing traditional agriculture in the Haouz prior to 1956, these were only vague and fleeting ideas, or else they only involved a few specific cases without general significance. There was really neither any training for the new form of agriculture nor any diffusion by 'imitation' on the part of Moroccans, though French colonialist leaders maintained these benefits were taking place, perhaps without really wanting them.

4 Half-Hearted Attempts at Modernizing the Moroccan Peasantry

Vague thoughts of modernizing the peasantry in the Haouz were not totally absent, but they were either promptly aborted or narrowly restricted to particular groups and places.

However dimly, the colonizers were aware of the necessity of involving the nearby small- and medium-sized peasantry with technological progress. This attitude was maintained mostly to guarantee their own acquisitions by distributing a few crumbs to the peasants. But the 'crumbs' could not be too large. To provide substantial aid to the peasantry in the Haouz would have involved allowing them irrigation. This would have meant reducing water supplies to the colons or eliminating their access altogether. Already the colons were expressing their anxiety on all sides at the slightest fall in water flow. Even though colonial farmers were not exactly in power, they still had influence. On the one side there was active greediness of the colons and on the other, passive resignation of the peasants. The colonial administration in the plain of Marrakesh was unaffected by pressure from peasants. Isolated incidents of resistance were limited to personal cases quickly crushed by el-Glaoui's efficient police force. There do not seem to have been any peasant revolts in the Haouz from 1920 to 1953. The exhorbitant privileges granted to or tolerated for el-Glaoui as the Pasha of Marrakesh made for economies in the march of modernization.

Anyway, what colonial justification could there be for helping the peasantry to modernize? In terms of capitalist market expansion, if Europeans had not been able to farm directly, they would have taken up the obligation of big companies to encourage the growth of a local capitalism dominated by themselves. But this was not necessary. Colonization oriented toward settling the French on the land, i.e. the middle range and large colonization, played its role to perfection: it was a large consumer of farming equipment, herbicides, fertilizer and manufactured goods. It created a veritable model of consumption.

Finally it provided agricultural raw materials that were easy to sell on the European market.

Much more time, care and expense would have been required to obtain the same result from the peasantry and the Moroccan bourgeoisie in the Haouz (and elsewhere). Direct colonization was profitable for big business. Until around 1945, the modernization of the Moroccan peasantry was a mythology included in a few sentences in the speeches of residents general; after World War II it was an homage paid to brave soldiers who had 'shed their blood for France'.[26] Any real association of the Moroccan peasantry with capitalist progress was opposed: by the colons, because they competed for the existing water supply, tractors, and loans; by the financiers, because it was not financially rewarding; by the Pasha and his rivals, for the same reason as the colons and because they feared that the portion of the population subject to taxation and corvée labor might be reduced.

Only a few 'visionaries' agitated, from time to time, in the proper political garb of the colonial administration, about the spectre of 'social problems'. These were timid gestures that were accepted as indispensable declarations showing that all views were being considered. Since there were people in the administration paid for following the peasantry, they occasionally had to 'take the pulse of this passive and dozing body' so as to 'record its merest quivering'.

But let us examine attempts towards modernization of the Moroccan peasantry, however timid they may have been.

A Could Moroccans Receive Colonization Lands?

According to the regulations, diversions of land from the Private Domain of the State for modern agricultural improvements did not exclude Moroccans from the distribution if it was demonstrated that they possessed sufficient technical expertise and adequate financial means. In practice, the eligibility of Moroccans was ignored; in the Haouz only two Moroccans obtained access to colonization land in the Targa: caid al-Ayyadi, on 128 hectares, and caid 'Abdi, on 120 hectares. All of the surrounding lands that were occupied by colons had been ceded by the two caids to the Private Domain of the State in order to cancel debts and mortgages. In a sense the caids became colons on their own lands.

When in 1941 the Director of Agricultural Production requested guidance on how to proceed with Moroccan candidates for land allotment, the Director of Political Affairs and his cabinet responded as follows:

> A movement toward obtaining access to colonization lands is emerging among young Moroccans, notably among those who have been educated in French schools. This development demonstrates a fortunate evolution among our protégés since it illustrates their desire to break with outmoded methods of cultivation and to comply with the technical requirements of the regulations. Consequently there is no ground to systematically oppose their participation in official allocation programs. However, in my opinion, it would be untimely for reasons as much political as social, taking into account as well as the lack of availability of domanial lands, to put them into competition with French applicants.

One could not find a clearer official statement. The 'reasons as much political as social' really refer to the attitude the colonizers themselves could adopt when confronted with distribution of lands to Moroccans. The discontent of Moroccans 'pushed aside' because they did not enjoy 'civil and political rights' and because they would compete with the French colonists did not seem to present any important problems for the administration.

Should one even mention the settlement of Moroccan war veterans — one in 1920 and fifteen who held military medals in 1932 — who were settled at the back end of the Tamesguelft sector, each with a plot of 20 hectares and less than 2,000 cubic meters of water per hectare per year? They rapidly became a part of the displaced people of neighboring villages and finally they became integrated into a fraction of the Oulad Brahim which had become a catchall for marginal people in that area. The ex-soldiers (only six of them remained in 1947) passed unnoticed until a survey of the regional Agricultural Service turned them up, cultivating 850 olive trees, 13 apricot trees, 4 orange trees, and 85 almond trees; they possessed no tractors among them.

Should one also mention the project formulated in 1948 for improving the lands of the Oulad Sidi Cheik tribe? This was to be done by regrouping the latter into pump irrigated districts. Encircled by the colonization farms of the Targa, the Souelah and the Saada sectors, the lands to which the Oulad Sidi Cheik had finally been confined represented the living image of the destitution of Moroccan farmers. In 1954, 1,100 hectares of border lands were irrigated by electric pumps which drew on underground water sources. The economic effects of the 1,100 hectare allotment were left, of course, only much later.[27] In sum, the total distributions to Moroccans were of little consequence; they comprised less than 2,000 hectares and fewer than 250 farmers!

B Wage Labor

From a naive perspective, the only positive consequence of colonialist modernization which benefited Moroccans was the opportunity of employment:

> If this region [the Haouz] had been farmed using the techniques most suitable to its climate, today it would be covered by plantations which could produce 200,000 to 300,00 tons of fruit per year, contribute 40 to 60 million francs for transport to the economy, and provide as much in salaries for native manpower.

Actually, the rural colonization has not done more than distribute some wages and create a thin social layer of rural workers.

If words are to keep their meaning, it seems necessary to avoid using the word *proletarianization* with regard to the Haouz during the period from 1920 to 1940. We would prefer to speak of *salarization*. We will reserve proletarianization for the well-known phenomena that occurred at the time of the monopolizing of collectively owned lands, for example, in the Rharb and the Beni Mtir, or for the establishment of ranches and concentrations of land.

Proletarianization is the process by which people, formerly possessing the means of production, are reduced by necessity to placing their labor at the disposal of those who have acquired the means of production. This phenomenon formerly involved foreign capitalist farms. The former landholders, mainly the state and some urban notables, did not end up working for the colons. The large majority of those who were hired as farm workers had not been landowners, but tenant farmers or people obligated to provide corvée labor to previous landholders. More precisely they went from the status of *quintenier* (a sharecropper who receives a fifth of the crop), tenant farmer, or shepherd to that of a more or less permanent salaried worker.

We have previously mentioned the drain on the relatively small pool of manpower that resulted from the clearing of the land and improvement of the Haouz.[28] At the dawn of the twentieth century, the free worker was a rare person. Population was not large and the growth rate small. But the sudden increase in the demand for workers not only increased wages, it also attracted the population of surrounding regions who escaped the 'iron grip' of the grand caids. As a consequence the grand caids had to rely on serflike labor from the southern slope of the Atlas and the Dra Valley. Then, after 1936, once the colonization lands had been developed, the seguias reconstructed, and the orchards planted, the demand for labor ceased growing as fast and even leveled off. This occurred with mechanization, beginning in 1947 and particularly after 1953, a period when the population was growing rapidly. Full production on the large plantations required an increasingly high level of seasonal manpower for short periods (e.g. in the case of apricots) or for a few months (e.g. in citrus), making it especially attractive to women and children.

For the period when a census was taken in the agricultural year 1964–1965, a detailed study of the labor employed and of the number of paid workdays permits the precise calculation of manpower employed. The following calculations illustrate the variety and types of workers and the number of days worked by various types.

Workdays — permanent labor force		522,600
Workdays — seasonal labor force		522,840
	of which	83,660 were seasonal workdays for men
	and	439,180 were seasonal workdays for women
	Totaling	1,045,440 workdays in 1964–1965
The number of permanent workers was		1,740 in 1964–1965 and comprised
		124 *caporaux* (foremen)
		165 tractor operators
		1,390 male agricultural workers
		61 female agricultural workers

It is difficult to determine the full-time equivalent number of salaried occasional workers because it fluctuates so greatly. By studying farm account books one can roughly evaluate the distribution by blocks of time of employment (see Table 2.18). There were more than 500 female (and some male) workers who statistically worked 300 days but were considered seasonal workers. In addition, nearly 1,000 worked half time and more than 1,500 worked at least 100 days during the year. The rate of working days per hectare of land was 31.7 per year if all hectares of land are counted as a basis. The corresponding figure per cultivated hectare was 63.7 working days. Half of this total was from genuine permanent workers and the other half from statistical equivalents of permanent workers. Traditional agriculture in the Haouz required directly productive employment time of only 26 working days per cultivated hectare. The difference is indeed significant. On the 33,000 foreign-occupied hectares, the system of colonial agriculture required a little less than 200,000 additional working days, that is, the employment of a little over 600 additional full-time equivalent permanent workers. However, it took more time because the working day in the traditional sector was a little less than seven hours while the working day in the capitalist sector averaged nine hours.

Table 2.8: *Full-time Equivalent Working Days of Salaried Occasional Workers in the Haouz, by Blocks of Length of Employment*

Number of days	Size of work force 1964–1965	Number of working days
30	1,708	51,240
100	1,620	162,000
150	940	141,000
300	562	168,600

Figure 2.2 illustrates the succession of the availability of manpower over three periods. Before 1920, colonial farms employed

only a few workers, for the most part on a permanent basis. The rural population at that time was still being employed largely by the traditional system as quinteniers, tenant farmers, and shepherds. The rural population was not really underemployed.

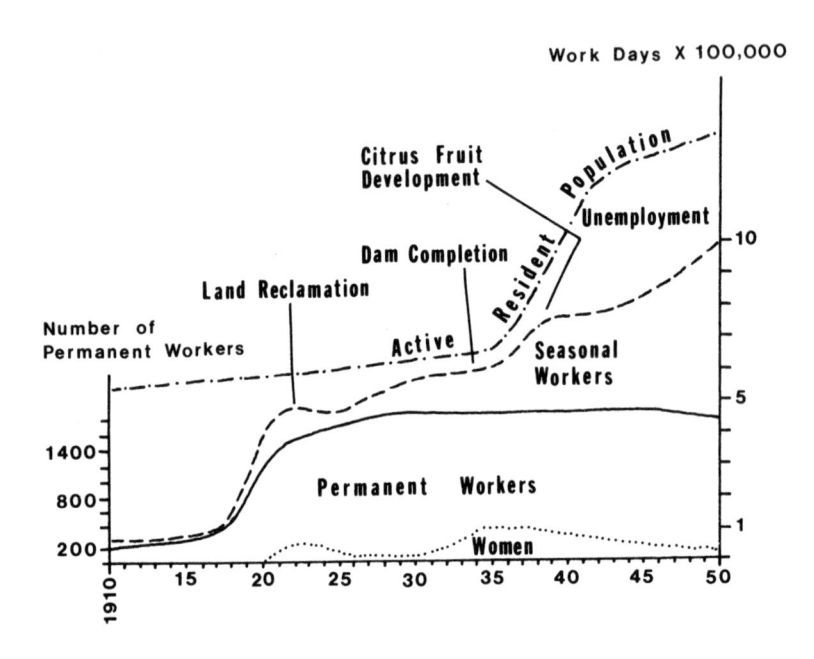

Figure 2.2: *Employment on Colonization Farms in the Haouz*
Source: Office of the Haouz.

From 1920 to around 1940, colonization drained almost the entire active resident population. The definition of 'active' even underwent change: women, who prior to 1920 did not work in the fields, were now working in gathering and harvesting. For a few years, during the period 1920 to 1930, there was a manpower shortage in the region; it was being recruited from neighboring regions. Wages increased. The competition among colons for existing manpower prompted them to make the majority permanent workers. The number of permanent workers for the period 1927 to 1964 remained remarkably stable.

After 1940, population growth, which was steadily accelerating, resulted in an increasingly pronounced divergence between the curves of available manpower and actual employment opportunities. In 1970, half of the active population was characterized by chronic unemployment in the zone of former colonial farms. To make the curves of available manpower and employment opportunity coincide after 1950, it would have been necessary to initiate further development of the greater Haouz.

It has not yet begun!

Chapter 3

The Progress of Capitalism After Independence

After World War II, internal pressures from diverse national interests and the development of popular awareness were in the process of bringing about, sooner or later, the independence of Morocco. The independence movement in colonial states pushing to come of age in the international community resulted in a broader perspective on these issues. These same conditions for political liberation were hastened in Morocco by an attack carried out against the legitimate sovereign and by the impatience of certain French political leaders when confronted by the refusal of the palace to accept an evolution toward direct French administration.

In these political crosscurrents, the question that arose was whether or not big business or indeed the capitalist mode of production as a totality had more to lose or gain from a direct French administration, which amounted to political colonization.[1]

From one point of view, it would seem to be in the capitalists' best interests for urgently needed reforms to be implemented, so as to increase their sphere of influence and restrict the traditional Moroccan sector. To gain this advantage they used the same procedures as they had in earlier times; in fact they were aided by the same men — el-Glaoui and Kettani — who had come to their assistance forty years earlier against Moulay Abd al-Hafid. From the perspective of business, the interest, thoroughly capitalist, of France was linked to increasing the institutional, judicial and material resources of French nationals in Morocco, obviously including the colons.

It does not seem that major financial concerns shared this viewpoint. A considerable number of bankers and representatives of international consortia correctly assessed the difference between the Morocco of 1955 and that of 1912. The evolution of nationalistic ideas in the entire Third World contributed to their assessment, but a more practical explanation for their position lies in the cost of management and supervision of a growing population. Such increasing expenses may have prompted big business to favor relinquishing the management of daily problems to local government. Finally, and this was the point of view of American financiers, the progress of technology and the development of the infrastructure accomplished by the French during the Protectorate provided good conditions for initial capital development to be followed by the deployment of low technology.

The French colonial community in Morocco was particularly irritated by the large companies that were only interested in nationalism as an arena necessary for capitalist accumulation. This arena was to fit within a larger process of integrating the Moroccan economy into a capitalist world economy. Nationalism had to assume the social and political costs of this latter achievement, and this, of course, could not come about without a few 'regrettable consequences': among them the eviction of small French businesses, the surrender of property by the colons to the Moroccan national bourgeoisie, temporary reverses, a cooling off of relationships, bitter anticapitalist protests, and even nationalization of industries. The most radical measures portended either success with the subsequent establishment of markets for the most sophisticated goods from the dominant countries, or alternatively, a resounding failure and an urgent appeal for profitable shipments of 'surplus' from developed countries.

Although the situation appeared favorable for big business, the outcome was not guaranteed. There were many factors that contributed to a large margin of uncertainty, and the banking interests were the first to express considerable caution.[2]

Thus, the political independence of Morocco sanctioned none of the alternatives: the ruin of the colonial interests, the liquidation of capitalist forms of business, or the immediate growth of capitalism. The situation was in reality far more subtle and complex. The process by which Moroccans assumed control of their own country was more visible than in any other country in the Maghreb and would, in itself, be worthy of a special study because it is so exemplary.

When we look specifically at the agricultural sector in the Haouz, the de-colonization process unveils the true nature of colonization: a chapter aimed at establishing the process of capitalist expropriation. A functionalist approach to these events would suffer from failing to consider the autonomous actions of individual actors, who did not always perceive the general trend of events to which they were subject. It is clear that the colons could not permit the growth of capitalism and its markets throughout the entire Haouz. If capitalism was to be extended, sooner or later they would have to leave. However, they were not powerful enough to entrench themselves. But if the colons were to leave Morocco too soon, the transitional process would have proven difficult and technological regression would have caused capitalists to forego possible profit; if they left too late it would have triggered an explosion itself regressive in terms of capitalist profit. The reality of the historical situation may not have led to the optimal outcome, but the protagonists did not complain too much.

At this point, we must confess the difficulty in trying to remain objective because we lived through these events, took risks, and shared hopes and disappointments while attempting to influence the outcome. We simply cannot remain neutral.

1 The Partial Liquidation of the Caidal System

The advent of independence did not result in the confiscation of the land and water that had been the colons' means of production. In the Haouz there were neither *vacances* (unclaimed lands) in the Algerian sense of that term, nor any occupation of colonial farms. Moroccans did not respond by putting the harvest to the torch or with other retaliatory measures.

A The Sequestration

Political action was taken against the caids, and it really developed only after the death of Pasha Haj Thami el-Glaoui. This chronology orders the sequence of events.

October 1, 1955	The government of Edgar Faure obtains the discharge of Mohammed b. Arafa.
October 25, 1955	The pasha has a photograph of Mohammed V posted on the door of his palace, while the sovereign, having returned from exile, arrives in France.
November 6, 1955	Declaration of Independence.
November 8, 1955	In Saint-Germain-en-Laye, el-Glaoui pledges obedience to Mohammed V.
November 16, 1955	The King returns to Morocco.
January 23, 1956	Death of Haj Thami el-Glaoui.
February, 1956	Numerous sites of revolt in Marrakesh and in the entire Haouz.[3] Caids and servants of the Glaoui are burnt alive with gasoline at Bab Doukkala; *azib* (farms) of el-Glaoui, notably his Buidda estate, are occupied by former Resistance fighters. Water thefts on el-Glaoui's seguias are reported in various parts of the Haouz.
April, 1957	Closing of the inheritance inventory of Thami el-Glaoui; the patrimony is assessed at three billion Fr. 1957 (540 million DH 1974) and the registration fees at 37 million Fr. 1957 (700,000 DH 1974).
May 1,1957	The Liberation Army kidnaps certain of el-Glaoui's sons.
July 20, 1957	Freezing of real estate transactions on the lands of those individuals threatened with loss of civil rights.
September 3, 1957	Publication of the list of names of persons whose civil rights have been revoked.
March 27, 1958	Confiscation and sequestration of land and urban property.
December 3, 1958	Release of el-Glaoui's sons.

April 21, 1959   Declaration of retroactivity of the sequestration law for those individuals deceased prior to March 27, 1958. This law is invoked to disown el-Glaoui's heirs.[4]

It was in fact the death of Thami that sounded the death knell of caidalism in the Haouz. Within a few days all of the practices associated with this mode of production disappeared: the corvée and *frida* (caidal tax) were gone. The tenants no longer brought the *mouna* (foodstuffs) to the homes of their masters. The peasants openly declared they would no longer pay the *dabit* (tax) and the hars crop share, and the sharecroppers said they would no longer accept the status of quinteniers. The caids and their vassals burrowed into their strongholds. Those who had escaped in time hid in the large cities, in Casablanca and Tangier, where they could be anonymous. Some notables remained secluded for several months in their homes, and we personally know of two caids who still have not crossed the thresholds of their homes ten years later.

If the actions and the executions of the Liberation Army were concerted and deliberate, without perhaps having been part of an overall plan, the spontaneity of the general uprising of the Haouz peasantry against the caidal exactions is an indisputable fact recognized by all observers.

The political discredit thrust upon the Pasha's allies and the collaborators of the Protectorate after the collapse of el-Glaoui was not, however, followed by an occupation of the lands of the former caid except in a few isolated cases. The main reason is that these lands were being cultivated by long-established tenant farmers who were strongly opposed to possible claims from outside competitors.

If the social relationships of caidalism were overthrown in a free movement of the peasantry, property relationships, on the other hand, were overturned by the administration and within a formal, judicial framework. In other words, the peasants rejected their serflike conditions, but they failed to challenge the ownership of the land they cultivated; they awaited legal remedies.

It is not easy to unravel the objectives and the actions of the various groups of the Resistance against the stronghold of caidalism after the Pasha's death. The victims said that the Liberation Army, or at least those who acted in its name, aimed at personal gain from the grand caids' property. The resistance forces maintained that they had to defeat a power, to reduce its arrogance, to free the humble. And this could not occur without reaching the feudal lords in their property by taking back the land and the money they had accumulated by means of their power.

The issue of the sequestration of these lands thus seems central. But after verifying the facts and meeting with all the protagonists, it seems to us that the condition under which 'emergency' sequestration legislation was carried out cannot be separated from the conditions surrounding the kidnapping and detention of el-Glaoui's sons. Without going into detail about this incredible affair, let us note that el-Glaoui's sons had been captured by elements of the Army of Liberation; they were then handed over to the public authorities, who assured their protection over a twenty-month period in a secret dwelling in the Chaouia. They were retained there until the time the sequestration was pronounced.

The new regulations resulted in the loss of civil rights and the sequestration of goods and property of those people who 'during the period of December 24, 1950, to November 16, 1955 have knowingly and deliberately: either played a dominant role in the preparation or the execution of the *coup* of August 20, 1953, to enforce the exile of the sultan, or committed acts of violence against the population or the Resistance forces'.

In the Haouz, twenty-two persons of note were affected by these new regulations. Ten of them owned a total of 26,391 hectares of registered land. This figure represented thirteen percent of the total area of the Haouz and twenty percent of the cultivated area. Not all of the recorded property of these individuals was confiscated, and less than one-fourth of the confiscated land was distributed to tenant farmers; the main portion was eventually restricted to the former owners or their heirs. Special mention must be made of the heirs of el-Glaoui. The sequestration effectively only involved living persons. It seems that, during the period of the negotiations between the Resistance and the State, it was agreed that el-Glaoui's heirs ought not to be the only ones or nearly the only ones not to be affected by sequestration simply because of their father's recent death. Under the government of Abdallah Ibrahim, a special decree was promulgated that was as unique as the fate of the Pasha Thami el-Glaoui — a decree tailored to the exact circumstances which flowed from his

Table 3.1: *Devolution of Haouz Lands Obtained by the State in the Sequestration of 1958*

Disposition	Hectares	Percent
Sequestrated	26,391	100
Confiscated	19,497	73
Distributed	4,961	19
Restored	21,430	81

unusual fate, namely making the law on sequestration retroactive.

Between the land that was requisitioned on the basis of the sequestration and the retroactive decree on the one hand, and the 1963 dahir on amnesty on the other, a considerable portion of the land of el-Glaoui's heirs was allocated to former Resistance fighters and people who lived near Glaoui property. Accordingly, the land most suitable for agriculture was not restored to the Glaoui inheritors following the amnesty. Nor has the Glaoui family recuperated the Pericardis and Baoubot properties at Tangier.

More unusual yet was the fate of El Biaz's property. El Biaz, the second largest landed power of the Haouz, was detained in the region of Zagora. First he was compelled to sign a proxy statement for the benefit of a broker from Marrakesh. The appearance of his name on the list of those people who lost civil rights and whose lands therefore were expropriated can be understood only as an effort to stop sales, and liquidate the property instead. El Biaz, having become useless from the point of view of some, was then executed. It appears that a confidential document not published in the official bulletin was later used to restore the sequestered property to the heirs.

When one considers that portions of this land, through marriage and other alliances, have become the property of new notables, who once occupied offices as prestigious as those of the former owners, one is forced to recognize that the system of caidal devolution was in fact perpetuated beyond 1958. Many land sequestrations were not carried out because of the considerable indebtedness of the caids.

However, it is especially with respect to water that the peasantry took its revenge on caidalism. The titled lands, which were as visible as if they were marked with billboards and coats of arms, could not be seized unless the people took power themselves. Caution, wisdom, and an awareness of their own weakness discouraged most peasant farmers from overly dramatic acts. Moreover, were they not themselves in the ambiguous situation of being both privileged and exploited? If they opposed the claims of their neighbors, they did not make major claims as owners. More secretive, and also more effective, was the diversion of up-stream seguias. This enabled residents of the foum, where rivers come out of the mountains and emerge on to the plain, to reclaim water that had been denied to them during the previous fifty years. As a result, the farms of the former notables dried up, and el-Glaoui's former tenants and the administration thereby became allied, the administration being the only possible source of authority to enforce the 'iron rule' that had assured the estates' irrigation.[5]

Even though, in the final analysis, the sequestration process only involved the redistribution of less than 5,000 hectares of land, the social and psychological impact of this sequestration was far greater. The discrediting of properties previously claimed, the end of traditional exactions, and the new stance of the farmers who 'held their heads high' resulted in unstable conditions for large estates. The absence of *mouna* (food payments in kind), gifts, services, and other deferential privileges compelled the lords to sell portions of their lands in order to sustain their lifestyle and pay their workers — as much for tilling the soil as for harvesting. All of a sudden, wage earning, albeit occasional and seasonal, became common throughout the Haouz. In order to meet the financial problems and escape the confrontations that resulted from the new face-to-face relationships with frequently hostile former tenants, the large landowners began to purchase tractors and trucks. The next step was to employ entrepreneurs from the cities as estate managers.

B *Allotment of Sequestered Land*

Although no specific policy and procedure had been developed with regard to free distribution of sequestered land, the administration had pushed for the rapid distribution of these lands for the benefit of the poor peasantry. But in the immediate wake of land seizures, the confiscated estates were added to the private holdings of the government and were offered for lease at public auctions. The history of land in the Haouz is perpetuated in this instance: the State's domain is always enlarged at the expense of political competitors who had either been unlucky or who had fallen out of favor. Thus sequestration always permits the state to award and grant favors to political personages who are in favor. In short, sequestered lands are quasi-appanage lands.

Table 3.2 shows how and to whom a little over 5,000 hectares formerly belonging to Haj Thami el-Glaoui were leased during the agricultural year of 1959–1960. It goes without saying that the tenants could not afford the rent and so had to endure new masters. The precarious position of the tenants, as one might suppose, did not encourage development. From the careful examination of the accounts of a few sequestered caidal estates, it is evident that the caidal system of production was the most advantageous for the estates in terms of net revenues. The intensified utilization of machinery to replace corvée labor led to a decrease in production and a decline in the remuneration of the former khammes. Table 3.3 illustrates this process for the Buidda estate. At the close of the caidal period, the picture is clear. The caids could no longer mobilize corvée labor, and machinery began to replace this labor. But the cost of acquiring and running machinery was thirty percent of the gross product. Consequently the number of tenant farmers decreased, and with it, their shares of the profit and produce of the land declined. However, the savings on manpower costs were insufficient to maintain the former standard of living of the landowners.

For the feudal landowner, the alteration of social and political structures resulted in a reduction of his net revenues: the weakening of his power cost him around 50 DH per hectare. The main beneficiary was the commercial and industrial technological sector which sold tractors. From this point of view, it can be argued without forcing the evidence that more local resources were siphoned off by capitalist interests through the replacement of corvée labor by machinery. This judgement is based upon calculations on farms in the Haouz. At the national level the effects are probably more complex and more difficult to assess.

When the caidal system was at its height, the surplus taken from tenant farmers may have gone to purchase Cadillacs or to enjoy the night life of Venice. In the declining period of the caidal system, the American worker, his employer, and the international economic networks benefited as much from the sale of agricultural equipment as

Table 3.2: *The Leasing of Lands Formerly Belonging to Haj Thami el-Glaoui, 1959–1960*

Lessee	Estate	Surface area (in hectares)	1975 Annual rent (in francs x 1,000,000)
A	Buidda	1,175	5.3
B	Tamesguelft	553	.72
	Hanout al Baggal	68	.85
C	Ain Jdida	537	1.35
	Sarro	226	.725
	Haj Omar Tazi	576	6
	Saada	1,147	
D	Targa Tacheraft	900	1
E	Trab el Maaden	210	.13
F	Ferdi	117	2.8
TOTALS		5,509	18.875

A was one of the pasha's main rivals in the Haouz. He represented the third landed, pastoral, and fiscal power of Marrakesh.

B is a big merchant in cereals and oil, a city dweller living close to the kasba.

C belongs to the category of 'absentee-farmers'; he is a civil engineer.

D is a former servant of el-Glaoui.

E is a former manager of el-Glaoui.

F is a foreign colon.

Table 3.3: *Estate Income and Its Allocation According to Means and Relations of Production*

	Caidal system				Peasant cultivation on allotted lands	
Allocation	Tenant sharecropping and corvée		Mechanized			
	Dirhams (x 1000)	percent	Dirhams (x 1000)	percent	Dirhams (x 1000)	percent
Landowner	310	75	260	79		
Tenants	80	20	50	15	121	93
State (taxes)	20	5	20	6	9	7
Total net product	410	100	330	100	130	100

they had from the previous sales of luxury automobiles. The main difference is that the mechanization of the process of production had structural consequences that were durable and largely irreversible, while luxury consumption is unstable, subject to change, and frequently delayed by hoarding of wealth.

A September 1959 report from the rural engineer stationed in Marrakesh, concerning the manner in which sequestered lands were to be allotted, stated, 'The people are anxiously looking forward to the allotment of the lands under sequestration! The utilization of these lands by the peasants is one of the most urgent national goals to be met.' The fire burns through even the bureaucratic language.

Prompt distribution seemed imperative to everyone. Within five months, 5,000 hectares were distributed to 255 landless peasants under the system of *colonat partiaire* (in which the farmer occupies land in perpetuity and gives a portion of the harvest to the owner). There was an attempt to group these lands in units suitable for cooperative production. This did not imply a wish to make the leap from feudalism to socialism; it simply aimed at replacing the collapse of caidalism with the framework of a modern State. Ideological rivalries were not absent from the administration: there were partisans of the theory that rapid change can skip stages of development, as well as those who favored a much more deliberate and gradual, step-by-step approach. Because of the centralized decision-making process, practical, pragmatic solutions were inherently ignored. Theories and practices all were determined from the perspective of the technocrats — the only views considered. Once again, the peasantry was absent from the debate!

However, the peasantry demonstrated its will, albeit negatively, by large-scale abandonment of land. Landless peasants, tenant farmers and other candidates for land allotments wanted land and the means to cultivate it, with no strings attached. The State had neither the patience nor the trust to grant their major wish: it was not satisfied with simply acting at the level of market control through manipulation of credit and prices. The State wanted the new landowners to be 'trainees', who would be modest and well-behaved, respectful of advice on agricultural matters and committed to the State's tutelage. Those who were allotted land, to the contrary, aimed at an increase in their food consumption, the assurance of security and economic stability, and liberation from usurers and landlords. Finally, they hoped to escape the conditions whereby the government indirectly controlled family farming. The bolder and more aggressive of the beneficiaries of land allotment (approximately twenty percent in the Haouz) abandoned their plots. The more astute gave them in partnership to tenants, thirty-five percent in the Buidda estate alone. Gradually, caidal social relationships were reestablished on most of the redistributed land. However, the excesses of caidalism were reduced, and the caidal relationships were precarious, for they were no longer legal.

The allotment process had been understood by the peasants as a reward, as a gain of privileges for services rendered to the national cause, or perhaps more to the point, as the price of appeasement. In the history of Morocco, supporters of the triumphant cause and faithful servants have always held land free from taxation — guich lands!

Thus, after the enactment of the regulatory laws of 1966 and 1969, when the government wanted to establish landholdings on a legal basis, certain beneficiaries produced booklets they had received which bore the image of Mohammed V; they reminded the government officials of the sovereign's majestic gesture when he had granted them, the former khammes of el-Glaoui, a plot to live on. These former sharecroppers have to this day refused to pay for the land, nor have they followed the agricultural directives and the advice of the civil administration. Their occupation of the land has no formal guarantee, but who could challenge it?

The most significant phenomenon of this whole episode was the complete and irreversible disappearance of any form of caidal exactions. The former tenants no longer contributed food, money, labor, or taxes to their former masters. The results of this process included: 1) the breaking up of most of the latifundia, either by the State or through the spontaneous sales of some large estates by indebted landowners who needed to satisfy mortgages or meet cash flow needs; 2) changes in the living standard of the formerly wealthy due to the disappearance of exactions; 3) the deconcentration of land; and, 4) the slow evolution of the *khamessat* sharecropping system toward *colonat partiaire* and seasonal wage employment. In sum, there was a broad and significant movement but not a revolution!

2 The Decline of Colonial Farming

Following the death of el-Glaoui in 1956, the colonial community in Marrakesh experienced some moments of intense anxiety. They thought they had lost their strongest benefactor. With the passage of time, they regained their former self-control and adopted an attitude of cautious expectation. They became convinced, beginning in 1959, that foreign-owned land would be quickly repossessed. This is where the French in the Haouz were wrong. Compared to other regions of Morocco, they benefited from the longest deadlines for the repossession of former colonial lands. They also knew enough to make the most of warning the government about the harmful consequences for Marrakesh of the massive exodus of colonial farmers that would occur if their lands were nationalized.

A Changes in the Production System
The colons in Marrakesh took every advantage of the warning they received and the continual postponement of deadlines. The following

six patterns of actions were characteristic of the colons in their precarious situation:

1. A decrease in the reinvestment in machinery, particularly for tractors and harvesting machinery, less so for pumps and transport equipment;
2. Abandonment of plans for replacing old trees and rejuvenation of citrus groves;
3. Progressive decline in the utilization of both permanent and seasonal male workers;
4. Increase of material advantages in kind to trained workers, such as mechanics and tractor operators, and to foremen (land plots given for cultivation, breeding cattle, barns, cottages);
5. Farming partnerships with 'most meritorious' workers and foremen on most of the annually cultivated land, in particular in the Aghouatim and Tassoultant sectors. The farming partnerships outside the plantation areas assumed vast proportions;
6. Obtaining and managing additional farm land from other colonialists who had already departed. Holders of official colonization lands were the principal beneficiaries of land left by private colons and company operatives. In 1966, out of 68 official colons, 24 took into management or leased private farms that they added to their own enterprises. This permitted them to widen the deployment of movable equipment and trained manpower. Consequently, when the anticipated confiscation took place, these colons were able to keep the best production equipment and labor while surrendering to the State the most wornout equipment and the least trained manpower. In response the State established inventory lists that, however, were never vigorously enforced.

Whatever the motivation for these actions, the result was a first ebb in the capitalist mode of production: it involved shorter term economic calculations, lower amortization, relative disinvestment, indirect farming, and the use of occasional manpower.

On the private colonization lands, there was broad agreement that the repossession of colonial lands would not occur for a long period of time. However, after 1961, observers noted an increase in transactions, not as much in the Haouz as in the lower Chaouia and the Rharb. The implementation of controls over real estate transactions seems to have led to an increase in private real estate transactions that were not reported to the authorities. The control procedures in no way limited the sale of land; they merely enabled the State to select the particular purchasers it wished to favor. It can be asserted that control over real estate transactions has been the second, at times the first, instrument of the agrarian reform.

All of the actions mentioned above altered the capitalist mode of production and moved into a form which some authors have called, for want of a better word, either semicapitalism or semifeudalism. It is not surprising that persons of note and high officials from the government gained access to the ownership of private colonization lands. Governors, pashas, super caids, and better yet, generals, colonels, ministers, and princes have acquired the bulk of the former colonial farms or taken shares in joint-stock companies and agribusiness. In Moroccan society it is a truism that landed property and the holding of political power are two confounded components. In a country and a society in which agricultural productions and the possession of land are of strategic importance, power, rather than capital or technology, leads to ownership of land, and possession itself is better than any other means of maintaining power.

It is also important to point out governmental reforms concerning property holdings of officials: property acquired during office is no longer seized from important governmental officials when they are removed from office, as under the *ancien régime*. Individuals sanctioned for unlawful acts during their terms of office, when prosecuted successfully, lose property only in the form of fines and indemnities in proportion to their wrongdoings. Individuals condemned for political rebellion have been threatened with regard to their property, but seizures have not been effected.

The sociopolitical system is evolving toward greater guarantees for property and towards a slight but noticeable distinction between power and possession. This must be counted as a sign of more secure ownership of land, and thus, of a reaffirmation of one of the essential components of the capitalist mode of production — the security and safety of capital. Observers should be cautious about the irreversibility of this trend: some recent land appropriations that have benefited

178 CAPITALISM AND AGRICULTURE IN THE HAOUZ OF MARRAKESH

the ascending classes are being challenged by most of the opposition parties.

B *The Decline of Colonial Land Ownership*
Figure 3.1 presents information on the devolution of colonization in the Haouz of Marrakesh from 1957 to 1974. Some comments are in order:

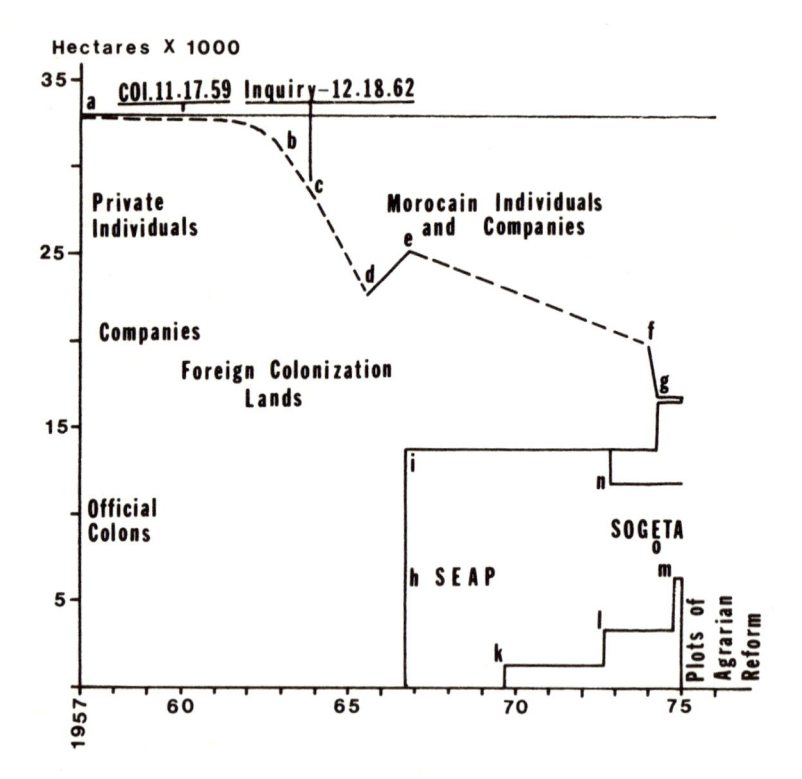

Figure 3.1: *Changes in Ownership of Former Colonization Lands in the Haouz of Marrakesh, 1957–1974*
Source: Office of the Haouz.

A The total area controlled by colonists on the eve of independence is not precisely known. It is estimated here at 33,000 hectares, based on a survey in 1952. Other transactions may have taken place without being formally registered. To simplify the graph, private and public colonization and company owned land were grouped together. Concerning individually owned land, the administrative distinction between official and private lands was extended beyond 1956 as follows: the individual farmers of official colonization land were not permitted to sell their land; they were repossessed en masse. In contrast, individuals with private colonization lands could sell their lands.

The relationships between the companies and the State concerning land distribution matters were characterized by compromise if not more. For example, a good number of companies involved in farming official colonization plots benefited from a seven-year deferment of repossession plans. The joint-stock companies 'Moroccanized' a portion of their shares and by so doing, in large part, were able to escape repossession prior to 1973. The official colonization lands that had been distributed to individuals appear primarily at the bottom of the chart, the private colonization lands at the top, while companies having official plots or private lands appear in the middle of the chart.

B On December 18, 1962, the registered transfers and transactions indicate that the colonization held a total of 31,068 hectares. I conducted this survey to demonstrate the 'melting away' of the property intended for Agrarian Reform. It was rumored that colons were selling their lands to Moroccan notables to get cash, in a manner similar to what went on before 1912. At that time, Moroccans might have sought foreigners for protection; now the situation was reversed. There were not many of these transactions but, if land reform were to succeed, it was necessary to block them. (The a–b curve is hypothetical; we have no precise data between these two points.)

Many decisions, public statements and signs warned the colonists of what was to come, including statements in the press, as well as official statements of public policy. One of the most important occurred in June, 1963, with the announcement of the repossession by the State of official colonization plots and the establishment of a Control of Real Estate Operations (COI). Also, at the end of 1959, the first five-year plan (1960–1964) announced the repossession of colonization lands, without indicating any deadlines. The dahir that announced publicly the approval of this plan was issued on November 17, 1960.

C   The point C in the graph is hypothetical. The line b–d has been assumed as a straight line between the two known points b and d. It is not known what happened between b and c (date of the publication of the document establishing the Control of Real Estate Operations), and between c and d (date of the May 1965 census). The announcement of the COI regulations (point c) may have both hastened transactions by causing people to predate them and increased the number of private sales.

D   On May 31, 1965, a decree from the Ministry of Agriculture ordered a census of properties owned by foreigners or companies. Although this inventory was simply a survey, it was rumored that it might become the basis for future indemnification, at the time of negotiations with the French government. Furthermore the Ministry of Finance and the Agricultural Credit Bank were enjoined to collaborate with the Ministry of Agriculture in order to obtain data as exact as possible on the holdings of foreigners. After processing all the data we found that 10,400 hectares that had been counted in 1956 were missing.

E   In September, 1966 at the time of the repossession by the State of official colonization lands, a legal audit of the conditions of all colonization lands was being held in the Haouz: it became apparent that 2,600 hectares had not been included in the preceding inventory because of nonobservance of the COI regulations.

F   From March 2 to September 20, 1973, private colonization lands were recovered by the State. A contradictory inventory revealed in Marrakesh that only 6,142 repossessable hectares remained. This drop resulted from excluding 3,155 disputed hectares that had been sold privately, and therefore illegally in terms of COI regulations.

G   The litigation was resolved through the restoration of 3,009 hectares to Moroccan buyers who were 'in good repute'. From February, 1974 onward, there remained in the hands of foreigners in Marrakesh only 42 hectares declared to be of nonagricultural use.

H   13,600 hectares of official colonization lands were repossessed in Marrakesh in September, 1966 as a result of the implementation of the dahir of September 26, 1963. The repossession was made for the benefit of the Center for Administration of Agricultural Enterprises (CGEA), an institution created on September 8, 1964.

I   The CGEA, dissolved on October 20, 1966, handed over the management of the farms to the Service for Provincial Agricultural

Enterprises (SEAP) which was placed under the authority of the Ministry of the Interior.

J On July 18, 1969, 1,477 hectares in the central Haouz (Tassoultant sector) were distributed within the framework of the 1966 Agrarian Reform.

K October, 1972: distribution of 1,986 hectares (Saada, Tassoultant, and Aghouatim sectors).

L October, 1974: distribution of 2,836 hectares (Saada, Tassoultant, Aghouatim and Tabouhanit sectors).

M Creation on October 30, 1972, of the Société de Dévelopment Agricole (SODEA) which subsequently managed the agricultural use of lands (1,850 hectares) that until then had been managed by the SEAP.

N The SOGETA, Société d'Etat de Gestion et de Travaux Agricoles, which was created on August 22, 1973, assumed responsibility for the remainder of the nondistributed arable lands.

O Following the litigation audit of the private colonization lands that were repossessed in September, 1973, SODEA found itself entrusted with 1,820 hectares of orchard, and SOGETA with 1,460 hectares.

The disposition of the colonization lands in the Haouz of Marrakesh as of December 1, 1974, is summarized by Table 3.4.

Table 3.4: *Devolution of Colonization Lands in the Haouz of Marrakesh, December 1, 1974*

	Surface area in hectares	Percent
Moroccan private citizens	16,100	48.4
Agricultural Reform assignees	6,268	18.9
SOGETA (State)	7,180	21.6
SODEA (State)	3,670	11
Foreign	42	a
TOTALS	33,260	100

a Less than 1%.

C Reclaiming Colonial Lands

Repossession of lands by the State came as no surprise to the colons; the event had been anticipated for a long time.[6] But awareness of the inevitability of a situation does not necessarily require good judgement about it. Many colons' memories were rooted in their farms, and as they now became more aware of the final outcome, those memories became more poignant.

On the early mornings of October 1966, the colons in the Haouz must have felt intense emotion as the members of the Inventory Commission jumped out of their cars and proceeded to strut around the orange groves on the former colonial farms with the assurance of new proprietors. Most colons looked on impassively. Some assisted the new officials while others justified the absence of this or that piece of machinery. Some were trying to prove that their small collection of tools was complete. Others acted arrogantly and simply waited for the new officials to pose questions.

What were these colons thinking? Was there even a single one among them who remembered the conditions surrounding the eviction of the former occupants? Were they able to compare their own emotions with the emotions of the former residents? Did they understand how the former residents often were forced to disperse more than a half century ago?

The general attitude of the colons was dignified and disabused: 'Our government is really the same as yours! We shall never be compensated: neither by the one or the other; they no longer need us!' The local authorities pretended not to understand French. The representatives of the French government looked on absentmindedly. The colons had no raison d'être any longer. Within the framework of France's broader designs, the former colons were even a bit troublesome, a bit too visible: they came from another age. There were, after all, other means to exploit the riches of a country than having colons in the Haouz established on thousands of hectares of land! The post-colonial French elite agreed that they merely had to contend with disposing of this cumbersome historic vestige.

On the eve of repossession, all the protagonists had agreed to control the movement of agricultural equipment and livestock. The gendarmerie had been alerted; its orders were vigilance, but no excess of zeal. The French consulate had recommended that its nationals act with decency and respect toward the agreements and the sovereignty of Morocco. But it had been known since June 18 that repossession would occur in October. The most skilful and the most dishonest had had time to effect transfers and to sell what they could. On the other hand, the most scrupulous and the most naive sought to justify their inventory in all its detail.

There were a few instances of despair; some colons suffered to the point of openly showing it. One suicide occurred: the commission had the widow facing them while the husband was hanging in the olive grove facing the Atlas. There were two other threats of suicide and one instance of armed resistance: a farmer awaited the arrival of the commission with a hunting gun loaded with buckshot. There was one desertion: one colon simply returned to his home country, leaving the house empty, the door ajar, while the workers in the courtyard awaited the arrival of the commission. On the table inside the house, a short note — 'I left just as I came.'

Within one week, the State had increased its property holdings by 13,600 hectares. The Center for Administration of Agricultural Enterprises (CGEA) was the new manager of these holdings. This agency was created on September 8, 1964 and was a state company entrusted with the management of the repossessed farms of the official colonization. The CGEA possessed all of the regulatory prerogatives and the autonomy that were necessary for management.

On October 15, after the first two weeks, the farm workers were paid as in the past. The resupplying of fuel stocks, the stocking of fertilizer, seeds, treatment products — the entire organization of centralized coordination of the largest set of holdings in the Haouz was gradually put into operation. Syndicalist organizations and representatives of workers' committees cooperated to provide the state managers with information about problems to be dealt with on each farm.

The exuberance that had been created soon dissipated. On October 20, 1966, the CGEA was dissolved. The colonization lands that had been repossessed went under provincial authority and were formally administered by the provincial assembly, under the close supervision of the Ministry of the Interior. The assembly was composed of businessmen, as well as leaders in the areas of religion, labor and the professions. Although he did not own the land, the governor of Marrakesh suddenly had under his control landholdings that were far greater and more productive than those of the former potentate of the

Haouz, Thami el-Glaoui. This episode would only be anecdotal except that it had durable agricultural consequences and revealed the fragility of capitalism's foothold in the Haouz.

The first result was the complete blockage of the administrative apparatus. At the end of sixteen weeks, the workers, not having received any wages, paid themselves from what was directly available on the farms. Since all the advantages in kind with which the former colons had rewarded their workers, such as a small piece of land or the permission to keep a cow in the barn, had been eliminated, the workers could only resort to making off with items that were either edible or not nailed down. At the end of 1967, it was well-known that the *joutiya* (fleamarket) of Marrakesh was stocked with tools from the farms. Then came a rash of petty crimes committed by vagrants. Grocers no longer gave credit to farmworkers. On some evenings one could see groups of workers armed with sticks wandering around on the roads and trails of the Targa: a substantial number simply deserted or became déclassé occasional workers. At the time of the reorganization of the farms into larger units, a large number of foremen refused to stoop to the rank of common worker, and elected to strike out on their own. The new managers found this development to their liking because they were confronted with an overabundance of manpower.

We will spare the reader any further detailing of these vicissitudes except to say that at the end of the year, the situation was assessed as follows: the farms would have reported 8.6 million DH profit, but depreciation had not been taken into account. In addition, the ordinary expenses of farming previously incurred by the colons — heaviest in the citrus groves and less for olives — had been ignored. Nor had the water dues been reckoned with. After these were taken into account, it seems that the actual profit did not exceed 6 million DH, that is, one half of the previous year's net profit.

At the national level it is difficult to make a rigorous comparison: the amount transferred from Morocco to France each year by the colons is not known. Furthermore, it is difficult to make a judgement after only one or two seasons about the decision to make widespread use of occasional manpower. The administrative statute dealing with managers, who hardly had an interest in the actual results, did not assure either a personal presence or a continuous vigilance on the farm. The leaders hoped to obtain more from the workers through negative incentives based on the workers' precarious position, rather than relying upon the formal skills of the new managers and the procedures to which they were held.

D *The Effects on Agribusiness and Marketing*

The repossession of the colonial estates proceeded legally by expropriation of shares and stocks that had been held by former landowners and companies and factories that were directly dependent upon those estates. In particular, this was the case for the shares of cooperatives, and especially for the Coopérative des Fruits et Primeurs and Le Bon Lait. Not only did the State become the largest producer, it also became the largest processor in Marrakesh. The year before, the nationalization of foreign trade in fruits, produce and canned goods had been announced.

In the spring of 1967 the conditions of the apricot harvest on the repossessed farms were as follows:
— production had been nationalized;
— processing industries belonged in large part to the private sector;
— marketing was nationalized;
— the wholesale distribution system in France depended primarily upon the industrial sector of the economy of Marrakesh;
— the price of primary commodities such as sugar and tin was dependent on French export merchants.

Without entering into details of the April 1967 auctions of apricots from repossessed farms, it is enough to say that after that event it became clear to everyone that amalgamation of public and economic power was the only means to get out of the impasse. At the same time, to some observers this solution portended the downfall of capitalist free enterprise. No one could really hold any particular link in the chain responsible. From the moment when any of the parties involved used the leverage available to it in business negotiations, others were left without 'respectable' profit margins, and governmental intervention was necessary to reestablish incentives.

The collusion between private capitalism and state centralism can only be regarded as a gigantic scheme to divide up the monetary value added at each stage in the process of production, according to the desires of a governor. For example, in the 1967 apricot sales operation, neither buyers from outside of the Province of Marrakesh nor small processors were able to buy, because apricots initially were priced too high. This resulted in industrial concentration with subcontracting appropriate to the market situation, followed by the expansion of the state role in the sector.

The situation that followed was ambiguous; business was neither private nor fully nationalized. Under these circumstances, the political involvement of certain individuals was considerable. For example, two influential members of the Provincial Assembly, thereby co-managers for the repossessed colonization lands, owned large factories in Marrakesh. Furthermore, the largest processor of apricots and olive oil in Marrakesh had been under the threat, from 1966 to 1973, of an anticipated 'Moroccanization' of his shares and lands (he managed close to 1,500 hectares of plantations in the Haouz). It is understandable that he could be of help to the political authorities in improving the productive activities of the Provincial Assembly.

If the management of the former colonial farms by the provincial government ensured a more immediate, more decentralized, and more 'Moroccanized' redistribution of benefits, the confused and covert character of management could lead only to a decline in production. 'Moroccanization of profit' can be considered to refer to any transaction that suppressed transfers of profit to Europe or reduced purchases of tractors paid for in hard currency, even if these actions resulted in lowering investment levels. Redistribution of wealth was also more immediate because produce was often taken from the process of production before it could be sold. Even seeds, fertilizers, and herbicides obtained through the government might be sold off to surrounding farmers. The farms thus were no longer capitalist enclaves within a feudal ocean. For once they were 'spreading progress', too much perhaps. But who could tell what impact this anarchy could have in terms of spreading progress to the masses?

The administration always has a ready answer to the problem: reinforce control mechanisms, that is to say, treat the ailment but not its cause. The resulting bureaucratic rigidity had as its consequences the stifling of farm operations and an increase in bribery, since favors were now more difficult to obtain. The State fairly rapidly came to the end of its experience of direct farm management. The cost of this effort can be placed at approximately 10 million DH in the area around Marrakesh. This was the acknowledged deficit: a high, but perhaps necessary, cost of recognizing the significance of the technical and legal framework of capitalist management.

The political events that occurred over the period of two summers at the national level accelerated both additional distributions of repossessed lands and the creation of organizations in the form of autonomous state companies to manage the best farms.

The attempted military putsch at Skhirat on July 10, 1971 was followed by a series of measures aimed at suppressing 'corruption' and speeding up land distribution. The attack on the royal airplane on August 16, 1972 was followed by a special land distribution, the creation of the SODEA (see below) and a speech by the King on the Agrarian Revolution. In our opinion, observers too often explain the control of land by the Ministry of the Interior in terms of the thirst for power and personality of the minister, General Oufkir.

Perhaps this phase was inevitable. Could the political powers spare themselves the pursuit of 'an impossible dream': coming full circle by returning to management of appanage land under state direction? What appears most interesting is not that this operation of land management was attempted, but that it failed. It was impossible to reverse totally the introduction of capitalism. As we mentioned above, the repossession of the former colonial lands resulted in a retreat of the capitalist mode of production. Inversely, we can add that management by the political authorities has proven that it was not possible to go very far in this direction.

The absence of a blueprint for society, of a clear hierarchy of objectives of a transition and future model could only lead to compromise. Beginning in 1961, it became obvious that a single solution applied to the whole territory and to all types of lands — in the tradition of French centralism — could not be viable.[7]

E Management by State Companies

The admitted failure of the formula for the farming of repossessed land by the provincial assemblies led to the adoption of three simultaneous formulas, each concerning a particular type of situation:
- management of orchard lands by a state agency, the SODEA, which was managed like a private company;
- temporary management of arable lands by a state company, again with private management and state funding, the SOGETA;

— the above temporary arrangement was to be replaced by a massive land distribution to the peasants. Officials 'closed their eyes' to a few instances in which highly placed political figures and dignitaries had simply taken possession. In the Haouz, eleven percent of the repossessed land (3,670 hectares), was assigned to the SODEA. Close to twenty percent (6,230 hectares) was distributed to landless peasants; close to twenty-two percent (7,130 hectares) was assigned to the SOGETA.

One might wonder whether the present devolution of repossessed lands is final; a brief glance backward (see Table 3.5) demonstrates the extraordinary succession of management entities for the same estates. On several occasions, the legal and financial liquidation of a given government organization had not yet been completed before its successor was being liquidated as well. When we remember that the state companies were often located in diverse places and that personnel changed frequently, it is understandable that complete archival records about these companies are not always available. We know of one farm that changed identification numbers in its government records four times and that successively belonged to three different administrative regions. Under such conditions it may never be possible to obtain complete data for the period 1960 to 1975. At best a balance sheet may be drawn up for the period immediately before and immediately after these fifteen years of frantic successions of managements and changes in government policy.

Table 3.5: *Length of Existence of Government Agencies Charged with the Management of Repossessed Lands*

Agency	Date of creation	Length of existence in months
SED (ONI)	Sept. 9, 1960	38
COMAGRI	Nov. 11, 1963	10
CGEA	Sept. 8, 1964	26
SEAP	Oct. 20, 1966	71
SODEA	Oct. 10, 1972	a
SOGETA	Aug. 22, 1973	a

a Authority continuing in 1977.

THE PROGRESS OF CAPITALISM AFTER INDEPENDENCE 189

The Allotment Process
The transfer of land to poor peasants was obviously a more permanent arrangement. The original purpose of the repossession had been to give land to poor peasants. State management was only regarded as a conservatorship while technical preparations were made by the proper departments for the allocation of land. The State accepted the former colonial lands. The expectant peasantry, absent from the social and political scene, awaited the august gesture of land redistribution.

On a broader scale, as early as 1959, provisions had been made to incorporate the colonization lands, along with many other types — collective, habous, dominal, even guich lands (what dreams!) — into a single resource for the Agrarian Reform. This would have permitted the land reforms to benefit the masses and eliminate certain anachronistic traditions. Land allocation was to distribute entire sectors to assure a wide-ranging land reform and a 'rational' organization of development.

Social Consequences
In the Haouz, there was no shortage of land to distribute, at least theoretically. In May 1965, 104,643 hectares potentially were available. This amounted to more than half of the useful agricultural area of the plain, divided as follows:

52,943 ha. from the Private Domain of the State
15,800 ha. from repossessed lands
12,900 ha. from public habous lands
23,000 ha. from guich land.

But the public habous and the guich lands only could be included in theory. Conflicting claims and acquired rights on them are inextricable. Only an expropriation with immense indemnities distributed with largess could bring this tangle of customs and traditions to an end. The Domain of the State was huge, but lacked water, which is why the colons never utilized it. It would have potential importance only with the transfer of waters from the Tessaout basin into the Haouz. All that remained were the repossessed lands. The regaining of private colonial lands would have increased considerably the potential for land redistribution, but we have seen already how quickly this mass dwindled, from 33,056 hectares in 1965 to 13,448 in 1974. Of these 13,448 hectares, nearly half were redistributed; the remainder (7,180 hectares) was still managed by the SOGETA and was to come up for redistribution in 1975 and 1976. It is expected that the final allotment in the Haouz will barely exceed 10,000 hectares, which is a little less than one third of the former colonial lands, comprising a total of only five percent of the surface of the Haouz.

Allotment of Repossessed Lands
The details of land redistribution in the Haouz is summarized in Table 3.6. By 1976 there would be more than 30,000 heads of families in the Haouz. If 10,000 hectares were distributed in minimum plots of five hectares, the portioning off process would involve 2,000 beneficiaries, slightly more than six percent of all family heads. It is possible to analyze the effects of the redistribution in several ways. However it is done, the conclusion is inescapable; land redistribution can have no significant social consequences.

Table 3.6: *Allotment of Repossessed Land, 1969-1974*

Year	Sectors of the Central Haouz	hectares	per year
1969	Tassoultant	1,447	1,447
1972	Saada	1,232	
	Tassoultant	754	1,986
1974	Aghouatim	1,608	
	Saada	956	
	Tabouhanit	271	2,836
TOTAL AND AVERAGE		6,268	1,045

But at least a few favored individuals have acquired some land! After the announcement was made concerning land distribution, some of the landless peasants, anticipating a rise in status, had jellabas made out of white cloth.

On the day of distribution, an entire village might go to the administrative center where platforms had been erected, with flags appropriate for the occasion. In the midst of a circle of cars, busy officials put the final touches to an improvised protocol. At some distance from the official platform decked out with carpets from the community, the hopeful assignees congregate in groups. Vague rumors reach them: 'It is the King himself who is coming!' 'No, it is the Minister of the Interior! Or the Minister of Agriculture!' There is banter about a man who supposedly paid much money but had failed to be included on the list. Some claim that the water rights will not be as important as officials had asserted. Others observe that some of the plots are quite distant from the village: 'What will we do if we are required to live on the premises?'

After many hours of waiting, everything happens very quickly. A police motorcade precedes an unusual parade of cars. The band plays while eager caids push the small groups of assignees toward the platform. Following a speech about how the State and the King are concerned about the poor, which includes some vague explanations about the obligations of landowners towards the State, names of the asignees are announced in rapid succession. Proceeding to the platform, each beneficiary receives from the bedecked official a piece of paper indicating the plot he is to receive and a booklet in which his name is inscribed. He resumes his former place in the line. Soon everything is over. What counts to him is that he has become an owner. He has proof, his name is in his booklet. He will wait until he reaches his own village to have someone read it to him. The officials are leaving and the Center for Rural Development (CMV) official tells the farmer that within three days he must call at the CMV office for the inspection visit that must precede the formal possession of his land, as well as for other useful information that may be available.

Within an hour after it is over the thoughtful peasant can be seen looking at his new plot, noticing the faults that had not been corrected, such as outcroppings of rock, improper drainage, improper slopes, etc. But so what! This was the long-awaited day; he now owns his piece of land! He is entitled to dream. In his reverie the peasant may be thinking: 'Here, I will put the house, there, the vegetable garden, and there the orange trees; I shall tap water here. But who will be my neighbors?'

Three days later at the Center for Rural Development, government agents explain to the farmer the clauses in the contract — the obligation to reside on the plot, to build a stable, to get plowing done by CMV, and to agree to certain planting obligations. The regulations specify the portion of land to remain fallow each year, crops to be planted, the crops to be under contract, the amount of fertilizer to be used, the outstanding debt for the cost of plot development, the amount of the lease-purchase agreement, the access to ownership in thirty years, the cost of water, etc.

At the end of the day the peasant has a clearer picture: he is not really the owner but a client, and under obligation at that!

The Size of Plots

The legislation dealing with agrarian land reform distribution involved dividing the former non-orchard colonization farms into plots of five hectares each so as to establish on these plots a peasant family which formerly had been insufficiently provided for in terms of land. The size of the plots had been determined much earlier, in an era when all family members worked the farm in a self-sufficient enterprise. The doctrine aimed at what can be termed self-sufficient family farms; this approach was not strongly oriented toward importing the necessary means of agricultural production nor toward export.[8] Thus satisfaction was to be given to the traditional dream of the peasant — to possess a piece of land sufficient to earn his livelihood. Sophisticated studies even sought to justify the five hectare parcel through the calculation of the labor required for such self-sufficient cultivation. This effort was doomed to failure because necessary parcel size for self-sufficiency depends too much on external factors such as the price of sugar, the price of wheat, or the allocation of water. At the same time that the farmer was consigned to self-sufficiency on his five hectares, factories were being constructed nearby for ginning cotton, extracting sugar from beets, and canning fruit and produce. As a result of all of these events, the average peasant was being forced into a situation where 'the garment being prepared for him would not fit'. Since, as has been shown, the allotment procedures could not have any significant social impact, the circulation of labor should have been encouraged in order to assure a more equitable distribution of wealth.

Another stated objective was to reach a net revenue of 2,000 DH per year per household, which was considered to be an absolute minimum. Studies had shown that an average of five hectares of irrigated land were needed to obtain this income.

Large commercial-sized farms of 450 hectares might be divided into 90 different plots. To mitigate the disadvantages resulting from this situation (economies of scale, plans for cultivation, depreciation of heavy equipment, accounting arrangements, and the provision of skilled leadership), the former pattern of land was to be preserved by grouping assignees at that level into cooperatives.

It is difficult to separate out the many variables that guided the land reallocation process: ones which stemmed from an outdated and old-fashioned vision of family substance, the unexpressed political desire to bind the peasant to his five hectares of land, and the intellectual construction game of the engineer with his irrigation schemes involving the repetition of combinations of five units of land (five times five hectares makes one set), etc. Finally, in Morocco we should not fail to mention the possible magical and conceptual selection of the number 5 that could have inspired the idea: 5 people per household, 5 factors of production, the sharecropper arrangement built around sharing fifths (khamassat), 5 fingers in a hand.

In the Haouz, the division of arable land into five-hectare plots would have provided each farmer with 3,000 cubic meters of water per year until water could be transferred from el-Akhdar. If the farmer invested 50 centimes per cubic meter, a five-hectare plot would have yielded less than 1500 DH. Under these circumstances, most assignees received a five-hectare plot under lease-purchase agreements, plus the use of an additional five-hectare plot under revocable conditions, as well as the cooperative use of almond and olive orchards. Apparently it was realized that five hectares under prevailing conditions were not sufficient. But after new irrigation development, there would be a return to five hectare plots. By the time increased irrigation is available, there will really be two families on one plot anyway! If we are to compare this distribution with that for the colons one half century earlier, one might conclude that a colon is worth twenty Moroccan assignees!

D Political or Symbolic Distribution?

The small amount of land distributed, combined with the low social impact of the distribution and the debatable economic advantages resulting from the division of the farms, might lead one to think that the goal to be reached was purely political. Some degree of land distribution would be a necessary sacrifice to the idea of social justice in a country and a region where agrarian inequality was remarkably accentuated.

At the highest levels of the State, political considerations proper were a part of the allotment decision. The close correlation between rapidly developing political events and the acceleration of the allotment process provides proof for this argument. Yet at the regional and local levels, we do not think the distributions had a political objective. In the first place, the allotment benefited only a very small number of peasants; the benefit would be symbolic and only in proportion to the amount of publicity and propaganda developed concerning the operation. Most of the assignees were former workers from the same farms. As was the case for the former soldiers of the Saadian army, they were being settled on lands when their employers could no longer pay them. The purpose was to erase the drain on state-financed companies!

Second, the distribution produced more dissatisfied than satisfied individuals. Because a complex and, in principle, completely objective point system was used to assign plots, there were many disappointed peasants. For example, 3,000 acceptable candidates might easily apply for only thirty available plots.

The rural commune, as the smallest legal territorial entity, is the only one able to be formally considered by the administration. However, the social space constituted by the rural commune bears no necessary direct relationship to housing patterns since the smallest has almost 10,000 inhabitants. Of course the neighboring villages would plead their case with the administrators, invoking their proximity to the redistributed land, even producing proof of their former occupation of these colonization lands. In addition, they would bring to the attention of the administrators the fact that some of their village people had worked for the colons and had participated in the improvements of the lands; they had in fact invested their own labor in them. But from the point of view of the State this was the worst approach for making a land claim. The State could permit no exceptions to the principle that former use or proximity did not create any basis for a legal claim. To do so would have opened a Pandora's box to uncontrollable wildcat land occupation and promoted unprecedented confusion over both the land and the social and political situation. It was necessary, as the State saw it, to demonstrate that only chance and the right of the Prince could play a role in the distribution process. To do otherwise would have been to encourage the immediate rebirth of the very local powers that the State was constantly trying to check.

The political authorities could not help but be impressed by the fiery debates concerning the moral character of those who received allotment parcels. In Morocco, regulations stated that only farmers with less than five hectares of land who lived in a rural commune where land distribution would occur had the right to apply. Since the announcement of the land distribution was public and general, there was no shortage of applicants, and emotion surrounding the final selection of the few 'lucky' ones was certainly more widely distributed than the land itself. Newspapers of the opposition were filled after each distribution with debates about the selection of the assignees. Several caids or super-caids in the Haouz were dismissed in the aftermath of allocation transactions.

Neither social, nor political, nor economic: what then is land distribution in the context of the Agrarian Reform? Without notable social consequences, without any significant economic profitability, without any political involvement at the local level, land redistribution in the context of the Agrarian Reform appears at best symbolic and ritualistic: a sacrificial gesture made during the month of September which allows the demonstration of concern for the 'common man' once each year. During the remainder of the year, without excessive publicity, a more extensive land reform for the benefit of the middle- and large-scale landowners takes place on the basis of state toleration of the purchase of former colonial lands and granting of preferential loans to the most 'solvent'. Only later will a more objective critique of these events be possible.

Concerning the establishment of capital Moroccan farms, we possess only inadequate and incomplete data, and at the most, some indication of trends. This is because the phenomenon is recent and the purchasers are just launching their enterprises. The Haouz, from this point of view, cannot be compared to the Rharb or the Tadla, for the latter are devoid of the established interests of urban elites enmeshed in pre-existing value systems. In these regions of new development, the modern farmer, the capitalist entrepreneur and the gentleman-farmer made their appearance very early and created a model to imitate. For example, one can point to the impact of a Nejjai or the M'chiche!

This was not the case in the Haouz. As far as we can observe today in the plain around Marrakesh, the Moroccan purchasers of former colonial farms tend to increase mechanization and readily utilize state credit, even bank credit. There is undoubtedly considerable improvement in farm equipment; also underway are expansion of citrus fruit plantations, increases in selective breeding, and improvements in animal husbandry practices. But at the same time, the size of the permanent wage-earning class has been reduced to an essential minimum of guards and tractor operators, at the risk of lowering technical expertise and equipment maintenance. The more rapid wear and tear of equipment is seen by the Moroccan capitalist farmer as a result of the choices available to him for financing. Since he has easy access to state credit at low interest, he believes it is always to his advantage to reduce his daily cash-flow problems by reducing the number of wage laborers and increasing equipment expenditures. In a time of inflation, such reasoning is valid so long as it is not concerned about impoverishment of the working class and increases in unemployment. On the level of social relationships, the present-day capitalist farmer prefers to brandish the threat of lay-offs rather than deal with a system of incentives for performance.

The colons experienced a different situation in 1920, when labor was scarce, and they developed a formula for an appropriate division of labor. In time they developed customary labor arrangements. From 1945 on they had somewhat modified their system for the new plantations by increasing the use of female labor without touching the nucleus of permanent workers. In taking over the land, the Moroccan farmers have attacked this last vestige of the '20s. The aging permanent workers were eliminated largely by attrition rather than lay-offs. The reduction in the permanent labor force significantly modified the relative negotiating strength of farmers and their employees.

Being fewer in number, the workers have more difficulty in organizing. The farmer tends to treat each individual as a special case, to establish distinctions, to divide in order to control. Union activity has been reduced substantially, and there is an evolution toward a division of labor and social relations of the caidal type. Large masses of occasional workers actively organize during their seasons of employment. Their salaries increase as a result. For short periods these workers hold the forefront of public attention; however, they are scattered and even absent throughout the remainder of the year. This situation only encourages the farmers to recruit occasional workers from the social and family networks of permanent workers. One result has been the influx of women and children into the harvesting of fruit and produce. This is an advantageous situation for the employer in more than one respect!

There has been, in short, an evolution toward a mixed system using a capitalist approach with a heavy investment in land on the basis of credit rather than cash flow, and associating it with a flexible and unstable compromise on the level of social relations between a caidal sort of attitude and the manipulation of kinship relations.

Some observers have termed this unbridled capitalism. The terminology is probably correct for the new urban colons, but for many others, the former land owners of the Haouz, there has been so much complicity with the recent past that it would be an injustice to think them so heavy-handed.

3 Social Structure Today

All too often concepts of social structure are patterned after agrarian structures. Agrarian structure? The fashionability of the concept should make us suspicious. There exists no precise single definition upon which specialists agree. One definition is, 'the sum of the land and social conditions of agrarian regions'.[9] Another, 'the sum of the data concerning the morphological aspects of a specific region and the qualitative relations upon which the farming system rests'.[10] Authors equally include the mode of land use, the relationships between man and the cultivation of land (the form of production), legal and social relationships between the individuals and landed property, and the relationships between people who own the land and those who cultivate it. For example, Sorre says: 'The agrarian structure is a complex of the second order within the global agricultural context with all factors interrelated.'[11] Thus the question is as much the mode of distributing agricultural land as the pattern of cultivations and the concrete indicators of ownership of plots.

For Derruau, agrarian structures are the projection of 'the legal infrastructure' (sic) of society[12] and are affected as much by the distribution of property as by the activity of farming the land. Finally, a more narrow definition would focus purely on the descriptive aspects of the management of land: the shape, the dimensions, the distribution of the plots.

We will not go into the advantages or disadvantages of this or that definition. It simply seems to us that because significant discontinuities mark the landscape, a geographic approach may usefully describe the agrarian structure of a region. It can also help in the analysis of the facts of geographic distribution (soil, water, energy, etc.). However, it is up to the historians and sociologists to analyze to what extent the relations of production, the social relations, legal relations, and political and ideological factors explain the discontinuities within the continuity of the agrarian fabric. Perhaps they can tell us whether or not agrarian structures have any broad degree of autonomy.

The Haouz illustrates the extent to which physical geography, topography, and water distribution establish an enduring framework for the distribution of cultures and people. But historical events have become intertwined with the physical geography and gradually modified it by the deeds of men. Especially important are the conditions which obtain on the basis of type of society: tribal, theocratic, caidal, Makhzenian, and capitalist. Changes, breaks are superimposed on the ancient regime without totally liquidating it: the past never disappears and new things are not created *ex nihilo*. Sociologically speaking, an analysis of agrarian structures can only lead to a focus on the various modes of production of material life that are competing in the social formation.

Most studies of agrarian structure too often limit themselves to a dissertation on the distribution of land ownership: such and such a percentage of landowners possess such and such a percentage of the land, etc. There are three legitimate criticisms to this approach:

— first, such an approach implicity suggests that only one variable, the ownership of land, is significant. It is a monofunctional analysis, the most serious consequence of which is that it leads to the conclusion that by modifying the arrangement of land distribution, the whole will be changed.
— second, in this approach the ownership of property is acknowledged as the strategic variable everywhere and at all times. As we have seen, in the Haouz water is a more

important variable than land. In other regions of Morocco
(e.g. Tarfaya) the availability of human labor is the
dominant variable. Elsewhere, and increasingly, the
availability of capital is the dominant variable.
— finally, the size of properties does not explain everything.
Large estates may be state farms, private capitalist farms,
caidal latifundia, or domanial land that is leased annually
at public auctions, all utilizing different systems of tenure
and cultivation.

Since some specialists might reproach us for not presenting charts of land distribution by surface blocks, we are including the results of an administrative survey conducted in 1974 by the Office of the Haouz (see Table 3.7). However, we know from personal experience, based on a study made on the Oued Tessaout basin, that such figures are not very useful as indicators as long as regroupings and legal audits of the landed estates have not been carried out. This is because it is difficult to know the meaning of figures in the reciprocal game of concentration and dispersion of ownership of land. For example, the statistics are based on rural communes. An owner may have land in several communes. He will then, according to this table, be counted as several different owners. In other instances, twelve joint owners of a plot may be counted as a single owner. In other situations, each landed title that involves nonprivate lands might collectively relate to several hundred or even thousand beneficiaries or they could be domanial estates of which the state is only the titular owner. But in this situation, hundreds of tenants may have long-standing de facto rights that ought to be acknowledged by those making allotments as soon as any legal audit is begun. It is clear that in the first case concentration is underestimated, in the second case it is overestimated, and in the third case the outcome depends upon the direction taken in the ultimate distribution of land.

Other authors use as their main variable in explaining the structure of agrarian societies, patterns of land status (domanial lands, collective lands, guich lands, habous lands, colonization lands, and *melk* [privately owned] lands). However, there is much that is not explained by these categories of land. We know of collective lands where intensive irrigation of crops is being practiced in a way that amounts to appropriation of the land, and we know of other such

Table 3.7: Distribution of Land of all Statuses in the Central Haouz by Size of Landholding, 1974

Size of landholding (in hectares)	Surface area			Landholders and landless tenants		
	Hectares	Percent	Cumulative percent	Number	Percent	Cumulative percent
Landless	—	—	—	1,021	3.67	3.67
less than 1 ha	4,363.18	2.62	2.62	9,030	32.44	36.11
1 to 3 ha	15,852.40	9.54	12.16	8,180	29.40	65.51
3 to 5 ha	14,036.48	8.55	20.71	3,535	12.70	78.21
5 to 10 ha	25,996.24	15.64	36.35	3,608	12.96	91.17
10 to 15 ha	12,686.67	7.63	43.98	1,046	3.76	94.93
15 to 50 ha	28,052.31	16.90	60.88	1,122	4.03	98.96
50 to 100 ha	11,686.13	7.02	67.90	173	.62	99.58
more than 100 ha	53,281.14	32.10	100	117	.42	100
TOTALS	165,954.55	100	100	27,832	100	100

Source: Office of the Haouz.

lands that are used for opening grazing. Colonial lands have been used both as microfundia for consumption needs and as agribusiness plantations. Furthermore, the solution does not deal with the melk lands, which tend to become the largest legal category.

The system of cultivation also is sometimes used to illustrate agrarian structures, or social relations, or even the organic composition of capital and its relationship to human energy. For example, it could be shown that olive cultivation on large mechanized colonial farms, where permanent wage labor predominates, is carried out with 100 to 200 trees per hectare (in squares or checkerboard pattern) distributed over continuous surfaces. Production is entirely commercial. Then there is the caidal latifundium, where olive cultivation is practiced in rows of trees which alternate with strips of cereals, with a tree density of 50 per hectare. There is a low level of mechanization and the crop is harvested with corvée labor; production is for the grower's own use as well as for commercial purposes. On the microfundium, on the other hand, or on rented domanial lands, olive trees are only planted haphazardly along the distributor lines of the seguia, with 20 trees per hectare. This method of cultivation, however, is only of significance for purposes of comparison, and the olives, which are harvested with family labor, are almost entirely consumed by the growers themselves.

The means of processing of the harvest could also be considered: the factories, small shops, communal mills and hand presses are exactly articulated with the characteristics of each mode of production. This conceptualization seems at first glance to be the most heuristic.[13] Table 3.8 illustrates the various modes of production used in olive cultivation and their social and economic features. This sort of analysis can be extended to an extreme, for example, as follows. In the Ait Ourir and many other areas of the Dir, there is an old technique of olive oil extraction in which the olives are pressed between enormous rocks lifted by levers. The olives are first crudely ground, then heated in the sun by placing them upon flat rocks that have slightly roughened surfaces which face southward. This ancient technique of harvesting olive oil is done during the winter solstice and only by women. We have carefully measured the yield from this means of extraction, and it does not exceed 8 percent of the gross weight of the olives. By comparison, the common mill provides an extraction rate of 15 to 17 percent, modern methods exceed 20 percent, and by the most recent techniques, one is able to recover 25 percent, completely utilizing the olive pulp. The traditional heavy stone mill preceded the arrival of Islam in Morocco; indeed, we have located more than a dozen prehistoric sites. Even today, it is not just an item of folklore. Upon being questioned, some solemn elders of the Ait Tinelli tribe of the Zat region told us: 'While we await the drying of the olives for the common mills, this technique is the only means we have to get fresh pure oil.'

There is a similar process for the threshing of cereals done by hand with a wooden beater, again a task performed by women. Vestiges of this technique can be found in the whole of Morocco. We have witnessed it recently in the foothills of the Rif in the vicinity of Quezzane. The productivity of this technique is extremely low compared to treading by men and hoofed animals, and even more so compared to the use of the threshing machine. But the process insures the viability of the family economy at times when its reserves are exhausted, the price of grain at the weekly market is very high, or all available cash has been utilized by the harvesting process (which is quite costly). Should this type of analysis be pursued on other levels? For example at the judicial, the cognitive, the ideological levels?

It would be easy to analyze the frequent interconnections between these several variables and it would be possible even to lead up to an analysis of the internal logical coherence between the different aspects of the several modes of production.

But then, what is the society of the Haouz? Does it have a holistic coherence to its social structure? Or is it really only the coexistence, the juxtaposition, the patchwork collection of several modes of production that have little connection between them?

A What Would a Homogeneous Society Be Like?

It would be an internally coherent society, one in which social facts could be deduced one from the other without having to appeal to facts extraneous to that society. Let us try to imagine one such example of a homogeneous society, patriarchy, which is the mode of organization that still dominates the rural family in the Haouz.

In such a society, technology is little developed. The energy utilized is mainly human: the woman carries the water jar and the man the bundles of wheat. The people do everything. The animals do little and there are no machines. The flour mills are hand operated. The wheel

Table 3.8: *Characteristics of Olive Production and Distribution*

Techno-economic characteristics	Mode of production		
	Capitalist	Caidal	Patriarchal
Grove density per hectare	100 to 120	50	20
Arrangement	continuous, square, quincunx 8–10x10	in line 10x20	network
Energy	mechanical, fuel	animal and human	human
Equipment	tractor	traditional plow	hoe
Social relations	permanently salaried and seasonal	tenant and corvée	familial
Processing	factory	communal mill and press	family stone press
Destination	international and national markets	regional markets	familial

is scarcely utilized; the animals do not pull carts but carry light loads on their backs. Productivity is low and human energy predominates. Survival depends upon the number of men bound together by mutual feelings of solidarity.

It is necessary to convince men that they are tied to one another, in order to organize against nature and produce wealth for consumption. Patriarchy is based upon the idea of the existence of a mystical tie linked to the procreation of the father. The fact of being a child of this or that father is the basis of patriarchal society and explains almost all of the social facts of that type of society. The agnatic lineage is a sort of nation; in it everything is subordinated to the family and the father is the source of all power. He distributes the rewards and the work; he defines the law: his will is the law. This relationship explains many aspects of the present-day Haouz and other patriarchal societies. It explains aspects as diverse as various forms of inheritance, the tendency toward the exclusion of women from inheritance, the taboo concerning virginity, the cult of the dead, the correlation between age and authority, the prestige of the elders, and a wealth of linguistic facts. (For example 'sharafa' is the Arabic root evoking the high lofty character of a given thing. Yet from that term has been derived connotations as different in a capitalist society as 'sage', 'old', and 'noble'.)

Let us take another case, that of the capitalist farm. Here the crystallization of labor around capital is the fundamental fact of social organization. Scientific and technical advancement have permitted human labor to be stored in machines. Technology requires concentration of increasingly skilled labor and the corresponding regularization of employment opportunities. The society then evolves toward the employment of regular salaried workers who increasingly become organized in labor unions for purposes of negotiation with management. At the legal level this is a society of contracts: it continually tends to formalize the relationship between producers and workers through laws, conventions, constitutions, institutions. Everything is organized to permit an increase in capital, to realize a profit. If patriarchal societies produce men, capitalistic societies produce profits.

But these two contrasting modes of production, as abstract types, are constructions of the mind. Each particular characteristic does exist, but there is no such thing as a society or group that is purely patriarchal, tribal, caidal or capitalist. Pure types describing the stages of agrarian development or modes of production are schematizations carried to the extreme. They have pedagogical value, but if pushed too far, they betray reality. When one calls a particular societal trait obsolete or outdated, it means that one is unable to place that trait conceptually within the ongoing social formation. But there are no 'residues'; all actual social facts are to be taken into account for what they are worth today.

Societies drag their pasts along with them; a society is not constituted without history, and that history is precisely the evolution of the modes of production, the social relationships, and the ideologies that shape it. Historical societies are complex and, at any moment in time, they are mixtures of the past societies that have succeeded one another. These composite forms of historical societies

THE PROGRESS OF CAPITALISM AFTER INDEPENDENCE

are the specific features of any given society.[14]

Algeria and Morocco are composites different from each other today because the vicissitudes of the histories of both societies have taken different forms. Likewise the Haouz is neither the Tadla, nor the Rharb, nor the Sous, etc. Present reality is neither the disorderly juxtaposition, nor the sum, nor the linear substitution of simple models. If in this study we have had to segment space and time, it is only because we lacked the skills to do otherwise. But we want to reserve the right to reject the necessary artificiality of discourse in reaching the conclusion of the study.

B Composite Society

When different modes of production coexist in the same society, the relationship is neither indifferent nor peaceful. There is, between the various modes of production that comprise Haouz society, permanent competition and a set of complex social relationships between the various social groupings. There are dominant social forms and subordinate ones, and they either resist one another or are allied and interrelated. Diversity in such arrangements plays a role according to the particular region and the particular time in history.[15] We shall examine three cases.

At the level of technology we will examine the use of *energy*. In the city of Marrakesh, electricity, natural gas, and fuel oil are the predominant sources of energy; hackney coaches are reserved for tourists and families of the petty bourgeoisie on Sundays. The flour mills are electric and more and more the ovens rely on fuel oil. These sources of energy have become dominant over animal and human energy; the entire society is organized in such a way as to insure their competitive success. Long-distance supplying and marketing are assured by international agreements. The technology that permits using electricity and natural gas for fuel is possible because there are schools to train the people, and so forth. Only a few kilometers from Marrakesh, electric power, fuel and gas are replaced by traditional forms of energy — animal, human, and simple hydraulic power. Using motor pumps presents problems because of the remoteness of any mechanics and the lack of spare parts. Given these problems, woodburning, animal and human energy compete with modern technology. A little farther from Marrakesh, as we enter the mountains, it is human energy that competes with animal energy for predominance. In the Haouz, among different forms of energy, there are thus concentric circles of competitiveness and levels of technology. At the level of *social relationships* the same parallels can be drawn. In Marrakesh there is a permanent, trained wage-earning class with assured employment, some degree of respect for unionism, social welfare programs, and in some cases medical and retirement benefits, etc. — all things necessitated by high levels of technology.

Outside Marrakesh the predominant form of labor is the seasonal wage earner who has no guarantee other than receiving fixed wages at the end of a day or a two-week period. Beyond that still there is the *sharika* (tenant farming) or the khamessat — with risky compensation based on the harvest, with the burden of debts that have to be paid off. Further away still from Marrakesh there are other forms of labor relationships including quasi-bondage or serfdom. In addition there is non-remunerative family labor.

At the level of *legal relationships* or at the level of *ideology*, in fact at all levels for all aspects of society, it is possible to make similar distinctions. We have used the variable of remoteness from Marrakesh to describe the successive patterns of domination of the various modes of production that are in competition. But they also coexist within the same city. Even within Marrakesh, there are examples of advanced capitalism (IBM, ITT, etc.) and of feudal or slavelike relationships. Did we say this occurs in the same city? It even occurs in the same family! The father may be a capitalist proprietor and he may have within his home a maid the equal of the feudal type and a son who is a militant progressive.

The study of composite society over a long period of its history conjures up the imagery of causalities that are so entangled that one is no longer able to isolate even the least significant variable. Jacques Berque has cautioned us:

> The life of society is complex; in this society, it is even more so. It is a texture with broad interlacing designs, a fabric with unexpected historical throwbacks, that defies any simplistic appraisals and descriptions.[16]

For the Seksawa tribe, Berque's work delivers us from those linear simplifications of Robert Montagne. Berque would not let us forget the extraordinary complexity of patrimonial relationships, of space, of holiness — even in the analysis of a single tribe. Berque refused to study the Seksawa except as a whole, as a durable, if not immutable, society. Should we not follow Berque's approach of replacing the complexity of the Seksawa society, for the person who is unable to go and look for himself, by the complexity of sociological discourse on this tribal society?

The scholar who does not have the gift of intimate and inspired discourse ought to work in the field from analysis to synthesis. What variables should one take into account in exploring the infinite planes of social reality?[17] During this entire study we have moved among political competition, emphasis on technology, judicial statuses and social relationships. These discourses wandered from concern to concern depending upon the directions of history — the flags raised by the protagonists at any period in time. In describing their quarrels or their utopias do we have a lesser chance of understanding their society? And by seeing that which we today think to be more fundamental in their unrest, is this not tantamount to shifting our ideas of causality into another age? This would be a serious anachronistic error!

We know that no society truly understands itself; behind the bombast and the rhetoric of each crusade there is an effort to make some more immediate gain. Accordingly, one of the tasks of historians is continuously to debunk the pomp that each society creates in its images of itself. The ceremonial activities as well as legal fictions are as much means as ends: they are neither totally determined nor totally autonomous.

Who is to decide definitely at all times and in all places which factors are fundamental? Why should not ideas, ideologies, religion, power or even technology be at this or that moment in time the initiating factor in social change or at other times the consolidating force in response to change being caused by other variables?

For example, it is not the redistribution of the caidal lands that altered social relationships; it is the change in the relationship between tenants and owners which modified the distribution of the land. This occurred when the caids were discredited by the national liberation movement and suddenly found themselves deprived of support by the foreign administration. Since the farmers rejected corvée labor and exactions forever, the caids were forced to sell portions of their land. The result was the distribution of land in a different manner, which in most cases benefited not the former tenants, but a new urban elite interested in profit from speculation. All of a sudden administrative power alone could not levy taxes. There was no longer a congruence between politico-administrative office and enrichment. But changes of social attitudes between protagonists and the establishment of new, binding relationships between owners and tenants, could only become permanent and durable with a broad and definitive redistribution of land and water rights. The Agrarian Reform was never carried out to the extent that the rhetoric suggested. The ineffective reform effort and the subsequent turning away from it simultaneously marked the limit of the political reversal of the old elites and the limit of the emergence of the peasantry. Still, there was to be no return to the former situation. What emerged was a precarious system of compromises based on anomalous aggregations of individual cases. There were well-known cases of regression and the reestablishment of serflike tenure. There was broad progress in salaries, primarily for occasional laborers, and for permanent workers, significantly altered by the caidal mode of production.

No inventory of concrete situations in balance at each moment would exhaust reality. In the interconnecting threads of social facts, it is just as well to show the continuity of the social fabric as the discontinuity of interrelations. The continuity which affirms the sociological coherence of society in the region of the Ait Ourir, and in many others, is the result of a refusal to give primacy to one of the knots in the warp of causality. 'Everything influences everything reciprocally' is the motto of continuity. Everything reacts on everything. The extreme complexity of the systematic delineation of causality, or just of interrelationships, is such a dense tangle that true comprehension is impossible. Whence the holism of Gurvitch, the poetics of Berque, the structuralism of Levi-Strauss.

If in theory a good number of analysts declare themselves objective in their search for continuities, in practice they have to accommodate their readers: when everything cannot be said at once, the ellipse is practiced with talent. Discourse necessarily gives primacy, at any given point, to one causal chain and some links. Thus the analysts are forced, after having affirmed the holistic vision, to establish the lawful basis of a chosen chain of causality as an exception, before returning anew to the totality. Through this window, they have been able to pass out a little rationalist and pragmatic 'merchandise', and thus put themselves beyond the reach of a crudely functionalist critique.

On the other hand, the schools of thought that assert discontinuity are continuously threatened by the mechanistic, cyclical, or linear visions of social causality.

C Domination and Hegemony

The various social facts vying within a society have a differential competitiveness within space and time. However, from a global perspective there are long-term irreversible patterns of domination, even though we may occasionally witness temporary setbacks. We already know that the Haouz society is a *composite*. It is not purely this or that; instead, several modes of production are competing in its social formation — patriarchalism, feudalism, tribalism, and capitalism. Socialism is also present but this type of social formation operates only at a level of ideology and political organizations. It has no material base, nor any institutions of production. How are these four modes of production linked, and what are the prospects from an evolutionary perspective?

The answers to these questions are not very simple. They hinge on the social factors under consideration and the relationship of Moroccan society to other societies. Industrial society predominates at the level of technology. The development of technology, from the use of machines to electrification, continues to progress and to make its presence felt in all areas of society — wages, modern law, education, political participation, and so on. It will result in a diminution of the khamessat, customs, illiteracy, tyranny, superstition.

However, there is resistance at other levels in this society. Other social factors have a degree of autonomy which gives them a certain competitiveness and capacity to reject the modern model. For example, some institutions sanctify feudalism and consequently distribute power not on the basis of technical skill, but upon faithfulness, a network of clientele, and land ownership. In the family, the patriarchal mode dominates and thus social relationships, the status of women and so on, create resistance.

Thus, if we are obliged to summarize the social situation of the Haouz today, we arrive at a formulation of the following complexity: the social formation in the Haouz is caidal-Makhzenian. Tribalism is being eliminated and patriarchal domination is being controlled. The latter finds refuge in the nuclear family with the accompanying overexploitation of women and children. But caidalism itself is dominated by international capitalism in the sphere of production and trade. Eight years ago we tentatively concluded some reflections on these issues with a question, perhaps based on our reading of the literature, concerning the necessity of nationalization of the whole process of production in an economically dominated country. We pondered whether one of the essential components in the economy of the Haouz was not the hydraulic character of its economy; consequently we asked if the nationalization of water distribution did not involve a perspective of hegemony. Today we are not ruling out this possibility. The present hegemony of capitalism will perhaps be unable to solve the problems associated with population growth. Perhaps formalized competition between self-conscious social classes will develop. At the present time it is dormant, informal; the feudal networks have not entirely given in. Tribalist reactions often adorn competition, which, if unveiled, might appear as class competition. The presence of the zaouia and the *moussem* (Islamic devotional holiday marked by sacred and secular fairs), for example, diverts the eye from seeing the hegemony of capitalism. But no matter how dependent and externally determined the zoauia and the moussem are, they maintain a sometimes more than negligible degree of autonomy. The possibility of a situation in which the entire social order would work for an international capitalist system, but which internally would be a centralized Makhzenian society, cannot be totally ruled out. It is, however, apparent to all observers that capitalism is on its way to victory in the Haouz.

The Haouz is not an island! The purely internal aspects of the development of international capitalism aside, the development of the Haouz involves increasingly marginal zones which require increasingly sophisticated and costly techniques for development. These can only be profitable within a larger economic framework on a national or international level. Such calculation of profitability, because of the scale of investment, can be made only in terms of time frames that are 'guarantees'. Only broad projections can justify certain investments which demographic growth will make inevitable. We can then ask if the capitalist mode of production, which those who live in the Haouz know only as deep-rooted foreign extension, will succeed in establishing the appropriate guarantees for its development,

THE PROGRESS OF CAPITALISM AFTER INDEPENDENCE 211

to respond to demand and to protect what it already has achieved.

D Man in the Composite Society

How do men live in this society? How can they adapt to a complex world where there at least four competing types of ideologies, conventions, mores, values, legal systems, technologies, and cognitive systems, three to four languages, three monetary systems, and four calendars in daily use? Each man has to work out his own internal equilibrium. He has to adapt himself to this complex society that presents itself to him daily in a thousand different manifestations, each one having its own logic, references, vocabulary, traditions, and, at times, even its own language.

Let us examine, for example, a peasant who has just learned that he is to be the recipient of an agricultural loan. He must proceed to the local office of agriculture to make arrangements and pick up the form to complete the arrangements for constructing a new barn. He leaves his home wearing his white jellaba and carrying his dagger in an obvious manner — a sign of a free man or a member of the peasant aristocracy. He invokes the name of God while straddling his small motorbike, both out of religious fervor and out of a desire to have protection on his journey. His motorbike will not start because the fuel line is clogged and he has to make repairs — a technical act. In the bike's saddlebag he places a chicken, whch he intends as a gift to the government official who will give him his application papers. Upon reaching the Rural Development Center, and, since he is not familiar with the various offices and feels he may not be recognized (an identity problem as well as a problem of social coming of age in a caidal socicty), he proceeds to the workshop where he locates a mechanic who happens to be a cousin. His relative explains to him that he is merely a worker and in that capacity he has no particular access to the office in question and that he cannot very well intervene on his behalf — division of labor in an industrial society. However, he, as a mechanic, has recently repaired an automobile for an office clerk who is accordingly in his debt: the clerk will be able to make an introduction.

Through a complex arrangement of referral, which from the point of view of the bureaucratic regulations have no raison d'être, and which could have been avoided by the peasant if he had chosen to spend a somewhat lengthy wait in front of the director's door, the peasant finally edges his way into the director's office. It would be interesting to find out whether or not the chicken has been accepted, but even more importantly one needs to understand the meaning of the proffered gift. Was this gift an understood part of the salary of the official or is it a form of corruption? For the peasant, the three questions — is the chicken a gift, a part of the official's salary, or a form of corruption? — are so inextricably enmeshed that one would have to delve deeply into his psyche to understand how he views the exchange. In the mind of the peasant, this official sitting in a large office, whose door is difficult to enter, ought not to be paid only by the State, but should receive some remuneration from the peasant as well. Finally, the discussion comes to the original plot, the loan itself. The discussion revolves around the complex nature of the loan and aid arrangements. The loan the peasant receives is to be paid back in full in a certain number of years at a specified, relatively low rate of interest. Of course the peasant is familiar with usurious situations where loans are made at high rates of interest, but here the State is making low-interest loans, formally and in writing; his loan is then matched by a grant from the state to build the barn. The peasant wonders, is this grant a gift, aid, perhaps a favor? All of these alternatives are so intertwined in his mind that we cannot say whether we are dealing with capitalism, feudalism, or even socialism. But our peasant friend is required to insure himself against fire hazards. He receives the explanation that his barn might possibly be struck by lightning or destroyed through negligence of hired hands. He is told that he cannot receive the loan unless he insures against such risks. How can we expect our peasant to understand the notions of probability and statistical projections, in a milieu where climatic hazards predominate and in a cultural setting where the future is viewed as unpredictable, where a man feels so helpless in front of nature and his fellow countrymen? Finally he must sign on the appropriate line, and the question of the name is no small matter, for though he is well known in his village by his own name and his father's, his village has lost significance beyond his own rural commune and means nothing to the directors and officials of the development office. It will be necessary to have witnesses as well as the physical presence of the *moggadem* (local government official), perhaps even the presence of the sheikh. The man just exposed to insurance policy requirements and probability tables is now, by these requirements, thrust back into a social relationship that is feudal and tribal.

This kind of situation occurs in real life every day. Our farmer never escapes participation in a society which he never fully grasps; since he cannot comprehend the full meaning of the society, he cannot behave in a completely logical way from the beginning of his course of action to the end. The only unity which governs his personal behavior is his self-interest. In this is to be found the source of possible explanations for the extraordinary development of individualism in Morocco and the accompanying complexity of Moroccan society.

Every society has its norms, its values, and its mores. But a person from a composite society plays on all keyboards, on all the registers. He pursues personal and sometimes collective objectives without examining whether any particular item or behavior reinforces or destroys any specific value system. In other words he makes use of values from each of the social systems, although he may claim to be 'modern' or 'respectful of tradition', or 'efficient' or 'socialistic'. For many people, these beliefs do not effect changes in behavior; ideas do not necessarily create obligations. However, to be in a society is to behave in a certain way. If one lives in a composite society, one has a personal tendency to abide by a set of morals and behavior patterns that are a composite of several value systems. These are the rewards and limitations of ambivalence!

4 Transition or Composite?

It can be asked whether the model sketched for the Haouz is applicable generally. Does our analysis apply to other regions of Morocco, to the country as a whole, and even beyond its borders? We do not possess the pretension necessary to attempt to answer such a question. But we will say this: the establishment of a more unified, more coherent social formation requires the liquidation of less competitive modes of production. This liquidation is not without cost: it must compensate for the conscious, and thus premature, dismantling of the partial competitiveness of subordinate and dominant systems. The ideological, political, social, and of course financial resources to cover the costs of transition are to be found in the design of a credible society — a society that mobilizes the wills, and ... the economic surplus as well. When the one and the other are confiscated and exported, the society no longer can marshal adequate means to assure the transition; it is then left to compose, i.e, to articulate among diversified instances that differentially frame the social order, which is unceasingly threatened by a growing proletarianization.

This is why the transition is only possible with national integration, independence and ideological mobilization. Only on this basis is it possible to counter the whole logic of short term individual interest, be it caidal, theocratic or Moroccan capitalist, so as to aim for and give credence to one model over another.

To change society is to choose a new mode of existence for a new society; it is to live a new morality, a homogeneous morality and ethic of action in a society which seeks homogeneity. This poses the problem of the historical *rupture*. The problem of such a break is not new. Ibn 'Ajiba, a sufi savant from Tetouan who died around 1810, protested against the practices of his contemporaries, and he recommended achieving the perfect unification of personality (*attawhid al khass*) by way of the people (*fi tariq al-Qawn*), by breaking with conventional customs (*bi-khargi al-'awaid*). This would have amounted to giving primacy to ideology. In the nineteenth century, as we have seen, ideology failed in the face of the competiton of material forces from abroad.

Afterword

Aside from a few minor changes, the preceding text is the second part of a Ph.D. thesis I defended at the University of Paris (Paris VII) on February 22, 1975. No doubt I could have improved it considerably at the cost of a fairly substantial recasting. I would also have liked to have been able to present first to the public, and especially to the Marrakchis, an inexpensively priced initial text, so as to take into account the indispensable critiques that this work will call forth. Those who know the Haouz more deeply and more intimately than I shall ever know it, do not write. They do not have the time, the occasion, the possibility. Moreover, it is a trait of this culture to avoid stepping foward and implying that one knows more than others do. In the Marrakchis' reserve, there is modesty, a sense of decency, and above all prudence. Outside the circle of close friends and acquaintances, anonymity is more sought after than it is transgressed. In select company, there is an eloquent charm to exchanging fierce and scathing remarks on minor and major issues alike; yet people avoid bringing into the open anything other than fitting words, using turns of phrases which are both friendly and emphatic: only the initiated decipher the silences and the innuendos that reflect strong personal opinions.

I am aware in part that in Marrakesh the publication of this work has a savage and unpolished, let us say 'uncivil', character. I do hope, although I dare not believe it too much, that my work will give rise to discussion. My greatest expectation is to receive critiques and rebuttals whether public or private, written or oral, signed or anonymous; only the formulation of such critiques will reduce the wide gap that exists between dispersed deep and intimate knowledge and our all too vast collective ignorance; it is thus that the human sciences can hope to advance.

I also would have liked to take up again the concluding chapter, which lacks vigor and conviction. I was extremely cautious in declaring in what way Haouz society, and hence, in a certain manner, the whole of Moroccan society, is a *composite* society. I have not been well understood by my peers. Some have countered by suggesting that composite society is the fate of every society in the world, and that the concept of *social formation* actually already contains complex configurations of modes of production which compete within it. But these arguments do not convince me. I maintain that there is a certain conceptual progress in distinguishing between various social formations that, I agree, are not all homogeneous and that practically never proceed from one single mode of production, even when one of them is absolutely dominant. I want to distinguish, on one hand, between societies of *transition* — those whose agents proclaim, desire, and designate the ideals they want to bring into being, and eliminate the rest and, on the other hand, the *composite* societies — those which, by contrast, refuse, are repugnant to, and shun a radically new direction and try to endure by acting on all fronts which offer them implicit competitions of past and new modes of production. I am not saying that, objectively, these societies will not be forced to change all the same. Little by little and irresistibly, they will see dominating, within a new social formation, that which they want to suppress, but with all the delays, all the costs, all the instabilities which attempts at suppression encourage.

Some will object that composite societies are all resisting progress and that the societies of transition want to do away with this past that lingers on. Indeed? Perhaps there is more complicity than one would think in this self-restraint, in this secret fear of breaking out of History's womb. Is this wisdom, prudence or cowardice?

And if in the final analysis all societies were composites, it would be necessary to start by stating what differentiates them from one another. It is the forms of competition, of resistance, of domination specific to each of the modes of production of the composites which specify those composites. And these are conjoined in a particular manner, at the level of such or such an instance of the social formation.

To expose that configuration, to take it apart, to prove it — this is the task of another work.

Notes

Editor's Introduction

1 The deficiencies of modernization theory were detailed by Immanuel Wallerstein in two essays, 'The present state of the debate on world inequality', published in 1975, and 'Modernization: requiescat in pace', published in 1976. Both are included in his (1979) collected essays. The clearest but also most self-consciously ideological statement of modernization theory is that of Rostow (1967), who in fact serves as the principal target of Wallerstein's critiques.
2 For example, in the analysis of 'development of underdevelopment', the central theorist is Gundar Frank (1967), whose cases are South American countries. Peter Evans (1979) moves from dependency theory in the work of Frank and others to describe 'dependent development' in Brazil.
3 See Bryan Turner's (1974) effort to distill a consistent analysis of Islam from Max Weber's diverse comments.
4 Hindess and Hirst (1975) dismiss the 'asiatic' as a conceptually inadequate specification of a mode of production, but they nevertheless show how it fits into Marx's overall development theory. Later (1977), they abandon the concept of 'mode of production' because they do not think it can exist independently of a social formation. So at least in Hindess and Hirst's version of structuralist marxism, perhaps Marx's 'asiatic' analysis is retrieved.
5 Turner (1978:6).
6 Turner (1978:5, 27).
7 Turner's (1978) proposed approach.

8   Wallerstein (1979) emphatically argues for the hegemony of the capitalist world economy. But he and Gutkind (1976) acknowledge the complex interplay of pre-colonial and colonial modes of production in their discussion of sub-Saharan Africa. For a study of Mexico comparable to the present one, but within the world-system perspective, see Frank (1979). For a critique of world system theory assumptions as a basis of substantive analysis, see Hall (1984). The work of John G. Taylor (1979) sets forth a theoretical framework for analysis of Third World social formations which more closely parallels Pascon's empirical approach, at the same time that it gives a critique of both development and dependency theories.

9   One logically distinct alternative stands out: Althusser and Balibar (1970) really want to speak of holistic social formations which are distinctly bounded. In Althusser and Balibar's scheme, one could perhaps speak of *succession* of one mode of production by another, perhaps of their co-penetration of the same territory, but not of a transition in the sense of the term used here. Interestingly, Pascon cites Althusser in the present volume. For a discussion of Althusser's theory of history in relation to the *Annales* school, see Hall (1980).

10 Pascon's (1977) thesis was published in Morocco in two volumes, as *Le Haouz de Marrakech*. The first volume deals with geography, climate, irrigation, and historical heritage; the second with the subject of the present volume.

11 Personal letter to the editor, and an interview with Pascon (1978).

12 See Hexter (1972).

13 Except where otherwise noted, the following account is based on Pascon (1977), volume I, though it is not intended by the editor to serve as a summary of that volume.

14 Hoffman (1967:20).

15 An excellent account of Moroccan prehistory is given by Bovill (1970).

16 For a discussion of a similar ecological and cultural boundary in the British Isles, see Hechter (1975:49–59).

17 On ecology and tribes, see Burke (1976:6–9). Hoffman (1967:98), Bidwell (1973:73ff.), and Burke (1976:14) all discuss the character of caids in different political situations and time periods.

18 Gellner (1969).

19 Gellner (1969:22ff.).

20 Scham (1970:94).

21 Gellner (1969:3).

22 Turner (1974) critically examines the nature of sainthood in Islam and Christianity, and the consequences of Islam for capitalism. On the latter, see also Rodinson (1978). Rabinow (1978) examines a case of

'sainthood', while Gellner (1969) and Eickelman (1976) provide studies of zaouias and their relations to the social order.
23 Gellner (1969:6).
24 Weber (1977:231-232); Burke (1976:16), against Gellner, typifies Moroccan domination as a kind of patrimonialism. See Roth (1971) for a general discussion of patrimonialism in the new states.
25 Bovill (1970) describes the Moroccan role in sub-Saharan trade. Chirot (1976) analyzes a parallel case, the relation of the Roumanian state to a local peasant and a long-distance trade economy. Morocco's efforts to limit internal commerce by foreigners up to the end of the nineteenth century are well known. On the suspicion of sultans toward foreigners as forerunners of expansionist European states, see e.g., the comments by Joseph Thomson noted by Rotberg (1971:245).
26 See especially Cruickshank (1935) and Bowie (1970).
27 Weber (1977:912-919) discusses English and other European stances toward imperialism at the turn of the century.
28 See Scham (1970).
29 For an assessment of Moroccan land reform, see Griffith (1976:73-115). Waterbury (1970) describes the post-colonial Moroccan political elite which undertook the reforms.
30 The overall ecology of the region fits well within Braudel's (1972:55ff.) description of the Mediterranean.
31 Aside from Pascon (1977: 1:92), see Hoffman (1967:88ff.). For an interesting discussion of irrigation and social organization around the town of Sefrou, in the Dir of the Middle Atlas, see Rosen (1979).
32 Gellner (1969:35ff.).
33 Weber (1977:909-910).

Chapter 1: Penetration of Capitalism into the Haouz of Marrakesh

1 Miège (1961a; 1961b; 1963; 1964; 1969).
2 On the technology, see Laoust (1920: 43-49).
3 See Jacques Caille (in Roscoat, 1956: 437-441) and Miège's (1963: 117n8) citation of additional sources.
4 Amédée de Roscoat (1956: 446).
5 In the words of Leon Godard (1859: 62).
6 Miège (1963: 132).
7 Schlumberger, 'Rapport mensuel'. April, 1894. Archives de la Guerre à Vincennes (French manuscript source) C8, Maroc 575.
8 Miège (1963: 131).
9 Miège (1964: 139, 301, 336).

10 The classic mercantilist position. See Miège (1961a: 82ff).
11 Miège (1961b: 83-85, 237-238). Cf. Ibn Khaldun (1968: 574-577).
12 See the account of Pierre Guillen (1967:505).
13 The European documents of the period use the term 'mkhalate' (or, in Guillen's [1967] spelling, 'mochalate') or 'censal'. The root of the Arab term, 'muhallat' means to mix, to associate diverse things without allowing their intimacy. Like 'intermediary', the term is somewhat disparaging. 'Censal' is an alteration of 'semsar', or courtier.
14 Letter of Madden to Lister, Casablanca, February 13, 1909. Public Record Office, London (English manuscript source) 174.257#25. Protection legally accorded for a long time (cf. Article 11 of the Treaty of May 28, 1767, concluded by the Count of Breugnon between France and the Empire of Morocco) to agents and associates of foreigners was only extended in practice with the development of commerce. Thus it could easily happen that protégés were subjected to local jurisdiction and the payment of personal charges demanded by functionaires. Protection was basically a 'safeguard' analogous to that assured by the *dahir* (decree) of 'tawqir wa ihtiram', with the notable difference that a foreign nation provided it.
15 See Ibn Khaldun (1968: 789-799). Concerning protection, see Miège (1961b: 401-402; 1963: 263ff).
16 Guillen (1967: 403-405).
17 For a chronology of the events, see Bouderbala, Chraibi and Pascon (1974: 9-10).
18 The pretext could have been the loan made by Paribas to the sultan in April, 1904, even though the Compagnie Marocaine was considered to have more longstanding rights to such commerce. See the *Bulletin du Comité de l'Afrique Française*, May-June 1904. The relations between the great French banks are far from being marked with the spirit of collaboration. The rivalry between the Banque de Paris et des Pays-Bas (Paribas) and Schneider — the Banque Protestante — was quite strong, each trying to tip the favor of the Quai d'Orsay [the French Ministry of Foreign Affairs] to its cause. At the outset of the 1902 considerations about a loan to Morocco, it seems that Théophile Delcasse, French Minister of Foreign Affairs at the time, supported Schneider and Company, notably through its subsidiary, Gautsch. But because Paribas united the banks into a consortium to oppose Gautsch, the Compagnie Marocaine could no longer obtain financing. Delcasse fell out with Schneider and aligned with Paribas, once Paribas demonstrated its greater strength and effectiveness. The loan of 1904 was prepared by Delcasse and Paribas. The Schneider group responded by proposing to Moulay Abd el-Aziz (sultan from 1894-1908) a rival loan contract involving themselves in conjunction with the Banque Protestante and

the Union Parisienne; an agent of the Compagnie Marocaine negotiated the matter. In Paris, a lively lobbying campaign developed in the press and in parliament. The agents of Schneider denounced the aims of the Ministry of Foreign Affairs and of Paribas; they discussed the specter of dependency in Morocco, as well as abroad. The Schneider group only retreated in the face of a threat by Delcasse to cease ordering war material through them. The arbitration of Rouvier was imposed on Paribas and the Compagnie Marocaine because these rivalries ran the risk of favoring the plans of the British and, more particularly, the Germans. My analysis is based on a search of the archives of the Compagnie Marocaine in Paris. It has been extremely difficult to obtain precise and documented information on this matter. Ultimately it is thanks to Lawrence Abrams (1977) that I have been able to obtain irrefutable documentation.

19 Miège (1964: 247-248) writes that the Compagnie Marocaine born of 'the association of Jazulot, Gautsch and Faberes [was] energetically supported by the legation'. But that was in 1902. In 1906, they thought they were not aided enough, or less than Paribas.

20 'G. Veyre [the agents of the Compagnie Marocaine in Fez] who played on the confidence of Moulay Abd el-Aziz, seems to have been one of the intermediaries between the Sultan and the French banks', according to Ayache (1956: 64).

21 Doutte (1901: 29).

22 Guillen (1967: 509, 512n2).

23 Miège (1963: 110) makes some analogous remarks about a period preceding by a quarter of a century the one with which we are concerned here: 'It would be incorrect to take as the basis of description the contemporary accounts, which constantly used such expressions as: reform party, liberal party, progressive party or reactionary party, lunatic fringe . . .' Granted that they existed, without further research it would be impossible to say exactly what was behind these 'parties'.

24 Up until now the single source for this whole affair is the extremely detailed report of Louis Gentil (1907) prepared for the French legation. Gentil's report seems very objective in the main body of the account, if not in the conclusion. There is also the official version, which essentially follows Gentil's report; it is contained in the letter of Regnault, French Minister at Tangier, to Stephen Pichon, Minister of Foreign Affairs in Paris, March 23, 1907. All the other commentaries — Arnaud (1952: 235-236), Weisgerber (1947: 156), Maxwell (1966: 97) and Ayache (1956: 67) — are taken from the same source. The consular reports of other foreign powers also follow Gentil's account. Beyond these, there are still some other sources which have not yet been studied, notably the correspondence between Kouri, French consul at Mogador

and Moulay Hafid, and the notebook of M'hamad Ibn At-Tawdi described by Allouche (1949). Curiously, these documents remain unedited.

Chapter 2: Development of Capitalism Under the Protectorate

1. In terms of qualitative analysis, the transcripts of the Committees of Colonization are indispensable. They have remained preserved in the vaults of the Ministry of Agriculture; the Office of the Haouz in Marrakesh has also established an almost complete basic archive on the history of land holdings. Finally, examination of newspapers is useful: one could consult the large dailies of Casablanca, but the interests of the colons of the Haouz are pursued and illustrated by five successive weeklies published in Marrakesh from 1916 to 1956 with more or less regularity: *L'Atlas* (1913–1914; 1928; 1933–1950); *L'Echo des Deux Villes* (1916–1917); *L'Echo du Sud* (1918); *Le Sud Marocain* (1917–1956); and *Le Réveil du Maghreb* (1933–1956).
2. Le Coz (1965).
3. *Le Sud Marocain*, no. 46, May 15, 1920: 3. Here it is a question of auctioning building lots in the Gueliz, the new (i.e. European) section of Marrakesh.
4. As comptroller, he was especially charged with overseeing the administration of customs. See Guillen (1967: 762). Interestingly, he was to be designated the trustee for the register of real-estate holdings of the Makhzen established to serve as collateral for the loan of 1910.
5. See the report of Trintignac (1936).
6. Cf. Berque and Couleau (1945).
7. According to Branquec (1945: 40B), who goes on to comment: 'the simple comparison of these two numbers sufficiently demonstrates the need to establish a better balance between these two categories of producers.'
8. Branquec (1945: 40A).
9. Branquec (1945: 133B).
10. This recalls the faithless remark of Jacques Gadille (1957: 152), that 'there are a few more failures among those holding diplomas in agriculture than among cultivators who work the soil without benefit of theory'.
11. The descriptive remarks of Ladreit de la Charrière (1910) and the quasi-ethnographic accounts of Troussu (1919) were at one time the only available works on irrigation problems of the Haouz. The difficulties encountered by colonial agriculture had the effect of multiplying the

scientific and technical works on the issue: see Parroche (1925), Celerier (1925), and Martin (1927). Equally worth consulting are Maria (1931), Duval (1933), Dresch (1934), and Fenelon (1941). More recently, see Pilleboue (1962), Ducrocq and Pascon (1973), and Pascon (1970).

12 The codification of customs by the Protectorate would be a chapter in itself. See Bouderbala and Pascon (1972).
13 A long and difficult procedure which, in the final analysis, can only succeed in areas dominated by dams, where the new distribution of a sizeable supply of summer water to native Moroccan farmers would justify the whole operation. On this point, see Ducrocq and Pascon (1973: 53B-56A).
14 This procedure was applied on the Oued Tessaout, where a gross coefficient of land quality was taken into account (Ducrocq and Pascon, 1973: 37A-37B). It is true that, in this case, the Moroccan administration depended on the existence of a reservoir created by a dam. Because of the extensive 'new' resources available, it did not have to engage in any ethnic or social discrimination.
15 Martin (1927: 11), emphasis in original. The author relates how he proceeded when he held the post of Bridge and Road Engineer at Marrakesh.
16 Trintignac (1936: 4).
17 Martin (1927: 8), emphasis added.
18 Martin (1927: 17).
19 J.R. Vaughan-Russell, 'Economic situation at Marrakesh at the end of March, 1936', Public Record Office, London (English manuscript source) F.O. 371/20495, file 20#3629: 336-337).
20 Berque (1962: 265-267).
21 Perhaps to adorn their memories or to appeal to ideas of conquest. On the contrast developed by Christian travelers between the 'generous land' and the 'evil people' in the Maghreb up to the sixteenth and seventeenth centuries, see Turbet-Delof (1973: 51-57).
22 Trintignac (1936: 6).
23 On agricultural industries in the Haouz, see Lahlimi (1963), whose basic analysis is summarized and augmented by Mandleur (1970). To these should be added the annual reports of the Office of Commercialisation and Exports and the 'Bulletins Economiques' of the Province of Marrakesh, as well as the promotional article by Bouquerel (1969), 'Marrakesh: industrial center of southern Morocco'.
24 Lachkar (1964: 8-10).
25 Referring to the Dahir of 1930 (the so-called Berber dahir). Berque (1962: 229).
26 Here of course, it is a question of the Haouz alone; the situation was

quite different in the Rharb and the Tadla, for example. See Berque and Couleau (1945).
27 Theron (1962).
28 On the problem and the methodology for measuring agricultural labor in the Haouz, see Pascon (1966a; 1966b).

Chapter 3: Progress of Capitalism After Independence

1 Evidently, even today it is necessary to look elsewhere than in French sources for a relatively objective and dispassionate approach to these political events. It seems to us that the best source of information is the work of Bernard (1963), and, less serious, that of Landau (1956).
2 'This situation led the French groups — Schneider, the Banque de l'Union Parisienne and even Paribas (the Banque de Paris et des Pays Bas) — to conclude that it was urgent to effect a political change which would safeguard their essential interests,' according to Ayache (1956: 360). See also the study of Pierre Viansson-Ponte, the then head of the political desk for *Le Monde*, on the attitude in financial circles in the face of decolonization in Morocco; the most significant extracts are reported by Bernard (1963: 243–247).
3 The work of Gavin Maxwell (1966: 266–268) is often quite general and novelistic, but it does contain a credible account of the revolt in Marrakesh.
4 Dahir 1.59.112. Bulletin Officiel (Morocco) #2429 (May, 25, 1958: 804). This dahir changed the allocation between el-Glaoui's sons effected some days after the death of Thami by the cadi of Marrakesh on the order of the Palace: the Sultan had given 'them two letters to the cadi of Marrakesh, authorizing them to divide their father's inheritance between them' (Maxwell, 1966: 263).
5 See our article (1963a) on the Buidda: the water 'thieves' of Tabadout themselves say, 'Let us admit that our diversion of water is theft. Thievery which lasts a hundred years is a right!' In order to preserve previous water rights on the Buidda estate, the State had to induce among the Oulad Said fraction upstream a fear as great as the amount of water el-Glaoui distributed downstream.
6 On the judicial and diplomatic aspects of repossession, see Azencot (1973).
7 See our (1964b) article on the State's initiative in land distribution, and especially the charts which show the need to take differences in land types into account.
8 Lazarev (1962) and Pascon (1962).

NOTES

9   Meynier (1958: 8).
10 George (1956: 72).
11 Sorre (1961: 113).
12 Derruau (1961).
13 Jean Le Coz (1965) comes to the same conclusion.
14 We link up here with a new current of marxist thought; see the special issue of *La Pensée*: Serini (1971: 40–41), Godelier (1971: 99–100), Labica (1971: 90–94), Dhoquois (1971: 70–71), Glucksman (1971: 54) and Herzog (1971: 81), as well as Dhoquois (1969: 168, and Althusser's (1966) formulation: 'an economic and social formation is a concrete, actual combinatory of modes of production hierarchically situated in that social formation.'
15 Beginning in 1967 we developed this theme in research in rural and urban contexts, as well as in relation to age groups and sex differences. For a summary statement, see Bouderbala and Pascon (1971).
16 Berque (1962: 277).
17 Terminology reminiscent of Georges Gurvitch! But who can escape this architectonic vocabulary of level, plane, infrastructure and superstructure? There is always a mechanical geometry in sociology; it seems that no one yet has really been able to escape it.

Glossary of Arabic and Berber Terms

Translation of Arabic and Berber words generally follows the French system employed by Pascon. The only exceptions involve French spellings which would lead to awkward pronunciation in English (e.g. the French 'cheikh' is changed to 'sheikh').

adoul: Notary public.
agdal: Royal garden (in larger cities), orchards, pasture or park of the nobility.
azib: Farm.
bled as Siba: 'Land of dissidence', or that portion of the Moroccan Empire which refused to accept government-appointed caids or to pay taxes. Tribes in siba could and did maintain a variety of relations with the government, however (Burke, 1976: 276).
bled el Makhzen: 'Land of dissidence', or that portion of the Moroccan Empire which accepted government-appointed caids, paid taxes, and sent delegations to the sultan (Burke, 1976: 267). More narrowly, lands which comprise the patrimonial domains of the Makhzen.
bour: Non-irrigated land, as distinguished from land served by a seguia.
burnoose: A popular one-piece hooded cloak.
cadi: Judge.
caid: Chief of tribe or of territory appointed by the Makhzen, or sometimes, recognized by the Makhzen as the effective de facto power in a territory, independent of legitimation by the Makhzen.
censal, pl. censaux: Moroccan intermediary who acted on behalf of Europeans in the pre-Protectorate period in matters in which Europeans were legally restricted.
dabit: Payment or financial settlement; that which is owed; regular (non-canonical) tax.

dahir: Sovereign decree, law, edict, announcement or rescript.
dir: Piedmont, foothills.
foum: Alluvial fan formed at the point where a mountain stream enters the plain.
fraction: Unit of tribal organization smaller than a tribe, usually involving a particular geographic district with perhaps four to twenty villages and numerous lineages.
frida: Tax assessment; share due based on debenture or traditional familial obligation, a caidal tax.
guich: Army; tribe subjected to regular military conscription, often in return for usufruct rights to land; land occupied by such a tribe.
habous: Property or land which is designated in perpetuity for sacred use and benefits (religious habous), or for perpetual use of male inheritors; property which is not to be further divided or removed from traditional family ownership.
Haouz (of Marrakesh): Plains and foothills around Marrakesh, from the Oued Tensift to the Atlas Mountains.
hars: Land tax which originally was equivalent to the canonical tithe; later, a seigneurial ground rent.
imam: Religious functionary; the individual who conducts prayer.
jellaba: Long hooded robe with sleeves; the traditional garment worn by both men and women in North Africa.
jihad: Effort, struggle, holy war.
joutiya: Fleamarket.
kasba: Government citadel: fortress of the Makhzen housing its rulers and their entourages, offices, and armed forces.
khalifa: Lieutenant, second in command, vicar; successor to the throne. In Morocco, a provincial viceroy or assistant to a government official (Burke, 1976: 268).
khamesat: Sharecropping arrangement according to which the harvest is divided into fifths allocated to various functions, such as ground rent, seed, planting, weeding and harvesting.
khammes: Sharecropper who participates in the khamesat (q.v.) allocation of shares; in France, a *quintenier*.
khettara: Underground canal which collects water from runoff and the water table at higher elevations, with wells connected to it to permit drawing off of water at various locations.
khobza: Form of sharecropping.
Maghreb: Muslim countries of the west, bordering the Mediterranean Sea.
Makhzen: Public treasury or storehouse; thus, by extension, the traditional Moroccan government administration.
marabout: 'Saint', or local holy person who possesses gifts of spiritual power

THE PROGRESS OF CAPITALISM AFTER INDEPENDENCE 229

— *baraka* — independently of the lineage charisma claimed by *sherifs*, descendants of the Prophet. Turner (1974) gives a thorough discussion of the term and possible misinterpretations of it.

meks: In general, a non-Koranic tax or occasional levy; especially, tax on transactions; market dues or fee; gate toll.

melk: Private property.

Mohtasseb: Accountant; market provost, or person entrusted with control of weights, measures and prices; regional treasurer of the Makhzen.

mokhalat: One who mixes, and by extension, one who frequents the company of foreigners, thus, a censal or protégé.

mokhazni: Person associated with the Makhzen; servant or employee of the state.

moqqadem: Supervisor, overseer, chief, administrator (Burke, 1976: 269); in recent usage, the administrator of the state who operates at the smallest jurisdiction, consisting of one or several villages.

mouna: Food, provisions; supplying of food as payments in kind to a caid, Makhzen official, or individual legitimized by the Makhzen.

moussem: Votive holiday; religious and secular fair.

oued: River.

pasha: Governor of a city; in the region of Marrakesh, additionally commander of the kasba and guich tribes, and by extension, the governmental authority for the Protectorate subregion, the Cercle de Marrakech-banlieue.

seguia: Irrigation main canal.

sharika: Partnership, sharecropping; a serf-like mode of farming in which the sharecropper and family are attached in perpetuity to the land they cultivate.

sheikh: Chief or 'old man', the head man of a village or tribe; leader of a brotherhood; mystico-religious leader.

sherif: Religious notable; putative or actual descendant of Mohammed the Prophet.

soukkane: Inhabitant of a locale understood to be without ethnic origin or tribal affiliation; immigrant; commoner.

tertib: Regular, non-canonical tax, a secular tax established in Morocco by the Madrid convention of 1881, based on fixed percentages of agricultural income, and applicable to all inhabitants, without exception.

urus: Canonical Muslim tax which must be paid on fixed terms.

ulama: Learned man, specifically a member of the formally constituted body of religious scholars (Burke, 1976: 267).

vizir: Minister of state.

zaouia: Lodge of a religious brotherhood; sanctuary; monastery.

Glossary of Government Agencies

Agricultural Service: Service de l'Agriculture et des Améliorations Agricoles. This service was part of the Direction Générale de l'Agriculture, du Commerce et de la Colonisation established in 1920.

Center for Administration of Agricultural Enterprises: Centrale de Gestion des Exploitations Agricoles. The agency created in 1964 to manage repossessed farms of the official colonization.

Cercle of Greater Marrakesh: Cercle de Marrakech-banlieue. The Protectorate subregional administrative area which included the Haouz (see Map C).

Cherifian Interprofessional Cereals Office: Office Chérifien Interprofessional des Céréales. The office created in 1937 to help stabilize commodity prices.

Cherifian Office of Exports: Office Chérifien d'Exportation. The office created in 1932 to encourage export agriculture.

Commission of Development: Commission de Valorisation.

Control of Real Estate Operations: Contrôle sur les Opérations Immobilières. The board created in 1963 to deal with post-independence property settlements.

Center for Rural Development: Centre de Mise en Valeur.

Council of Government: Conseil du Gouvernement. The council with representatives from various chambers and population segments which advised the Residency of the Protectorate on budgetary and economic matters (Scham, 1970:75).

Service for Agricultural Production: Service de l'Agriculture et des Améliorations Agricoles.

Department of Agriculture, Commerce and Colonization: Direction Générale de l'Agriculture, du Commerce et de la Colonisation. The Protectorate Direction Générale which included, among others, the Service de l'Agriculture et des Améliorations Agricoles, the Service de l'Elevage and the Service de la Colonisation (Scham, 1970:62).

Department of Indigenous Affairs: Direction des Affaires Indigènes. The bureau of the Protectorate that handled tribal affairs, including property (Scham, 1970: 65).

Department of Political Affairs: Direction des Affaires Politiques.

Department of Public Works: Direction Générale des Travaux Publics. This Direction of the Protectorate included two services relevant to agriculture: the Service de l'Hydraulique Agricole and the Service des Travaux de Colonisation (Scham, 1970: 63, 68).

Information Service: Service des Renseignements. The Protectorate service charged with overseeing native judicial and police administration, as well as providing military and political intelligence (Scham, 1970: 65, 70- 71).

Joint Chamber of Agriculture, Commerce and Industry: Chambre Mixte d'Agriculture, de Commerce et d'Industrie. The combined (i.e., in Marrakesh) chamber which acted as a liaison between the represented groups and the Resident General (Scham, 1970: 74).

Liberation Army: L'Armée de Libération.

Department of Finance: Direction Générale des Finances.

Ministry of the Interior: Ministère de l'Intérieur (post-Independence).

Private Domain of the State: Domaine Privé de l'Etat. The lands owned by the Makhzen, used directly or through leases to generate commodities and income for the Makhzen,

Region of Marrakesh: Région de Marrakech. The Protectorate administrative region which included the Cercle de Marrakech-banlieue, the Haouz, and Marrakesh.

Section for Modernization of the Peasantry: Secteur de Modernisation du Paysannat.

Service for Provincial Agricultural Enterprises: Service des Exploitations Agricoles Provinciales (SEAP). A post-independence government service created in 1966 to manage official colonization lands.

Service of Domains: Service des Domaines. The Protectorate government bureau under the Direction Générale des Finances which collected proceeds from state domanial lands, and prepared plans for colonization (Scham, 1970: 66).

Bibliography

Note: the original edition in French (Pascon, 1977: 11) of the present volume contains footnotes documenting sources of historical and statistical data, with the author's extended commentary on the sources and other detailed issues. Footnotes in the present edition are included only for quoted material, for all published sources on history and sociology, including those concerning Morocco and the Haouz, and for other widely available works. The following bibliography, on the other hand, contains all sources cited by the author in the original edition, whether or not they are cited in the notes of the present edition, as well as works cited in the Editor's Introduction. The bibliography is divided into five sections: manuscript sources in Arabic; in French; and in English; contemporary periodicals; and finally, books, journal articles and other scholarly works.

Editor

Arabic Manuscript Sources

Archives Marocaines de Rabat
    Mohtasseb Boukili: file
    Moulay Hassan: dahirs to the Mohtasseb of Marrakesh
    Moulay Abdel Aziz: letters (File no. 1695)
    Miscellaneous materials (File no. 1690)
Bibliothèque Royale de Maroc
    Sherifian letters
        Moulay Ismail: 1/4
        Sidi Mohammed b. Abdallah: 1/11
        Moulay Tazid: 1/13

Moulay Slimane: 1/15, 1/18, 1/19
Moulay Abderrahmane b. Hicham,
Bousalham: 2/101, 1/127
Sidi Mohammed b. Abderrahmane: 1-2-2/201, 2/102, 2/105, 2/108
Family Archives

	Number of Documents		
Family	Author's Collection	Public Files	Comments
Goundafi	405	44	Complete, including Tazerwalti estate
Tamesloht	124	89	Complete
Mennou	34	1	Partial
Mtouggui	33	0	Partial
Ayyadi	26	0	Partial
Guich	18	8	Complete
Msouber	12	0	Complete
Grawi	7	0	Partial
Ouriki	6	6	Partial
Abdelhamid	5	5	Partial
Other	16	0	

French Manuscript Sources

Archives Générales de Rabat
    File no. A 16/1-A 16/6: Correspondence with vice-consulates, consular agents in Marrakesh, Mogador, Safi, and Mazagan.
Archives du Consulat à Mogador
    File no. Am 4/1-Am 4/5: Correspondence with French consular agents in Safi and Marrakesh.
Archives du Ministère de la Guerre, Vincennes
Archives du Ministère des Affaires Etrangères, Paris
Archives du Ministère des Affaires Etrangères, Nantes
Centre des Hautes Etudes d'Administration Musulmane
Archives des Renseignements Généraux à Marrakesh, Rabat
Archives des Travaux Publics et du Génie Rural (Office du Haouz), Marrakesh
Archives de la Municipalité, Marrakesh
Archives de la Chambre d'Agriculture, Marrakesh
    Proceedings of the Committees of Colonization

English Manuscript Sources

Public Record Office, Foreign Office, London
Documents pertaining to the Haouz of Marrakesh

Contemporary Periodicals

Bulletin Officiel de Maroc, 1913–
Bulletin du Comité de l'Afrique Française, 1891–1908
L'Afrique Française, 1909–1940
Renseignements Coloniaux et Documents, Bulletin du Comité de l'Afrique Française and Comité du Maroc, 1895–
L'Atlas, 1913–1950, with interruptions
L'Echo du Sud, 1918
Le Sud Marocain, 1917–1956

Books, Journal Articles, and Other Scholarly Works

Abrams, Lawrence, *French Economic Penetration of Morocco, 1906–1914* Ph.D. dissertation, New York, Columbia University, 1977.
Adam, André, *Bibliographie Critique de Sociologie, d'Ethnologie et de Géographie Humaine de Maroc*, Mémoires, Centre de Recherches Anthropologique, Préhistorique et Ethnographique, Algiers 20, 1972.
Akansus, Mohammed, *al-Jays ar-aramram al-humasi ji dawlat awlad mawlana ali as-Sijilmasi*, 2 vols, Fes, lithograph, 1918.
Allouche, I.S., 'Lettres Inédites de Mawlay 'Abd al-'Aziz', *Hespéris* 36(304):463–464, 1949.
Althusser, Louis, *For Marx* [1966], Tr. Ben Brewster, London, New Left Books, 1977.
Althusser, Louis and Etienne Balibar, *Reading Capital* [1968], Tr. Ben Brewster, London, New Left Books, 1970.
Arnaud, Louis, *Au temps des Mehellas ou le Maroc de 1860 à 1910*, Casablanca, Editions Atlantides, 1952.
Ayache, Albert, *Le Maroc: Bilan d'une Colonisation,* Paris, Editions Sociales, 1956.
Azencot, Préciada, *La Récuperation par l'Etat des Terres Agricoles ou à Vocation Agricole*, Diplome d'Études Supérieures, Rabat, 1973.
Belhoucine, Drissi, *La Reprise par l'Etat des Lots de Colonisation et leur Exploitation Actuelle*, Diplome d'Études Supérieures, Rabat, 1973.

Bernard, Stephane, *Le Conflit Franco-Marocain, 1943*-1956, 3 vols, Études de Conflits Internationaux, II, Brussels, Centre Européen de la Dotation Carnégie pour la Paix Internationale, 1963.
Berque, Jacques, *Le Maghreb entre Deux Guerres*, Paris, Editions du Seuil, 1962.
Berque, Jacques and Jean Couleau, 'Vers la modernisation du fellah marocain', *Bulletin Economique et Social du Maroc*, no. 26, July 1945.
Berthier, Paul, *Les Anciennes Sucreries du Maroc et leurs Réseaux Hydrauliques:* Paris, Centre National de la Recherche Scientifique; Rabat, Centre Universitaire de la Recherche Scientifique, 1966.
Bidwell, Robin, *Morocco under Colonial Rule*, London, Frank Cass, 1973.
Bouderbala, Negib, Chraibi, Mohammed, and Pascon, Paul, 'La Question Agraire au Maroc', *Bulletin Economique et Social du Maroc*, nos. 123-125, August-December 1974.
Bouderbala, Negib, and Paul Pascon, 'De droit et le jait dans la société composite: essai d'introduction au système juridique marocain', *Bulletin Economique et Social du Maroc*, no. 117, 1972.
Boulet, 'L'aménagement hydraulique de la region de Marrakech, inauguration de canal lateral au Nfis', *Le Maroc Quotidien*, February 13:4, 1934.
Bouquerel, Jean, 'Marrakech, centre industrial du sud marocain', *Bulletin*, Société Languedocienne de Géographie 3: 321-340, 1969.
Bovill, E.W., *Golden Trade of the Moors*, second ed., London, Oxford University Press, 1970.
Bowie, Leland. *The Impact of the Protégé System in Morocco, 1890-1912.* Papers in International Studies, Africa Series no. 11, Athens, Ohio University Center for International Studies, 1970.
Branquec, Yves,'La propriété rurale et la colonisation dans la zone française', *Bulletin Economique et Social du Maroc*, nos. 26, 27, July, October 1945.
Braudel, Fernand, *The Mediterranean and the Mediterranean World in the Age of Phillip the Second* [1966], 2 vols, Tr. Sian Reynolds, New York, Harper and Row, 1972.
Brunot, Louis, 'Le moulin à manège à Rabat-Salé', *Review Henri Basset*, Institut des Hautes Études Marocaines, Paris 18:91-116, 1928.
Burke, III, Edmund, *Prelude to Protectorate in Morocco*, Chicago, University of Chicago Press, 1976.
Caille, Jacques, 'Un Français á Marrakech en 1851', *Hespéris* 43:437-441, 1956.
Caix, Robert de, 'Report', *Bulletin de l'Afrique Française*, 275A, October 1906.
Celerier, Jean, *Contribution à l'Etude Hydrogéologique du Haouz Occidental et de la Plaine de Haouz; Les Eaux de Marrakech*, Lyon, 1925.

Cenival, Pierre de (tr. and ed.), [16thc.] *Chronique de Santa-Cruz du Cap de Gue* (Agadir), Paris, P. Guethner, 1934.

Chapi, Mustapha, *Quelques Grandes Familles du Makhzen Marocain à XIX Siècle d'après Ben Zidane*, Diplome d'Études Supérieures, Rabat, 1973.

Chirot, Daniel, *Social Change in a Peripheral Society*, New York, Academic Press, 1976.

Clerc, René, 'Renseignements coloniaux', *Bulletin du Comité de l'Afrique Française*, Supplement No. 8, August 1905.

Compagnie Marocaine, *La Compagnie Marocaine, 1902–1931*, Paris, La Compagnie Marocaine, 1933.

Cruikshank, Earl Fee, *Morocco at the Parting of the Ways*, Philadelphia, University of Pennsylvania Press, 1935.

Delilez, Jean-Pierre, Feuille, Pierre, and Pascon, Paul, 'Les lotissements de terres domaniales et collectives dans les périmètres de l'Office National des Irrigations', Rabat, Library of the Office National des Irrigations, 1961.

Derruau, Max, *Précis de Géographie Humaine*, Paris, A. Colin, 1961.

Deverdun, Gaston, *Marrakech, des Origines à 1912*, 2 vols, Rabat, Editions Techniques Nord-Africaines, 1959, 1966.

Dhoquois, Guy, 'Propositions pour une classification nouvelle des sociétés humaines', *L'Homme et la Société II*: 159–178, 1969.

'La formation économico-sociale comme combinaison de modes de production', *La Pensée* 159 (October): 67–71, 1971.

Doutte, Edmond, 'Rapport politique sur les points d'appui de l'influence française dans le Haouz', *Archives Marocaines des Affaires Etrangères* 187:129–163, 1901.

Dresch, Jean, 'Cartes des grands travaux d'hydraulique agricole et industrielle au Maroc', *Bulletin Economique et Social du Maroc*, July 1934.

Ducrocq, Michel, and Paul Pascon, 'La mise en valeur du périmètre de la Tessaout', *Hommes, Terre et Eaux: revue de l'ANAFID* 6(1):19–25, 1973.

Duval, Georges, *L'hydraulique au Maroc*, Diplome d'Études Supérieures, Paris, University of Paris, 1933.

Eickelman, Dale, *Moroccan Islam*, Austin, University of Texas Press, 1976.

Evans, Peter, *Dependent Development: The Alliance of Multinational State and Local Capital in Brazil*, Princeton, N.J., Princeton University Press, 1979.

Fenelon, P., 'L'irrigation dans le Haouz de Marrakech', *Bulletin de l'Association Géographique Française* 139:63–70, 1941.

Flouriot, Jean, 'L'oléiculture dans la région de Marrakech', *Revue de Géographie Marocaine* 9:85–119, 1966.

Frank, Andre Gundar, *Capitalism and Underdevelopment in Latin America*, New York, Monthly Review Press, 1967.

Mexican Agriculture 1521–1630; Transformation of the Mode of Production, Cambridge, Cambridge University Press, 1979.

Gadille, Jacques, 'L'agriculture européene au Maroc: étude humaine et économique', *Annales de Géographie* 66:144–158, 1957.

Gatell, Joaquin don, *Viages por Marruecos, el Sus, Úad Num y Tekna*, Ed. J. Gavira, Madrid, IEA, 1949.

Gellner, Ernest, *Saints of the Atlas*, Chicago, University of Chicago Press, 1969.

Gellner, Ernest and Charles Micaus, (eds,), *Arabs and Berbers: from Tribe to Nation in North Africa*, Lexington, Massachusetts, D.C. Heath, 1972.

Gentil, Louis, 'Rapport sur le meurtre du Docteur Mauchamp', *Bulletin du Comité de l'Afrique Française (April): 131B ff.* 1907.

George, Pierre, *La Campagne, le Fait Rural à travers le Monde*, Paris, Presses Universitaires de France, 1956.

Girard, Georges, *L'Equipement hydraulique du Maroc*, Marrakesh, Direction des Travaux Publics, 1954.

Glucksman, Christine, 'Mode de production, formation économique et sociale: théorie de le transition', *La Pensée*, no. 159 (October): 50–58, 1971.

Godard, Léon, *Le Maroc, Notes d'un Voyageur (1858–1859)*, Algiers, A. Bourget, 1859.

Godelier, Maurice, 'Qu'est-ce que définir une "formation économique et sociale"?' *La Pensée*, no. 159 (October): 99–106, 1971.

Griffith, Keith, *Land Concentration and Rural Poverty*, New York, Holmes and Meier, 1976.

Guillen, Pierre, *L'Allemagne et le Maroc, 1870–1905*, Paris, Presses Universitaires de France, 1967.

Hall, John R., 'The time of history and the history of times', *History and Theory* 19(2):113–131, 1980.

'World-system holism and colonial Brazilian agriculture: a critical case analysis', *Latin American Research Review* 19:43–69, 1984.

Hechter, Michael, *Internal Colonialism: the Celtic Fringe in British National Development, 1536–1966*, London, Routledge and Kegan Paul; Berkeley, University of California Press; 1975.

Herzog, P., 'Le point de vue d'un économiste', *La Pensée*, no. 159, (October):78–83, 1971.

Hexter, J.H., 'Fernand Brandel and the *Monde Brandellien*', *Journal of Modern History* 44:480–539, 1972.

Hindess, Barry and Paul Q. Hirst, *Pre-Capitalist Modes of Production*, London, Routledge and Kegan Paul, 1975.

Mode of Production and Social Formation, London, Macmillan, 1977.

Hoffman, Bernard G., *The Structure of Traditional Moroccan Rural Society*, The Hague, Mouton, 1967.

Ibn Khaldun, [14thc.] *Muqaddima: Discours sur l'Histoire Universelle*, 3 vols, Tr.

V. Monteil, Beirut, Commission Internationale pour la Traduction des Chefs-d'oeuvre, 1968.

Ibn Zidan, Agd al-Rahman, *Ithaf a'lam al-nas bi-jimal ahkar hadirat Miknas*, 5 vols, Rabat, 1929.

Labica, Georges, 'Quatre observations sur les concepts de mode de production et de formation économique de la société', *La Pensée*, no. 159 (October): 88–98, 1971.

Lachkar, Charles, 'L'agriculture étrangère et les industries alimentaires de Marrakech', Marrakesh, Office du Haouz, 1964.

Ladreit de la Charrière, J., 'Les procédés d'irrigation dans la plaine de Marrakech', *La Nature*, 1149 (January 10): 273–274, 1910.

Lahlimi, Ahmed, 'L'oléiculture dans le Haouz', Marrakesh, Office du Haouz, 1963.

Lakhdar, Mohammed, *La Vie Littéraire au Maroc sous la Dynastie 'Alawide (1075–1311/1664–1894)* Rabat, Editions Techniques Nord-Africaines, 1971.

Landau, Rom, *Moroccan Drama, 1900–1955*, London, R. Hale, 1956.

Laoust, Emile, *Mots et Choses Berbères: Notes de Linguistique et d'Ethnographie, Dialectes du Maroc*, Paris, A. Challamel, 1920.

Lazarev, Grigori, 'Les charactéristiques des exploitations agricoles', *Bulletin of the Office National des Irrigations* 2:53–71, 1962.

Le Coz, Jean, 'Les tribus guichs au Maroc: essai de géographie agaire', *Revue de Géographie Marocaine* 7: 1–50, 1965.

Levi-Provençal, Evariste, *Les Manuscrits Arabes de Rabat*, Bulletin, Institut des Hautes Études Marocaines 8, 1921.

Les Historiens des Chorfas: Essai sur la Littérature Historique et Bibliographique au Maroc du XVIe au XXe Siècle, Paris, E. Larose, 1922.

Lyautey, Louis-Hubert-Gonzalve, *Lyautey l'Africain, Textes et Lettres du Maréchal Lyautey*, vol. I: 1912–1913, Ed. Pierre Lyautey, Paris, Plon, 1953.

Mandleur, A., 'Les industries alimentaires de Marrakech', *Revue de Géographie Marocaine* 17: 53–67, 1970.

Maria, 'Note sur les eaux et l'irrigation dans la région de Marrakech', *Arts et Métiers*, no. 130 (July): 245–250, 1931.

Martin, M., 'La question hydraulique dans la région de Marrakech', *Revue de Géographie Marocaine* 6:1–25, 1927.

Mauran, *Le Maroc d'aujourd'hui et de demain*. Rabat Études Sociales, Paris, H. Paulin, 1909.

Maxwell, Gavin, *Lords of the Atlas: The Rise and Fall of the House of Glaoua, 1893–1956*, New York, Dutton, 1966.

Meynier, André, *Les Paysages Agraires*, Section de Géographie no. 329, Paris, Collection Armand Colin, 1958.

Miège, Jean Louis, 'Coton et cotonnades au Maroc au XIXe siècle', *Hespéris* 46:219–238, 1959.
Le Maroc et l'Europe (1830–1894), vol. 1, Paris, Presses Universitaires de France, 1961a.
Le Maroc et l'Europe (1830–1894), vol. 2, Paris, Presses Universitaires de France, 1961b.
Le Maroc et l'Europe (1830–1894), vol. 3, Paris, Presses Universitaires de France, 1963.
Le Maroc et l'Europe (1830–1894), vol. 4, Paris, Presses Universitaires de France, 1964.
Documents de l'Histoire Economique et Sociale Marocaine au XIXe Siècle, Paris, Centre National de la Recherche Scientifique, 1969.
Moreux, René (Ed.), *Annuel 1958–1959*, 51st ed., re-edited, Paris, Annuaire des Entreprises d'Outre-mer, 1967.
al-Nasiri, Ahmad Ibn Khalid, *Kitab al-istiqsa fi akhbar al-maghrib al-agsa*, 9 vols, French tr. E. Fumey, in Archives Marocaines 9, Casablanca, Dar al-Kuttab, 1956.
Parroche, *Contribution à la Connaisance des Eaux de la Région de Marrakech*, Diplome d'Études Superieures, Bordeaux, University of Bordeaux, 1925.
Pascon, Paul, 'Les systèmes d'exploitation du sol dans le Haouz de Marrakech: essai de typologie des exploitations agricoles,' *Revue de Géographie Marocaine* 1–2:97–113, 1962.
'La Coopérative d'Ain Talmast, expérience ou utopie?' *Bulletin de l'Office National des Irrigations* 6:226–240, 1963.
'Buidda Mers al Bghel', *Bulletin de l'Office National des Irrigations* 7:293–313; reprinted in 'La Question Agraire au Maroc', *Bulletin Economique et Social du Maroc* 123, 124, 125 (1974):279–337, 1964a.
'La distribution localement massive des terres à l'initative de l'Etat'. *Bulletin de l'Office National des Irrigations* 7; reprinted in 'La Question agraire au Maroc', *Bulletin Economique et Social du Maroc* 123, 124, 125 (1974):257–277, 1964b.
'Les terres distribuées dans le Tadla en mars 1964', Rabat, Office de Mise en Valeur Agricole, 1964c.
'Analysis et restructuration des terres de colonisation officielle du Haouz et Project de distribution', Marrakesh, Office du Haouz, 1966'.
'La main d'oeuvre et l'emploi dans le secteur traditionnel et methode de calcul du sous-emploi apparent', *Bulletin Economique et Social du Maroc* 100–102 (April–September): 46pp, 1966b.
'Le que disent 296 jeunes ruraux', *Bulletin Economique et Social du Maroc* 112–113 (June): 144pp, 1969.
'Theorie générale de la distribution des eaux et de l'occupation des terres

dans le Haouz de Marrakech', *Revue de Géographie Marocaine* 18:19pp, 1970a.

'Les ressources naturelles et la mise en valeur de la plaine du Haouz', *Revue de Géographie Marocaine* 17, 1970b.

Le Haouz de Marrakech, 2 vols, Rabat, Centre Universitaire de la Recherche Scientifique, 1977.

'Interview: Paul Pascon', *Lamalif* 94 (January/February): 16–25, 1978.

Pilleboue, Jean. *Aspects de l'Irrigation dans le Haouz de Marrakech*, Diplome d'Études Supérieures, Paris, 1962.

Rablinow, Paul, *Symbolic Domination; Cultural Symbols and Historical Change in Morocco*, Chicago, University of Chicago Press, 1978.

Rodinson, Maxime, *Islam and Capitalism* [1966], tr. Brian Pearce, Austin, University of Texas Press, 1978.

Roscoat, Amédée du, 'Relation', ed. Jacques Caille, reprinted pp. 441–447 in 'Un Français à Marrakech en 1851', *Hespéris* 43: 337–447, 1956.

Rosen, Lawrence, 'Social identity and points of attachment; approaches to social organization', pp. 19–122 in Clifford Geertz, Hildred Geertz and Lawrence Rosen, *Meaning and Order in Moroccan Society*, Cambridge, Cambridge University Press, 1979.

Rostow, Walter W., *The Stages of Economic Growth*, Cambridge, Cambridge University Press, 1967.

Rotberg, Robert I., *Joseph Thomson and the Exploration of Africa*, Oxford, Oxford University Press, 1971.

Roth, Guenther, 'Personal rulership, patrimonialism and empire-building', pp. 156–169 in Reinhard Bendix and Roth, *Scholarship and Partisanship: Essays on Max Weber*, Berkeley, University of California Press, 1971.

as-Salam b. Suda, Abd, *Dalil Mu'rij al-Magrib al-Aqsa*, Tetouan, Morocco, 1950.

Sanchez-Giron Blasco, José Maria, *Monedas de Marruecos, 1879–1971*, Ceuta, 1972.

Scham, Alan, *Lyautey in Morocco*, Berkeley, University of California Press, 1970.

Secretariat Général du Protectorat, 'Note sur l'évolution du patrimoine rural français au Maroc mai 21', Rabat, Archives Générales, 1955.

Serini, Emilio, 'De Marx à Lenine: la catégorie de "Formation économique et sociale",' *La Pensée* no. 159 (October): 3–49, 1971.

Sorre, Maximilien, *L'homme sur la Terre*, Paris, Hachette, 1961.

Taillandier, G. Saint-René, *Les Origines du Maroc Français: Récit d'une Mission (1901–1906)*, Paris, Plon, 1930.

Taylor, John G., *From Modernization to Modes of Production: A Critique of the Sociologies of Development and Underdevelopment*, New York, Humanities Press, 1979.

Theron, D., *Types d'Exploitations dans les Périmètres d'Irrigation du Haouz*, Diplome d'Etudes Supérieures, Rabat, 1962.

Trintignac, 'Rapport sur la situation de la colonisation dans la région de Marrakech', Marrakesh: Génie Rural à Marrakech, 1936.

Troussu, 'Les Retharas de Marrakech', *France-Maroc:* 246–249, 1919.

Turbet-Delof, Guy, *L'Afrique Barbaresque dans la Littérature Française aux 16e et 17e Siècles*, Geneva, Droz, 1973.

Turner, Bryan S., *Weber and Islam*, London, Routledge and Kegan Paul, 1974

Marx and the End of Orientalism, London, George Allen and Unwin, 1978.

Wallerstein, Immanuel, *The Capitalist World-Economy*, Cambridge, Cambridge University Press, 1979.

Wallerstein, Immanuel, and Peter C.W. Gutkind, (eds.), *The Political Economy of Contemporary Africa*, Beverly Hills, California, Sage Publications, 1976.

Waterbury, John, *The Commander of the Faithful; the Moroccan Political Elite*, New York, Columbia University Press, 1970.

Weber, Max, *Economy and Society* [1921], ed. G. Roth and C. Wittich, Berkeley, University of California Press, 1977.

Weisgerber, Félix, *Au Seuil du Maroc Moderne*, Rabat, La Porte, 1947.

Index

Ab der-Rahmane, Moulay, 43
abandonments, 122, 123, 174
Abbas al Harbili, el Haj, 67
Abd as-Salem el Warzazi, 76, 77
Abd er-Rahmane b. al-Hassan al-Alaoui, Moulay *see* al-Kbir, Moulay
Abdallah Ibrahim, 168
Aferiat family, 48
agencies, 48
Aghouatim sector, 124, 139, 141, 142, 143, 144, 145, 176, 181, 190
agrarian reform, 179, 189, 192, 195, 208
agrarian structure, *see* social structure
agribusiness, 18, 145-50, 185-7; *see also* Compagnie Fermière
agriculture, 36; capital Moroccan farms, 195-7, 204; colonial, 139-45, 175-97; commercial, 58-71; crop cultivations, 152; cultivation and social structure 201; farm characteristics, 144; modernization, 43-5, 115, 152-3, 154-61; native, 149-50, 150-4; origin and destination of goods, 53; plot size, 99-100, 192-3; production characteristics, 142-3; research, 140-1; state control, 18, 32, 183-4, 186-8; surface area of cultivation by crops, 151; *see also* agribusiness *and* production
Ait Imour tribe, 39, 89, 92, 117
Ait Ourir, 201, 208
el-Akhdar waters, 150, 193
alfalfa, 140

Algeciras, conference of, 60, 61, 88, 105
'alien to the tribe', 90
Allal ben Ahsan, 74
almonds, 56, 193
Annalists, the, 22-3
appropriation of surplus, 16, 17, 18
apricots, 140, 141, 147, 185-6
arabs, 27, 28, 38
arboriculture, 140-1, 145, 150, 152
Argoub, 66, 68, 92
asiatic mode of production, 16
Atlas mountains, 27, 33, 36, 38, 40
al-Ayyadi, caid, 68, 91-2, 101, 152, 155

Banque de Paris et des Pays-Bas (Paribas), 63, 64, 103
Bedouins, 27
beef, 140; *see also* cattle
Ben Dhan, 94
Ben Dhima, 94
Benhamou of Saada, 146
Beni Mtir area, 83, 157
Berber tribes, 27, 28, 29, 38
Berque, Jacques, 138, 150, 152, 206-7
el-Biaz, 169
bled as Siba, 28, 29
bled el Makhzen, 28, 29, 85, 87, 89, 93
Boubker, Moulay, 87
Boubker Rhanjaoui, 50-1
Bour el Raf, 115, 117
Brand-Toel, 69
Braudel, Fernand, 23
Braunschwig company, 56
Brulard, General, 97

Caidal system/caids, 18, 20, 28, 39-40, 80, 210; as protégé, 31; decline after independence, 165-75, 207-8; wage labour and, 102, 158
candles, 57; *see also* wax
de Caqueray, Gaston, 63
cattle, 47; *see also* beef
Cazes, Mr. 117
cementing of sequias, 129-30
Centre for Administration of Agricultural Enterprises (CGEA), 180, 183, 188
Centre for Rural Development (CMV), 191, 192
cereals, 141, 152
Chaouia region, 110, 177
Cherarda tribe, 115
Cherifian Interprofessional Cereals Office (OCIC), 138
Cherifian Office of Exports (OCE), 138, 145, 146
citrus fruit, 140-1, 149
civil rights, loss of, 168
cochineal, 47; *see also* dyes
coffee, 47
'colonat partiaire', 173, 175
colonial agriculture, 139-45; decline after independence, 175-97
colonization: capitalist, 16, 17, 18; lands *see* lands, during Protectorate; private, 97-8
colons, 107, 109; customary labour arrangements, 196; debts during slump, 136-9; production after independence, 175-8; relations with administration, 96-7; repossession of lands, 182-5; technical ignorance, 121-2
Compagnie Agricole et Industrielle de Marrakech, 58
Compagnie Fermière Marocaine d'Exploitation Agricole, 58, 100, 102-13, 139-40
Compagnie Marocaine, 51, 52, 53, 56, 63-7, 70
Compagnie Marocaine d'Arboriculture et d'Elevage, 145
composition, 20, 205-9, 211-13, 214, 216
contractual processing, 146
Control of Real Estate Operations (COI), 179-80
Coopérative des Fruits et Primeurs de Marrakech, 145, 146, 185

cooperative production, 173-4
cooperatives, 145, 146, 185, 193
corvée labour, 101, 102, 167, 171, 173
cotton, 44, 45, 57, 68, 94, 139, 140
credit, 98, 137-8, 196, 197
Crédit Foncier D'Algérie et de Tunisie, 105
Cruchet, Mr, 110
cultivation *see* agriculture
cumin, 56, 152

dams, 113, 130-2, 145
Dannenberg company, 69
debts: during slump, 136-9; liquidation through land transfer, 90, 91-2
'decrees of water distribution', 128
Demnat lands, 87
dependency, 16, 17-18
Derruau, Max, 197
dissidence, 29, 38, 39; *see also* resistance
Djebala region, 29
domanial (estate) lands, 85, 86, 89, 91, 92, 115, 170-1, 189; misappropriation of, 87-8; new types of lease, 90; population of, 117
Doutte, Edmond, 65, 105
dyes, 56, 152; *see also* cochineal, henna

eminent domain, right of, 92
employment *see* wage labour
energy *see* power
Engels, Friedrich, 17
England *see* Great Britain
esparto, 56
experimental farms, 140-1
exports, 55-6

Fernau, (J.H.) and Co., 49
feudalism, 28, 209; semi-, 177
Ficke, C., 69
fiscal reform, 72-3
flax, 140, 152
Fondère, Mr, 98
forage crops, 152
foreign trade: control by Makhzen, 30, 31; penetration and protection, 47-57; protégé system *see* protégés; seizure of, 46-58; *see also* exports *and* imports
Fournier (of Marseilles), 57
France, 32, 57; colony in Marrakesh, 51-3; military intervention, 75, 77; Protectorate *see* Protectorate

INDEX

Gellner, Ernest, 28, 29
Gentil, Louis, 75, 76
Germany, 32, 57; colony in Marrekesh, 49-50; land acquisition, 68-70
Ghanjaoui family, 48
Gharb, 83
Glaoua tribe, 40, 48, 70, 96
el-Glaoui family, 51, 166, 168, 169; *see also* Madani *and* Thami el-Glaoui
Goundafa tribe, 38, 40, 48
grain, 47
grand caids, 40, 48
'grandfather clause', 125
Great Britain, 31, 50-1, 57; land acquisitions, 67-8
groundwater, 132-6
guich lands, 90, 92, 113, 174, 189
guich tribes, 29, 38, 39
gunpowder, 44, 45, 47

Hafid, Moulay (Sultan), 60, 61, 65, 75, 77, 87-8, 89, 98, 103, 164
al-Hassan, Moulay, 90, 93
hemp, 55, 140, 152
henna, 47; *see also* dyes
Hexter, J.H., 23
Hmad ben Aissa L'Abdi, 93, 155
Hmed El Krissi hajib, Haj, 87
Homad al-'Abdi, 90
hydraulic power, 42, 43

Ibn 'Ajiba, 214
Ibn Zidan, Agd al-Rahman, 45
immunity *see* protection
imports, 56-8
improvement of land, 98-9, 100-1, 139
independence, 163-214
inheritance inventory, 166
innovation, barriers to, 44-6
insurrections: Mauchamp affair, 75-7; shoemakers' revolt, 73-5
intermediaries *see* protégés
irrigation *see* water resources
Islamic Brotherhood lodges *see* zaouias
Isly, 47
isolationism, 47
Italy, 32

Jaap, W., 69
el-Jadida, 48
joint-stock companies, 179

al-Kbir, Moulay, 58, 103, 104, 105, 108, 109, 112, 139
Kettani, Mr, 164
khettara *see* wells
khobza, khobzataires *see* sharecropping
Krupp, 50

Lagnel, Mr, 43, 45-6
Lalla Takerkoust dam, 130-1, 145
Lambert, Mr, 150
lands: *after independence*: abandonment, 174; allotment, 170-5, 189-93; categories of, and social structure, 199-201; colonial, state control of, 183-4, 186-7; decline of colonial ownership, 178-81; distribution, political, 193-7; formerly belonging to el-Glaoui, 172; holdings of officials, 177; ownership distribution and social structure, 198-9; plot size, 192-3; private transactions, 177, 179; quasi-appanage, 171; reclaiming colonial, 182-5; regulatory laws, 174-5; repossessed, 190-2; sequestration, 166-70
during protectorate, 81-120: abandonment, 119-20, 122; acquisition by colonization, 81-3, 84; allotments, 96-102; confiscation and seizure, 85, 90-1; debt liquidation by transfer, 90, 91-2; failure to expand after 1930, 113-20; improvements, 98-9, 100-2, 139; lease, new types of, 90; Moroccan candidates for allotments, 155-6; native occupation, 93-6, 105, 106-8, 110-12, 116; owned by sovereign, 86; search for, 83, 85-96; sequestration, 88; size of tracts, 99-100; tenure system, 85-7; transactions, 117-19; tribal boundary establishment, 89-90
pre-colonial: British acquisition, 67-8; French acquisition, 58-67; German acquisition, 68-70 *see also* bled as Siba, bled el Makhzen, domanial (estate) lands, guich lands
Lassallas, Jean Denaut, 51, 52, 53, 63, 65-6, 67, 77, 150
Le Bon Lait, 145, 146, 185
Le Coz, Jean, 92
lead, 47

lease-purchase agreements, 193
Lebon, Mr, 105
lessees, 172
Lhaj, Meslohi, 45
Lhaj, Meslohi, Moulay, 65
Liberation army, 167, 168
Loukkos, 103, 110
Lyautey, Louis-Hubert, 32, 88, 97, 104, 108, 109
Lyautey policy, 79

Ma el'Ainin, 76
Macaire, Robert, 89
Madani el-Glaoui, 40, 51-2, 53
Madrid, conference of, 31-2, 59-60
Mahjoub *see* Sidi El Mahjoub Ould Mekki
Maigret, Mr, 52
Makhzen, The, 18, 28, 30; dependent on European money, 32; dissidence, 38, 39; failure of sugar refinery, 44-5; land *see* bled el Makhzen; monopolization of commerce, 30, 31, 47-8; opposition to land acquisitions, 59-60; position on exporting, 46-7; register of property, 86, 87; seizure of property of, 90; weakness of, 80
Mangin, Colonel, 59, 77
Mannesmann, 43, 50, 66-7, 70, 139, 150
manpower, salaried *see* wage labour
Mansouri family, 48, 152
marketing, 185-7
Martin, M., 130-1
Marx, Karl, 16, 17
Marx, W., 50, 57, 69, 70
Mauchamp, Emile, 66, 75-7
mechanization, 158, 170, 171, 173, 196, 204
Meknes region, 97
Menabha tribe, 67
Mesfioua tribe, 38, 55, 83, 91, 96, 98, 114
Mhamdia, 92
Miège, Jean-Louis, 41, 44, 45, 47
military service, 29, 38, 39
mills, 42, 43, 44-6
Mjat(t) tribe, 70, 117
modernization: of agriculture, 43-5, 115, 152-3, 154-61; orientalist view, 16-17, 22
Mogador, 48, 50, 53, 66
Mohammed V, 166

Mohammed b. Arafa, 166
Moinier, General, 87-8
Mokri *see* Taieb el-Mokri
monarchy, 28; expropriation of colonial lands, 32
Morocco: geography, 27; history, 27; pre-Protectorate, 23-32
Montagne, Robert, 206
Moulay Ab der-Rahmane, Moulay Hafid *etc, see* under name not title
moussem, 210
Mrabtine region, 113
M'Tougua tribe, 40

Nairn, C., 67
Najem, caid, 67
nationalism, 164
native agriculture, 149-50, 150-4; modernization, 43-5, 115, 152-3, 154-61; state control, 183-4, 186-8
Nfis river, 55, 68, 90, 127, 128; dam, 113, 130-1
Nicholson, Sir A., 72
Nier, Herr, 65, 67, 70, 150

OCE *see* Cherifian Office of Exports
olive oil, 43, 45-6, 47, 141, 148, 193, 201, 203
Omar Tazi, Haj, 90, 93, 94
Omar Tazi, Si, 70
orientalists, 16-17, 22
ostrich feathers, 56
Ouarzazate roses, 56
Oudaia region, 113, 114, 117
Oudaya tribe, 39, 89, 92
Oujda, 75
Oulad Abdesiam, 117
Oulad Brahim, 117, 156
Oulad Gaid tribes, 70
Oulad Hamadi, 117
Oulad Hussan, 117
Oulad Said tribes, 70
Oulad Si Ahmed, 117
Oulad Sidi Cheik tribe, 39, 156-7
Oulad Yacoub, 70
Ourika river, 127
Ourika tribe, 38, 55, 128-9
al-Ouriki, caid, 110

PARIBAS *see* Banque de Paris et des Pays Bas
partnerships, 80, 110; farming, 59-60, 61-2, 176; forbidden, 98-9; German

INDEX

firms, 69; ranching, 61; *see also* protégés
Pascon, Paul, 21-3
pastoralism, 16
patriarchy, 203-4, 209
patrimonialism: prebendal, 16, 28, 29; sultan and, 30
peasant agricultural economy, 16
penetration, 47-53; capitalist, 16, 23; condemnation of foreign, 46; resistance to, 71-7
Phillippar, Mr, 112
plot size, 99-100, 192-3
Pointcarre, Mr, 109
population growth, 161, 210
portage, 42
power: pre-colonial scarcity, 42-4; uses in composite society, 205-6
pre-Protectorate Morocco, 23-32
prebendal patrimonialism, 16, 28, 29
processing, 145, 146, 149; as social structure variable, 201-2; contractual, 146
production: agrarian tribalism, 30; asiatic mode, 16; changes after independence, 175-8; characteristics, 142-3; cooperative, 173-4; income and allocation according to, 173; indigenous pastoral, 30; *see also* agriculture *and* mechanization
profitability, 210
proletarianization, 157-8
protection, 50-1; of protégés, 31, 48-9
Protectorate, 32, 79-161
protégés, 31-2, 48; for land acquisition, 59-61; of German firms, 69; protection, 31, 48-9

quasi-appanage lands, 171

'reform of the colonization', 138
Regnault, Eugène, 103-13, 139-40, 150
Rehamna tribe, 29, 38, 66, 67, 68, 70, 77, 83, 91-3
relocation, forced, 110-11
resistance: cultural, 16, 17; to foreign intervention, 71-7; to innovation, 44-6
retroactive sequestration, 169
Rharb, 97, 103, 110, 157, 177, 195, 205
Rhirhaia tribe, 55
Richter, M., 69

Rocade canal, 150
de Roscoat, Amédée, 44
Rothschild family, 67-8
Rouvier, Maurice, 64

SFCI Dar Glaoui, 146
Saada sector, 124, 142, 143, 144, 156-7, 181, 190
Safi, 48, 77
Saint, Resident General, 129
Saint-René Tallandier, Mr, 104
salarization, 157
Scham, Alan, 29
Schlumberger, Mr, 44-5
Schneider and Company, 63, 64
Section for Modernization of the Peasantry, 115
Seggara sector, 92
segmented lineage tribalism, 18, 37-8
seguias *see* water resources
Seksawa tribe, 206-7
Sektana tribe, 38
semicapitalism, 177
semifeudalism, 177
sequestration, 88; after independence, 166-70; retroactive, 169
serfdom, 206, 208
Service for Provincial Agricultural Enterprises (SEAP), 180-1, 188
Sgharna tribe, 70
sharecropping, 20, 39, 93, 94, 95, 96, 158, 160, 167, 173, 175
shepherds, 158, 160
sherifs, 28, 72
shoemakers' revolt, 73-5
'shorn colons', 138
Sidi El Mahjoub Ould Mekki, 65
Sidi Mohammed, 43-5, 47
Sidi Mohammed b. Rachid, 93-4
silk, 44
skins, 47, 55-6
soap manufacture, 43
social structure, 197-213; allotment of land to peasants, 189-90; composite society, 20, 205-9, 211-13, 214, 216; cultivation system as variable, 201; geographic approach, 198; homogeneous society, 202-5; land categories as variable, 199-201; land ownership distribution as variable, 198-9; processing methods and, 201-2; resistance, 16, 17, 44-6, 71-7, 209; transition, 19-20, 213-14, 216

Société de Development Agricole (SODEA), 181, 187, 188
Société d'État de Gestion et de Travaux Agricoles (SOGETA), 181, 187, 188, 190
Société Fruitière d'Emballage, 145, 146
Société Immobilière, 63
Société Industrielle et Agricole de Marrakech (SIAM), 91, 94
Société Oléicole de Marrakech (SOM), 145, 146
Sorre, M., 197
Souelah sector, 92, 156
Souihla sector, 68
soukkanes, 108
Spain, 32, 75
sugar, 44-5, 56, 108, 139, 140
sulfur, 47
surplus, appropriation of, 16, 17, 18

Tabouhanit sector, 124, 129, 142, 143, 144, 181, 190
Tadla area, 195, 205
Tagouramt seguia, 133
Taguenza sector, 142, 143, 144
Taieb el Mokri, 87, 88
Taieb el Mokri, Si, 94
Talougart seguia, 133
Tamesguelft sector, 115, 116, 156
Tamesloht, 45, 46, 115
Targa sector, 67-8, 92, 124, 128, 133, 139, 142, 143, 144, 155, 156
Tassoultant sector, 44, 114, 124, 139-40, 142, 143, 144, 176, 181, 190; Compagnie Fermière in, 102-13
Tassoultant seguia, 127, 128-9, 130
Taza, 103
Tazi *see* Omar Tazi
tea, 44, 47, 57
Tekna tribe, 65, 117
tenant farmers, 93-6, 105, 106-8, 158, 160, 167, 173; forced resettlement, 110-11
Tensift river, 33, 36, 55, 68
Tessaout river, 33, 70, 150, 199
Tetouan, 47
textile factories, 43-4
Thami el-Glaoui, 40, 58, 77, 91, 98, 101, 128, 152, 154, 164; Compagnie Fermière and, 104-13; death, 166, 167
tobacco, 47
Touggani family, 48

trade: balances, 54; foreign *see* foreign trade
transhumance, 38
transition, 19-20, 213-14, 216
transportation, pre-colonial, 42
tribalism, 20, 28-9, 80, 209, 210; circles of kinship, 37; establishment of boundaries, 89-90; monarchy and, 28; pastoralism, 16; pre-Protectorate, 36-40; segmented lineage, 18, 37-8; *see also under individual tribes and guich tribes*
Trintignac, Mr, 113-14, 121, 129-30, 133, 137, 141
Turner, Brian, 16-17, 22

unemployment, 161, 196
union activity, 196, 204
usufruct, right of, 92

Vaffier, Mr, 52
Vaughan-Russell, J.R., 134
Voinot, Colonel, 92, 106

wage labour, 99, 101-2, 157-61, 170, 184, 196, 197, 199, 204, 206; *see also* corvée labour
water resources, 33, 36, 42, 81, 105, 112, 113, 120-1, 122, 124-36, 193; after independence, 169-70; colonial priority on seguias, 126-7; establishing rights, 125-6, 128; irrigation allotment per farm, 124; irrigation pumping, 133-6, 156, 157; monopolization by colons, 114, 128-9, 133-6; nationalization of, 210; regulation of seguia flow, 127-8; regulation of stream flow, 130-2; social structure and, 198; water losses on seguias, 129-30; wells and groundwater, 132-6
wax, 47, 56; *see also* candles
Weber, Max, 16, 30
Weiss and Maur, 49, 50, 69
wells, 132-6
wireless telegraph, 75-6
wool, 44, 47, 56

Youssef, Moulay, 87

zaouias, 29, 36, 46, 210
Zemrane tribes, 70
zinc, 47